what
to
eat

To Jane, who introduced me to health foods.
To Allison, who wanted a book like this.
And to my mother, Lucille, who is always
with me in the kitchen.

what to eat

eat

to

99 super ingredients
for a healthy life

RENÉE ELLIOTT
FOUNDER OF PLANET ORGANIC

PAVILION

Contents

Foreword

I question convention. Not to be awkward or difficult, but because I have come to believe that just because many people are doing something does not make it a Good Idea.

This started when I was little and really wanted to do something that my parents didn't. After several ineffective arguments, I tried the old, 'But mom, everyone else is...' which my mother quickly countered with, 'If everyone jumped off a bridge, would you?' This, repeated through my teen years, was frustrating and annoying.

But I am a thoughtful person. I grew up. By the time I reached 19 and had started to realise that everything isn't as it seems, I was beginning to agree with her. As part of my nutrition degree at university, I had read a book about the horrors of the American beef industry and realised that the pretty pieces of meat in the little packets from the supermarket were not as harmless as they appeared.

The label said nothing about the intensity of beef production, the routine overuse of antibiotics, the growth promoters, the cheap and inappropriate feed, the lack of outdoor grazing and basically the absence of a fairly normal life for a cow. So I promptly became a vegetarian, as organic meat was not an option then. This wasn't because I did not want it, but because I no longer saw conventional meat as healthy food.

I had trusted that someone was looking out for me, ensuring that if food was for sale, then it was good for me. Not just not harmful, but GOOD for me. I suddenly realised how naïve that was. Now I do my own research. Needless to say, I don't take my health advice from the government. They don't appreciate ancient wisdom or modern nutritionists, and because they look after the masses, their advice is often fear-based, like 'bean sprouts are dangerous', and broad, like 'eat less fat'. Neither of which is accurate or helpful.

So I developed a questioning attitude in earnest. And I learned. I learned that food is farmed, processed, refined and distributed in some ways that have nothing to do with whether it is good for you. Instead, these practices are to make food last longer than it should, taste better than it does, look brighter than it can. And this has nothing to do with whether or not it is good for us. There are actually many people in the food chain who don't care about your health. I do.

Over the years, I concluded that 'conventional wisdom' is not always smart. And I looked for another way. I care about my health, and as a child of the Sixties I have a huge sense of social responsibility so I care about other people's health, too. In time, I forged my path and opened Planet Organic to provide another way to shop. We sell the best-quality foods in order 'to promote health in the community'. This is my mission.

Introduction

My Mission

Having studied health and nutrition since 1982, I have concluded that many of the illnesses that plague us today, such as obesity, diabetes and heart disease in all of its forms, are the result of poor eating habits. And I believe the six main culprits, contrary to what the government may propose, are the following:

1. Junk food and fizzy soft drinks
2. Refined carbohydrates, including:
   white sugar – especially if combined with
   white flour white wheat flour in all of its guises
   refined grains like white rice
3. Too much bad fat, including:
   hydrogenated fat
   partially hydrogenated fats
   polyunsaturated fats
4. Poor-quality meat
5. Farmed fish
6. Chemicals in our food and body-care products

Most of what I do fits my mission: 'To promote health in the community'. I have been on that mission publicly since 1995, but privately it's motivated me for a great deal longer, probably even through my childhood and education while I was observing, studying, researching and learning. I opened Planet Organic in November 1995 as an antidote to conventional supermarkets: to provide the best-quality food and give people the choice of health.

Fast-forward to June 2006, when I made a new friend named Allison. As an American transplanted to London, she was already a shopper at Planet Organic. Alison, said, 'I stand there staring at barley on the Planet Organic shelf. I know I should eat it, but I'm not sure what is the best way to cook it.' Maybe you have bought coconut oil because you know you should use it, but it's been sitting in the cupboard getting old because you're not using it quickly enough? Perhaps you keep finding beetroot in your organic veg box and can't be bothered to look up a recipe? Or you find yourself staring at baobab powder in your local health-food store and can't remember why you're supposed to eat it.

This was the seed of the idea for this book. But at the time, sales of cookbooks were declining as more and more people went online for recipes. Today, though, that trend has reversed: with so many bloggers and so much information online, it's become difficult and time-consuming to sift through the mass and find valuable and reliable data and recipes.

The time feels right for an authoritative reference book and cookbook based on all that I have learned about food and ingredients over these 30 years.

So here it is. What you should eat and – oh so importantly – how you should eat it. When you arrive home after a busy day, do you want to search countless websites because you heard someone say that quinoa should be soaked, or something you can't quite remember, and the recipe you're reading online doesn't mention this, so...?

Quite simply, I take you through the best ways to eat the most wonderful ingredients. You don't have to follow best practice always, but mostly is good.

I set out options that save time when preparing ingredients. And I avoid many of the time-consuming and largely unnecessary pre-steps, like pre-steaming vegetables or sautéing, that so many chefs seem to have time for but I certainly don't. Some of these steps also diminish the nutritional value of ingredients because they end up being overcooked in the final dish.

I like the whole food and I don't like waste, so I'll never say, for example, scoop out the tomato seeds – because what are you then supposed to do with them other than throw them away? So I'll recommend that you eat the broccoli stem and leaves, and include the cauliflower leaves in with your roasted cauli and garlic.

Eating well is so unavoidably important. My progress on this path has taken time and thoughtfulness. A major turning point for me came when I was pregnant and read in a pregnancy book to make every mouthful count. The book advised me to have one little treat a week like a wholegrain carrot muffin and one big treat a month like a honking piece of cake. That made so much sense to me that I decided to always make every mouthful count. And that's what this book is all about.

Middle-agers or Millennials?

This book is a no-brainer for women and men of my age (fiftyish) because it's an extension of me, and it's simple, informative, helpful and useful. When I asked some of my friends what they would want in a new kind of cookbook a local friend, EB, said, 'I want a list of what to have and what not to have in the house. And I'll do anything for the good of my children.' I get what she's saying, and I understand women with kids because I am one.

But this book is also for millennials who are into their health and wellbeing, and are using all kinds of great ingredients. I don't understand millennials as well, so I sat down with Laura, my goddaughter, and asked her if she would be my muse. Happily she agreed. So while writing the book, I would send her questions about what she would be willing to make or do, and whether it would fit with her twenty-something urban lifestyle. 'Would you create a rye starter and make sourdough bread?' I would ask. She would answer, 'Hmm, I like that it's an ongoing project, kind of like a plant you're slowly nurturing and then you get the good bit at the end!'
See? Who knew? So Laura helped shape this book for millennials.

Which Foods Create Good Health?

Then it came to deciding what went in the book. The underlying premise is that good health is created by eating well most of the time using a broad range of ingredients in their unrefined state, from vegetables to grains to meats. There is a lot of hype now about superfoods and many people writing and blogging about how great they are. But creating good health isn't just about mixing some expensive powder into your smoothie. It's about lightly steaming that broccoli, soaking seeds and sticking to wholegrains. It's about eating your ingredients at their best.

Good Health Recipe

The broad guidelines for basic healthy eating rest on simple ideas. Reduce and avoid junk foods, refined or highly processed foods, and sugar. I don't believe in calorie counting or portion pondering. I do believe in buying the best ingredients and eating as wide a range of foods as possible.

For a foolproof recipe, use the ingredients below and follow the method.

seeds
nuts
fruits
vegetables
pulses
beans
wholegrains
dairy
meats
healthy oils and fats
good water

Eat some raw; eat some cooked. Soak some. Ferment some. Eat certain things organically. Balance complex carbs with protein, vegetables and oil/fat.

Get enough sleep, do some exercise, take care of yourself and do things that make you happy.

Eat Foods Whole

I have a passion for eating foods whole. The more you take off, take out and process food, the less nutritionally valuable it is. Consider a carrot. First of all, don't peel it. A lot of the beneficial fibre and nutrients are in or just under the skin. Don't juice it. When you juice, you leave behind a wealth of goodness. Eat it or blend it.

Sugar in its many forms, including white flour and all the products made from it, as well as juices, are all extractions or parts of a better whole. If you chew on sugar cane, it's pretty unlikely you will get tooth decay, but extract the juice and refine it into cane sugar and a whole host of problems arise.

It is better for you to do the following:

- Eat fruits unpeeled, even kiwi fruit.
- Eat vegetables unpeeled, including carrots, beetroot, pumpkin, squash, sweet potato and Jerusalem artichokes.
- Blend smoothies instead of juicing.
- Bake with wholegrain flour and eat wholegrain snacks.
- Eat nuts with their skins on.

General Guidelines

I'm sure you'll have heard at least some of these points before, but if you're not doing them, it's worth reading and considering them again.

- Steam or sauté vegetables until just cooked. Please don't ever boil them. Buy a good veg scrubber and leave the skins on your vegetables instead of peeling the goodness and fibre away.
- Eat as many different-coloured foods each day or week as you can.
- Buy/try something new every week.
- Don't count calories, but make every mouthful count (most of the time) so that when you don't or can't, it's no big deal.
- Your body needs good fats and good salt, so make sure you're eating the right ones.
- Eat good-quality oil and fat, not low fat.
- Eat wholefoods whenever you can and avoid extractions like white sugar, flour, pasta, bread, biscuits and refined or processed foods.
- Avoid the sweet stuff: it's not doing you any good.
- Organic food is about healthy soil, healthy plants and animals, and a healthy you.

What Next?

When someone tells you that you can improve your life by changing what you're doing, it can be both exciting and overwhelming. If in this book I'm telling you that you can improve your health by changing the way you eat, just take it slowly. Change takes time. We all have very busy lives.

I suggest you pick one thing that you feel excited about changing or improving and do it for a month. Embed it in your life and make it a habit; then pick something else and do the same again. Correct one of the Six Mistakes (see page 7). Try something new – like leaving the peel on your vegetables and not boiling them – for a month. Then try something else the next month, perhaps a new ingredient such as seaweed. It doesn't sound like too much, does it?

But incorporating small changes creates great habits. If you do this for one year, you'll have 12 new habits in 12 months! And on and on, year after year.

So I invite you to join me on this journey of discovery. Nutrition is complicated and there are many different opinions out there. I believe firmly in doing the research, listening to my gut and then doing things that make sense. I also like keeping things simple: people are too busy and have enough to think about.

My job is to make this easy for you. This book is about eating good food – and making good food better.

How to use this book

This book takes 99 brilliant ingredients and helps you use them in the best way possible, while making it as easy as possible for you to do so.

Why These 99 Ingredients?

This is not a definitive list of everything that's healthy for you, nor is it a list of the only foods that you should eat. It is basically foods that you should eat if you don't already, and foods that you could eat more of. It's a mix of great, ordinary ingredients that you may be taking for granted – like apples, nuts and beans – and ingredients you may have heard of but haven't yet included in your diet – like miso, spelt and sumac. Plus some superfoods that may have little or no supporting research, but have been held in esteem in different cultures for decades or centuries, like goji berries, acai and maca.

I have arranged the ingredients mostly by their biological and taxonomical groupings, some of which may be unfamiliar to you. So to help you quickly find what you're looking for, I have included an index of ingredients on page 21. The book offers a broad mix of recipes for breakfast, lunch, dinner, soups, sides, dessert and drinks, with lots and lots of ideas for other ways to use and eat these wonderful foods. You'll also find a useful at-a-glance recipe index on page 22, in addition to a general index at the back of the book.

For most of the ingredients, there are clearly defined sections on benefits, ways to eat them and how to use them (and, where relevant, why it's best to go organic), although the format does vary a little from ingredient to ingredient, depending on its qualities.

Benefits

This book is not meant to be an encyclopaedia. It doesn't list all of the benefits an ingredient has. Instead, I have tried to emphasise the main highlight of a food – the reason it is in the book. I tried not to continually list the impressive vitamins, minerals and nutrients in each ingredient, as I know that to many people this is fairly meaningless. But I have done so more than I intended, because for so many of these foods, the list is just so exciting.

The Organic Advantage

Although I eat everything organically and wish the whole world would, I understand that it's not everyone's priority. One of the questions I'm most frequently asked is, 'If I don't buy everything organically, what should I focus on?' The answer is as follows:

- whole grains
- meat, dairy and eggs
- whatever you or your kids eat the most of

As you go through the book, the first two are reflected in individual pages. The last, you can decide for yourself, but to help you I have highlighted the products that are most heavily sprayed in the United Kingdom and America. For now, the lists are as follows. They change a little year to year, but you can look them up.

Pesticide Action UK's List:

apricots • apples • beans in a pod • carrots • cereal grains • citrus, soft (clementine, mandarin, minneola/tangelo, nova, satsuma) • courgettes and marrows • cucumber • dried fruit • flour, wholegrain • grapes • herbs • lettuce • nectarines and peaches • parsnips • peas in a pod • pears • pineapple • rice • strawberries • sweet potatoes • tomatoes • yams

Environmental Working Group US List, with the worst at the top:

strawberries • apples • nectarines • peaches • celery • grapes • cherries • spinach • tomatoes • sweet (bell) peppers • cherry tomatoes • cucumber • hot peppers • kale and collard greens

It is widely thought that the following are also heavily sprayed and should be purchased organically as well:

- berries
- spring greens and leafy greens

Ways to Eat

This incredibly useful section suggests different ways to use an ingredient. So, if you've decided to use almonds more and have bought a big organic pack, you'll find many ideas and ways to include almonds in your diet – and help you finish that bag. Sometimes these are simple recipe ideas and other times they are suggested dishes for you to try, with the understanding that you will be able to look up those recipes in other books or on the internet.

How to Use

Because friends and acquaintances know that I'm, well... a food freak, I am constantly asked questions like, 'Should I soak chia? Is it okay if I don't', and so on. There are so many voices out there, that it's not always easy to find someone who knows their stuff, so this book is a practical 'how to' handbook.

This section includes how to get the most nutrition from the ingredient that you're eating. This may mean eating it raw or cooked. Or that you need to soak it. Or that it should be cooked below a certain temperature or for a maximum amount of time.

There are also general tips like not to store tomatoes in the fridge because they go spongy, and to leave the peel on sweet potatoes to utilise all the fibre and nutrients, and that seeds and nuts are best eaten soaked and raw or dehydrated.

These tips are to help you understand the best way to eat a food, although you may not always want to eat it that way, which is fine. For example, blueberries are best eaten raw. But I love pie, and you may too, so it's not meant to stop you from making blueberry pie. The idea is to support you in educating yourself about foods so you can make informed choices. If you have a sweet tooth, for example, it's better to eat blueberry pie than a chocolate bar.

The Recipes

I've included at least one main recipe or recipe idea for every ingredient. Where an ingredient requires some extra preparation before it can be used in a recipe, such as activating a nut or a seed, for example, I have provided a short Base Recipe in addition to the main one.

I know that time is precious, so most of my recipes take 30 minutes or less. But as I have had family and friends double- or triple-test recipes in the book, I've found that some people are quicker or faster because of how quickly they chop or because they throw stuff in a food processor. So, the specified times are just a guide. Please don't yell at me if the Turmeric Scramble takes you 20 minutes instead of 15!

Some useful points about the recipes:

- Tablespoon and teaspoon measures are not the utensils you eat with, but are measuring spoons that can be bought in good kitchen shops or online. The same goes for cups.
- All vegetables are medium unless specified otherwise.
- Butter is salted.

When you have bought the ingredients listed and are ready to make something, do this:

Put ingredients on the worktop.
Prep ingredients.
Follow method.
Read through ingredients at the end to ensure you've included everything.

Finally, you'll make beautiful food for a beautiful you. A little attention to the table creates peace and beauty that add to your eating experience, whether you are on your own, having an intimate meal for two or are feeding a chaotic family of five. When time is more relaxed, I try to lay the tablecloth, napkins, fruit water jug, fresh flowers and candles. But even when I'm in a hurry, a little jar with whatever I can find in the garden – like a sprig of rosemary and a few dandelions – still makes all the difference.

Why eat organic?

I like things that make sense. Organic makes sense. Conventional farming does not make sense. Does it make sense to grow produce with chemical poisons that pollute our food, land and water – with poisons that aren't even necessary? No, is the answer. And yes, they are poisons, because the pesticides, herbicides and fungicides used in conventional farming are chemical poisons designed to kill bugs, weeds and diseases.

Some people ask me, 'Is organic really worth it?' Once we start talking, I usually find that they have a conception of organic foods, but very little factual understanding of conventional agriculture. I have studied organic and conventional farming since 1991. Let's just say that conventional farming does not resemble the childhood pictures you may have in your head of a jolly farmer's wife collecting eggs from her chickens in a wicker basket.

I think it's easy for people not to bother buying organic because they are not confronted with the unpalatable realities of conventional farming. It's easy not to worry about what you can't see or don't know. It's like covering your ears and closing your eyes while singing 'La la la la la la la la'. But having worked in the food industry for 25 years, I can't ignore the truth and am driven to tell it.

Organic farming is a system of agriculture where quality is key. By comparison, conventional agriculture has largely focused on quantity.

In April 2009, the European Union finished the largest-ever study on organic food and farming. It cost 18 million euros, involved 31 research papers and 31 research and university institutes. So far, more than 100 scientific papers from the study have been published – with hundreds more to come. The research programme concluded that:

- 'Levels of a range of nutritionally desirable compounds (e.g. antioxidants, vitamins, and glucosinolates) were shown to be higher in organic crops.'
- 'Levels of nutritionally undesirable compounds (e.g. mycotoxins, glycoalkaloids, cadmium and nickel) were shown to be lower in organic crops.'

Here are my reasons to eat organically:
- Organic food is free from the chemicals used in conventional farming and is grown in rich soil. No food has higher amounts of beneficial minerals, essential amino acids and vitamins than organic food. Organic food contains higher levels of vitamin C and minerals like calcium, magnesium, iron and chromium as well as cancer-fighting antioxidants. Organic milk has 68% more omega-3 essential fatty acids. And nutrients aside, would you rather eat an apple that has been sprayed up to 16 times with as many as 30 different pesticides – or an organic one?
- Organic processed foods contain no artificial additives and preservatives. Some chemical additives that preserve food or add colour or flavour affect individual wellbeing, for example, tartrazine food colouring is linked with hyperactivity. All controversial additives are banned in organic food, which means you avoid a wide range and large quantity of potentially allergenic or harmful substances. Organic processed foods are also better for you because they don't contain hydrogenated fats. (Hydrogenation drastically changes good oils by heating them to very high temperatures. The result is a solid fat that is easy to work with and has a long shelf life, but the process destroys the good oils and turns them into trans fats.) The trans fats present in some non-organic processed foods have no known nutritional benefits and because of the effect they have on blood cholesterol, they increase the risk of coronary heart disease.
- Let's face it: we live in a toxic world, from exhaust fumes to chemicals in our carpets to vaporisers in public toilets. With so much that you can't control, it makes sense to manage what you can. Don't overload your already exhausted liver with yet more toxins.
- And when it comes to the next generation, give them the best possible start in life. Create a foundation of wellness that will enable them to live well and follow their dreams.
- The biggest problem facing humanity today is probably water. In organic farming, the soil is not only able to

retain more water, but it also reduces the speed and scale of run-off after heavy rain.

- We are also no longer able to clean everything out of water. Certain pharmaceutical drugs and chemicals remain even in 'purified' water, reducing the amount of usable water in the world. The sprays used in intensive agriculture are in our soil and water and are present in the most far-flung parts of the world. Organic farming reduces pesticide use by 98% and artificial fertiliser by 95%.

- Conventional farming routinely adds antibiotics to animal feed to speed up animal growth and because many animals in conventional farming are stressed and become ill. Antibiotic residues in meat and dairy products are creating antibiotic resistance in bacteria that make people sick, thereby reducing the effectiveness of our antibiotics.

- Organic farming increases jobs on farms by 73%. It also contributes more to the economic and social wellbeing of rural areas.

- Without topsoil, little plant life is possible. Intensive conventional farming contributes to the depletion of topsoil with little effort to prevent erosion or protect topsoil. Organic farming conserves and builds fertile soil.

- Over 20% of the UK's greenhouse gas emissions come from industrialised food and farming. To produce just one tonne of nitrogen fertiliser takes one tonne of oil and one hundred tonnes of water – and produces seven tonnes of greenhouse gasses. This is not sustainable and seems pretty stupid. There is now evidence that organic farming produces more beneficial soil organic matter and soil carbon than conventional farming. By choosing organic, we can significantly reduce our carbon footprint.

- Organic farming is better for wildlife and allows bugs, butterflies and birds to thrive on farmland. This is because organic farming relies on wildlife to help control pests, so wide field edges are left uncultivated for bugs, bees and birds to flourish. The UK government's advisors found that insect, bird and plant life is up to 50% greater on organic farms.

Yes, organic food is generally more expensive. Quality always is. You will spend money on what you value. It's that simple.

Soaking & Sprouting

Foods in their whole state are nutritionally superior. But when it comes to beans and pulses, nuts and seeds, and cereal grains, they are best for you after soaking. And even better if you sprout them.

Grains, beans, pulses, nuts and seeds all have two things in common that make it hard for us to digest them and access the full spectrum of nutrition that they offer. Firstly, they have phytic acid in their outer husk which binds with calcium, magnesium, iron, copper and zinc in our large intestine, meaning we don't absorb them. And secondly, they contain enzyme inhibitors to prevent them from sprouting at the wrong time, which can neutralise important enzymes in our digestive tract. To neutralise both of these, you need to soak them.

The basic principle is that you soak them in acidulated water – water mixed with either yogurt, kefir or lemon juice (if you are dairy-free) so that enzymes, lactobacilli and other beneficial organisms can do their job. For soaking beans, see page 131; for grains, see page 143; for nuts, see page 169; for seeds, see page 183.

Soaking & Activating
The soaking process also 'activates' the little powerhouse inside, so soaking achieves the following:
- neutralises phytic acid
- neutralises enzyme inhibitors
- increases helpful enzymes
- increases vitamins, particularly B vitamins

Sprouting
Sprouting grains, legumes, beans, nuts and seeds takes them a step further. To sprout anything follows the same process of soaking, rinsing and allowing to grow. The only variable is the amount of time it takes for some things to sprout. Sprouting jars are excellent for this, but you can use a regular jar with a colander for draining.

Here's how:
- put about one-third grain, legume, bean, nut or seed in a Mason-sized jar
- fill to the top with good water
- soak overnight
- the next morning, pour off the water
- fill the jar again, pour off the water and drain in a colander
- rinse at least twice a day – more if you are able
- sprouts will be ready in 1–4 days

Rinse the sprouts thoroughly and let them drain in a colander until they are fairly dry. Then store them in the fridge for up to three days. It is not necessary and is difficult to sprout linseed, which becomes too mucilaginous to rinse. Nuts will sprout, except for pecans and walnuts, which should be soaked as above. Grains will sprout, except for oats, because they have been removed from their outer hull. Sprouted grains are best if lightly steamed.

Alfalfa sprouts, which are very common in health-food stores, contain an amino acid called L-canavanine. This amino acid stimulates the immune system, which can increase inflammation in people with lupus or other auto-immune diseases.

Sprouting does the following:
- neutralises phytic acid
- neutralises enzyme inhibitors
- increases helpful enzymes
- increases vitamins, particularly B2, B5, B6 and beta-carotene
- increases vitamin C
- breaks down complex sugars in beans and legumes that cause wind

Fermenting

Even in our time-pressured lives, I love products that take time to make. I like sourdough bread or properly soaked and cooked beans. I can manage some of those preparations, but with work and three kids, most of my cooking and baking needs to be quick. Fermenting doesn't require standing over something, so it's easy preparation-wise and then you leave the magic of fermentation to do its work.

Fermentation does the following:

- breaks down food to aid digestion and assimilation
- provides enzymes to aid digestion
- supplies and nourishes correct intestinal bacteria
- helps heal leaky gut and IBS
- boosts immunity
- removes cyanide

All functions in the body require enzymes and the enzymes in many foods are damaged or destroyed by the time we eat them. The more enzymes we have, the more easily we digest food, cleanse, heal and build.

It's great to include fermented foods in your diet on a regular basis. Remember the following fermented foods (and see pages 222–241):

amazake
apple cider vinegar
kefir
kimchi
kombucha
mirin
miso
pickled ginger
sourdough breads
tamari
tempeh
umeboshi plums
shoyu
yogurt

Fat

Fat is a BIG subject. There has been much misinformation and bad advice over the years. You have to wonder why anyone would think that hydrogenated margarines were ever going to be better for us than grass-fed organic butter? So, forgive me if I'm not convinced of the government's party line on fats.

As I said earlier, I question convention. There isn't enough space here to deal with all the issues around fat, but the following are the areas I most want to highlight.

Animal and vegetable fats and oils give our bodies concentrated energy and are building blocks for cell membranes and hormones. Fats are satisfying, make us feel full for longer, carry fat-soluble vitamins and are necessary for mineral absorption and other important processes in the body. Also, two-thirds of your brain is fat. Don't eat less or low fat; eat good fat. Fats basically divide into the following types:

• Saturated fatty acids (SFAs)
• Monounsaturated fatty acids (MUFAs)
• Polyunsaturated fatty acids (PUFAs)

A traditional diet based on fresh, unprocessed foods would have primarily contained saturated fats and monounsaturated fats. But as the medical world warned us away from butter, we shifted toward industrial fats, produced at high heat, containing little nutritional value and mainly polyunsaturated fats.

PUFAs, which feature much more in modern diets, are a problem because they are unstable and become oxidized or rancid when affected by heat, light and oxygen. Oxidation causes inflammation – and inflammation, whether acute or chronic, is at the heart of many diseases such as diabetes, obesity, rheumatoid arthritis, stroke and Alzheimer's, to name but a few. PUFAs cause free-radical damage and a host of problems in our bodies if eaten in excess.

Bad Fats

Rather than watch your fat consumption, a better idea is to stay away from truly bad fat – trans fats in fried foods, fried snack foods like crisps, and processed foods like doughnuts. Always avoid hydrogenated and partially hydrogenated fats, which are found in cheap foods. Oils high in PUFAs are often sold as 'vegetable oils'. These generically labelled oils are cheap, volatile and often rancid. They include soy, corn and sunflower oils and should be avoided (of these, sunflower oil is more stable, but should not be used for cooking or baking).

Cholesterol

For some people, the jury is out about whether cholesterol is a bad thing. Here are a few interesting points. Cholesterol comes from eating saturated fats. Cholesterol is crucial for the normal functioning of your body. It is in every cell membrane and is vital in hormone systems and other functions.

What you may not know is that only a small amount of cholesterol comes from what you eat. Around 85% of the cholesterol in your body is made by your liver. It is therefore impossible or incredibly difficult to control cholesterol by changing what you eat. And when people do cut down on fats in an attempt to reduce cholesterol, there can be problems with energy, concentration, depression, weight gain and mineral deficiencies.

One of the most amazing foods – human breast milk – has a higher proportion of cholesterol than almost anything. Fifty percent of the calorie content of breast milk is fat and 48% of that is saturated. This is because cholesterol and fat are vital for growth in babies and children – especially for the developing brain. Also, cholesterol and saturated fats are the most healing substances in the body.

The other point about fat – and any food, really – is that not all foods are equal. Fat from an intensively reared animal is different from an organic, grass-fed one. Because of the Lipid Hypothesis, we have been told to eat little saturated fat, but animal fats are not 100% saturated anyway. The ratio of fats in human fat is similar to lamb and pork. Pork fat is 44% saturated, 45% monounsaturated and 11% polyunsaturated. When animals are grass-fed, the proportion improves.

It has been reported for years that people with high cholesterol live longer and that older people need more cholesterol. When people eat less fat, they eat more of other foods, and ultimately do not lose weight. I think it's because when people reduce fat in their diets, they feel so unsatisfied that they overeat. Eating good fat won't make you physically fat if you eat a balanced diet that includes quality fat and oil.

Low Fat Sounds Good?

Okay, to put it simply, low-fat foods:
- have no flavour, so are often high in sugar or salt.
- aren't working as a strategy, because obesity is increasing.

- make even less sense when applied to dairy products like milk and yogurt. At 4% fat, these are not high-fat foods in the first place! When you take the fat out of milk, it has no flavour, which is why people end up drinking café lattes and eating yogurt loaded with sugar.

In my recipes, I often say to use healthy oil. This is to give you the choice of using, say, coconut oil instead of butter. Or if I use sesame oil and you only have extra virgin olive oil, it's not a problem for you to use that.

Grains

Across the globe, about half of our calories come from wheat, corn and rice. But because we eat them as refined foods, they provide less than half of our nutrients. To get the best of what nature provides, we need to eat the whole food, and for grains this means wholegrain rice, wholegrain flour and all of the products made with flour.

Many people know the problems created by eating sugar. But most people don't know that your body cannot tell the difference between a teaspoon of sugar and a teaspoon of white flour. The metabolic response is the same (see Sugar, page 18). So, you could almost think of a bowl of white pasta with tomato sauce as a bowl of sugar with some tomatoes.

If your diet comprises a lot of white flour and white rice, you would transform your nutrition by switching to wholegrain. You can try wholegrain breads, cereals, pastas, biscuits and snacks. Be aware that many breads may appear wholegrain, but are not. Brown bread and multigrain breads are white-flour based. Check the ingredients for wholemeal or wholegrain flour.

One of the easiest switches to make is to swap out white flour in baking. Although you may think that wholegrain baked goods are heavy, think again. First of all, in items like cookies, traybakes and brownies, wholegrain flour really makes no difference at all. And I have the best Cinnamon Cake recipe in the world (see page 109) and

perfect wholegrain pastry (see page 228), both of which will open your eyes.

It's impossible to talk about flour and not talk about wheat. Wheat is not my favourite ingredient. In fact, it's nearly at the bottom of my list. Wheat has been so hybridized over thousands of years that it no longer resembles the grain that nature gave us. It has been modified not to create a better food for us to eat, but to make it easier to harvest and to change the gluten to produce fluffier bread.

Many people just eat too much wheat. Toast for breakfast, biscuits at 11:00, a sandwich for lunch, cake in the afternoon and pasta for dinner could mean five servings a day. Do this every week and month and year, and it's not a pretty picture. Not only are there alternative grains for healthy baking, like spelt (see page 158), but there are also a wealth of other grains used in cereals, biscuits and pasta/noodles, such as amaranth, barley, buckwheat, Khorasan, millet, oats, quinoa and rye (see pages 140–165).

Another important point here is that although it is always better to eat wholegrains, they should be organic because chemical farming residues concentrate in the outer husk, and when possible, you should soak them. Soaking grains and flour gets rid of the phytic acid and makes them more digestible (see page 14).

Sugar

Sugar has to be the worst ingredient in our diets. So the question is: how do we eat it and be smart about it?

Our bodies are designed to run on carbohydrates, so we are attracted to the sweetness of them. If we eat complex carbohydrates, like wholegrains, beans, legumes and vegetables, the body functions properly, digests our food slowly and releases energy over a prolonged period of time.

Believing that sugar gives you energy is not smart. It's true that if we eat concentrated sugar – white sugar, brown sugar, glucose, honey and syrup – our bodies digest them quickly for a short burst of energy. But the pancreas then releases insulin to lower blood-sugar levels. This causes a drop that makes you tired – called the sugar blues.

This rapid increase in blood-sugar puts a strain on your adrenals, immune system and other body systems. Repeated over and over for months and years, it can cause more serious problems like tooth decay, obesity, heart disease and *candida* infections, and is thought to lead to type 2 diabetes.

The other problem with eating sugar is that if you don't use the energy from the sugar, it is stored in the body and becomes fat. Also, sugar seriously affects a child's ability to concentrate and learn.

These days there are many different types of sweeteners and syrups and sugars. Are some better than others? I think the bottom line is that sugar is sugar. There is minimal nutritional benefit from 'unrefined' sugars and the whole glycaemic index and glycaemic load thing is complicated.

There are now many sweeteners like stevia and xylitol. They may not have many calories, but they are very highly processed and they are expensive. The worst sugar has got to be high-fructose corn syrup, which is used in a huge multitude of products in America on an unsuspecting public. Coconut sugar is being touted as the best sugar at the moment. It is minimally processed, with some fibre and nutritional value. But, it is still sugar, and being less unhealthy than regular sugar does not in

fact make it healthy. Honey shouldn't be heated and is a simple carbohydrate. Agave is highly refined. I could go on, but it's more of the same.

The point is that you don't get anything for nothing.

So...I think the most important thing about sugar is how you eat it and how often. If you eat sugar in white flour cakes, this is a double whammy to your system because you are consuming two refined carbohydrates. If, however, you eat sugar with protein, fibre and fats, you slow down its digestion and soften its impact on the body. So, baking with wholegrain flour completely changes baked treats from being a damaging drain on the body to a nutritive delight.

I think that for most people, trying to cut sugar out of their diets is unrealistic. Or pinning your hopes on some new sugar that's the answer to your sugar prayers is fooling yourself. A simple, practical solution is to reduce how often you eat sugar and when you eat it, and to be really conscious about it. Try avoiding sugar when you don't actually need it, like cutting out sugary breakfast cereals. Or have an apple instead of biscuits. Then, when you really want a sweet treat, eat sugar baked smartly into something, from this book or elsewhere, that uses wholegrain flour with sugar no more than half the weight of the flour. Or make raw treats that contain Manuka or raw honey.

Useful Sweet Options
Brown rice syrup and barley malt syrup are probably the best sweeteners because they are fermented and are complex carbohydrates. But brown rice syrup is hard to find and of course as a liquid you must use it differently in baked goods. Amazake (fermented rice) is also a good sweetener (see page 240). Baobab powder is good, but expensive (see page 216). Coconut sugar may be better for you, but it's expensive, and needs more research. If you are swapping coconut sugar for other sugar, you must do it by weight, not volume (as in cups) as it is lighter than regular sugar. Good old blackstrap molasses is rich in minerals,

but has a strong flavour. It is good for baking gingerbread biscuits, flapjacks and spice cookies.

Yacón is the latest craze in America. Yacón is a tuber grown from Colombia to Argentina in the Andes mountains. It comprises mainly water and fructooligosaccharides, which have a prebiotic effect and are food for beneficial bacteria that enhance colon health and aid digestion. Fructooligosaccharides taste sweet, but they pass through the human digestive tract unmetabolised, so have few calories.

Lucuma is the fruit of a tree that grows in Peru, Chile and Ecuador. The pulp is dried and ground into a powder that is a less refined and delicious sweetener containing some nutrients.

Many people think they only need to avoid sugar if they're trying to lose weight, but really everyone should reduce or avoid sugar for better health. If you eat sugar five times a day, you could look at reducing that to three. Or if you eat sugar once a day, reduce it to twice a week. It's a different challenge for different people.

Umami

Playing with flavour is essential to good cooking, but umami, although discovered in 1908, is only now attracting attention from the rest of the world. There are not only four tastes – sweet, sour, salty and bitter – but five.

The Japanese scientist Professor Ikeda discovered the primary taste in dashi (seaweed stock made from kombu, see page 210) to be glutamate and dubbed it 'umami'. This is the fifth taste. These five 'tastes' cannot be created by combining other flavours.

The main components of umami are glutamate, inosinate and guanylate, which create a pleasant savoury taste. Glutamate is found in foods including meat, fish and vegetables. Inosinate is found in meat and fish. Guanylate is found in dried mushroom products.

Foods that are considered umami include meat, aged cheese, fermented products, shiitake mushrooms and matcha. It is a flavour that often comes with ageing, as in meats that are well hung, and the time involved with fermenting various products and ageing cheese.

After the discovery of glutamate in kombu, artificial monosodium glutamate (MSG) was created and used in processed foods as a flavour enhancer. Many people report headaches or feeling unwell after eating MSG and it is not allowed in organic processed foods.

Index of Ingredients

Index of Recipes

Vegetables

Asparagus

Asparagus are the young shoots of a lily plant, which nature gives us in spring as a delicious detox after the heaviness of winter. They have a short season and are a real delicacy. White asparagus are grown under the earth and picked before they reach the sun.

Benefits

Asparagus are considered one of the most nutritionally balanced plant foods. They have a great spectrum of vitamins and minerals, and contain high amounts of glutathione, a detoxifying compound that assists in the breakdown of free radicals and carcinogens. They have notable amounts of fibre, folate (one of the best sources), vitamins A, C, E and K, and the mineral chromium, which helps insulin transport glucose from the bloodstream into cells.

Asparagus are one of a few vegetables that contains inulin, a prebiotic that provides health benefits for our digestive tract.

Ways to Eat

• Include in quiches.
• Steam and try on pizza.
• Roast in the oven with oil and Parmesan cheese.
• Add to omelettes.
• Mix into green, pasta, rice, bean, grain and mixed salads.
• Use in wraps.
• Add to stir-fries.
• Grill or griddle as a side dish.

How to Use

Hold the middle and the stem end of each asparagus and bend. Asparagus will snap at a natural breaking point where the stem is no longer tough. Discard the ends. Steam the tips for 3–5 minutes until just tender.

Asparagus with Chilli Eggs

Perfect for a leisurely Sunday brunch – and a treat for guests – this is a wonderful way to enjoy eggs. Serve with wholegrain yeasted or sourdough toast and you have a meal. If you're serving it to children, you can reduce the amount of chilli flakes, or increase if you like spicy foods.

Serves: 4
Prep: 15 minutes
Cook: 10–12 minutes

300g/10½oz/1½ cups plain Greek yogurt
1 garlic clove, crushed
¼ tsp fine sea salt
4 tbsp extra virgin olive oil
½ tsp dried chilli flakes
3 asparagus bunches, ends snapped off
5 tbsp cider vinegar
4–8 eggs

In a small bowl, mix the yogurt, garlic and salt and set aside.

Heat a small saucepan to a medium-low heat, add the oil and chilli and cook for 3 minutes until the chilli begins to sizzle. Remove from the heat and leave to cool.

Steam the asparagus over simmering water for 3–5 minutes until al dente. Add the chilli oil to the yogurt mix and beat with a fork until combined.

Bring a large pan of water to a simmer. Add the vinegar and poach the eggs for 3 minutes. Remove the eggs from the water with a slotted spoon and dry on paper towels.

Divide the asparagus between 4 plates, cover with the chilli yogurt and top with 1–2 eggs each.

Carrots

Carrots, which have been around for thousands of years, used to be purple, red, yellow and white, like we're beginning to see on sale again recently. Orange carrots are relatively new, dating to the Netherlands in the 1600s. The word 'carrot' comes from the Greek *karoton,* where *kar* means 'horn-shaped items'.

Benefits

Carrots are famous for their ability to improve vision. This bears out in studies showing that women who eat carrots two times a week as a minimum have much lower rates of glaucoma than women who eat carrots less than once a week. Add to that carrots' beta-carotene and general antioxidant nutrients, their risk-reducing ability for cardiovascular disease and their anti-inflammatory and anti-clot properties.

The Organic Advantage

Carrots are a favourite with young and old, and are the most widely eaten root vegetable. Carrots carry so many chemical residues that years ago the FSA in England advised the public to top, tail and peel carrots. This doesn't help with systemic chemicals that are used in intensive farming. Carrots are so good at absorbing heavy metals from soil that they are sometimes grown as a throw-away crop to rid a field of lead or arsenic contamination. Buy organic, don't peel them and eat the whole thing.

Ways to Eat

- Grate into scrambled eggs or use in omelettes.
- Eat Carrot Cake Baobab Bircher (see page 217).
- Instead of juicing carrots, blend them if you have a high-speed blender, or if not, grate and add to smoothies and smoothie bowls.
- Dip carrot sticks or rounds into hummus, other bean dips or nut butters.
- Enjoy carrot soup.
- Grate or chop into green, pasta, rice, bean, grain and mixed salads.
- Mix grated carrots into egg or tuna mayo and chicken salad.
- Add into sweet potato mash.
- Use in sushi and nori hand rolls.
- Add sliced carrots into rice or other grains you are cooking for the last 5–10 minutes.
- Include in sautés and stir-fries.
- Make carrot muffins and carrot cake.

How to Use

Carrots are great – and different – raw and cooked, and the beta-carotene in carrots is heat-stable. It may also be more absorbable if you steam carrots until they are just soft. Cut 5mm/¼ inch thick and steam over simmering water for 5 minutes until just tender.

Don't peel carrots! The peel contains fibre and nutrients, so you don't need to waste time and money peeling it off and throwing it away. Simply scrub carrots with a good natural bristle vegetable scrubber.
Look for different coloured carrots to add variety and interest to your table. Aside from orange, there are purple, yellow, white and red. You can enjoy them whole, in sticks, rounds, julienne or grated.

Infused Carrot Sticks

These are fun at parties or at home, either for snacking or dipping in hummus.

Serves: 4
Prep: 5 minutes
Cook: 1 hour

480ml/16fl oz/2 cups boiling water
1 tsp coriander seeds
1 tsp cumin seeds
1 bird's eye chilli
4 carrots, cut in half lengthways, then into sticks

Put the boiling water in a measuring jug, add the coriander seeds, cumin seeds, chilli and carrots. Leave to soak for 1 hour, then drain and serve.

Carrot Rice

When you feel like rice, here's a great side dish. You can use any rice – remember red, black and wild – and for a change, substitute coconut milk or broth for the water. For a dairy-free version, swap coconut oil for the butter.

Serves: 4
Prep: 10 minutes
Cook: 35 minutes

200g/7oz/1 cup wholegrain rice of choice, soaked if time (see page 143)
480ml/16fl oz/2 cups water or stock
1 tsp fine sea salt
100g/3½oz/1 cup grated carrots
55g/2oz butter or healthy oil
40g/1½oz/½ cup flaked, toasted almonds

Bring the rice, water and salt to a boil in a medium saucepan. Reduce the heat to low, stir, and simmer, covered, for 25 minutes. Add the carrots on top and simmer for another 10 minutes until the rice is al dente. Add the butter, mix well and top with the toasted almonds. Serve warm.

Watercress

Grown for millennia as a food and medicine, watercress was considered a healing herb as early as 400 BC when Hippocrates built the first hospital on Kos island near a stream in order to have fresh watercress for his patients. It is part of the cruciferous Brassica family and is a rapidly growing, dark, leafy-green aquatic or semi-aquatic plant.

Benefits

One of the oldest-known leaf vegetables eaten by people, watercress is valued for its strong-tasting leaves, so it's no surprise it is botanically related to garden cress, mustard, radish and wasabi. Scientists have identified over 15 essential vitamins and minerals in watercress. It contains more iron than spinach (and is more absorbable), more calcium than milk (and is more absorbable) and more vitamin C than oranges.

Watercress is best known for bone-building and strengthening vitamin K and eye-supporting beta-carotene. Vitamin K also limits neuronal damage in the brain, making it helpful in combatting Alzheimer's.

Ways to Eat

- Include in smoothies.
- Mix into cooked scrambled eggs.
- Add to egg, chicken, potato, green, pasta, rice, bean, grain and mixed salads.
- Use in wraps and sandwiches.
- Make watercress pesto.
- Create chilled watercress soup.

How to Use

Watercress should be eaten raw. If you are whizzing watercress into pesto, soup or dip, you can use the crunchy stems. Try them to see how much of the stem you are happy to include in salads and such in case they are too tough.

Watercress Avocado Salad/Spread

This is absolutely delightful as a side dish or eaten on wholegrain or gluten-free crackers. If you want more of a spread, you can pulse it in your blender. It may seem like a big amount, but it disappears quickly when served. You can make this with rocket (arugula) instead of watercress, too.

Serves: 4
Prep: 10 minutes

200g/7oz watercress, chopped
2 avocados, mashed
2 tbsp extra virgin olive oil
3–4 tbsp lemon juice
1–2 tsp ground cumin or turmeric
¼ tsp fine sea salt
crudités and Romaine leaves, to scoop/fill
wholegrain or gluten-free toasts or crackers, to serve (optional)

In a medium bowl, combine the watercress, avocados, olive oil, lemon juice, cumin or turmeric and sea salt, and mix well. You can purée in a food processor or blender if you prefer.

Kale

Kale is so good for you and so easy to grow that it should be a must in your vegetable garden. Kale is a member of the Brassica family, along with collard greens and Brussels sprouts, which are becoming more and more known for their health benefits. When buying kale, look for different varieties for a range of flavours and colours like green, red curly kale, black kale (cavolo nero), red Russian and purple kale.

Benefits

Because of its high antioxidant levels, like other cruciferous veggies, kale's relationship with cancer has been studied the most. Kale's fame rests on three things: its antioxidant richness, its anti-inflammatory nutrients and its cancer-fighting glucosinolates. Kale also plays an important role in our body's detoxification process, which is essential to health and wellbeing.

The Organic Advantage

Dark greens grown in artificially fertilised soils can concentrate nitrates that become harmful in the intestine. Seeing as it's a cheap vegetable anyway, buying organic kale makes sense.

Ways to Eat

- Whisk with eggs and make kale scramble.
- Sauté kale for 5 minutes in olive oil, put on toast and top with poached, fried or scrambled eggs.
- Make kale pesto.
- Add to soup or stew 5 minutes before it has finished cooking.
- Add raw or roasted kale to green, grain, bean, pasta or mixed salads.
- Steam kale and add to pasta or grain dishes.
- Use it in frittatas.
- Sauté on its own or with other greens and add grated ginger, crushed garlic, olive oil and sea salt.

How to Use

If you don't cook kale or other dark leaf vegetables, you will not neutralise the oxalic acid and be able to absorb the calcium they provide. There are, however, benefits to eating kale raw and cooked, so eating it both ways may be your best bet.

Cut the leaves off the thick stems and discard the stems. Roughly chop the leaves and sauté in healthy oil or steam over simmering water for 5 minutes until just tender.

Crispy Kale

You can make this in your oven or in a dehydrator if you have one. Crispy kale is a super-nutritious and delicious snack that can be munched on before a meal, as a side or as an afternoon snack. Move over crisps, for this inexpensive and nutritionally exceptional food.

Serves: 4
Prep: 10 minutes
Cook: 30–40 minutes

100g/3½oz kale, washed and roughly chopped
2–3 tbsp extra virgin olive oil
¼ tsp fine sea salt

Spin the kale dry or leave to dry as water makes it soggy in the oven. When the kale is ready, turn the oven on to 50°C/120°F or its lowest setting.

Put the kale in a large bowl, add the oil and salt and toss well or rub the oil onto the leaves to help evenly coat with oil. Bake for 30–40 minutes until crispy.

Kale & Spinach Patties

These have a lot more spinach in them than kale, but they are so great and so green that they are included here. These make a tasty dinner, served with salads or sides. You can omit the Parmesan for a dairy-free version, but increase the sea salt a bit to compensate.

Serves: 4
Prep: 30 minutes
Cook: 10 minutes per batch

400g/14oz frozen chopped spinach
150g/5½ oz/½ cup fresh wholegrain breadcrumbs
60g/2¼oz finely chopped kale
60g/2¼oz finely chopped onion
60g/2¼oz grated Parmesan cheese (optional)
5 large eggs, beaten with a fork
½ tsp fine sea salt
pinch of cayenne pepper
2 tbsp healthy oil

In a large bowl, add the spinach, breadcrumbs, kale, onion, Parmesan, if using, eggs, salt and cayenne pepper and mix until combined.

Heat the oil in a large frying pan over a medium heat. Once hot, drop dessertspoons of the mixture into the pan. Cook for 5 minutes on each side until browned and crisp.

Beetroot

Beets grew along the coast of Europe, Asia and North Africa long, long ago and are considered an ancient food. At first, only the beet greens were eaten, but today, we enjoy the whole vegetable.

Benefits

Beets belong to the Chenopod family along with chard, spinach and quinoa, which are showing growing health benefits. Research has proven that beetroot (beet) is good for sports players, as it increases the oxygen-carrying capacity of the blood. It will lower blood pressure, boost stamina, fight inflammation, make you run faster and may help ward off cancer. Beets are a source of nutrients called betalains that provide antioxidant, anti-inflammatory and detoxification in the body. These nutrients are in the flesh – and concentrated in the peel. In general, beets are rich in nutrients and fibre. You should eat the greens, too (see page 66). Don't be alarmed that they will create red-coloured bowel movements.

Ways to Eat

- Steam, purée and add to hummus.
- Grate into salads or smoothies.
- Add julienne strips into sushi.
- Put thin slices in sandwiches.
- Roast with other vegetables.
- Enjoy beetroot risotto.
- Add to kebabs.
- Use in savoury tarts.
- Look up beetroot fritter recipes.
- Roast small chunks until tender, then add goat's cheese, hazelnuts, put on a bed of rocket (arugula) and add lemony dressing.
- Make chocolate beetroot cake or grate into cake instead of carrots.

How to Use

Scrub beetroots with a good vegetable brush, cut the ends off and trim the rough, thick skin off the end. The betalain nutrients are lost from food as the cooking time increases, so cook beetroot for a maximum of 15 minutes.

Borscht

I prefer to eat beetroot (beet) raw, but if you're cooking them, for me it's either beetroot chips or borscht. There are endless iterations of borscht, some of them with quite complicated flavours, but this is a simple classic. It is a dairy-free version, but you can thicken and richen it up with Greek yogurt, which also makes it pretty pink.

Serves: 4
Prep: 10 minutes
Cook: 15–20 minutes

3 beetroot (beet) (700g/1lb 9oz), unpeeled with tough skin at the end removed, washed and roughly chopped
1 onion, chopped
950ml/33fl oz/4 cups water
1 tbsp lemon juice
1 tsp Worcestershire sauce
½ tsp celery salt
½ tsp fine sea salt
Greek yogurt, to serve (optional)

Put the beetroot, onion and water in a medium saucepan and bring to the boil over a high heat. Reduce the heat to low and simmer, covered, for 15–20 minutes until the beetroot is tender.

Remove from the heat and whizz in a food processor or blender until smooth.

Add the lemon juice, Worcestershire sauce, celery salt and salt. When cool, put in the fridge to chill. Serve with Greek yogurt if desired.

Onions & Leeks

Onions and leeks are related and share many beneficial, health-promoting compounds. Held in very high esteem, onions were prized by the Egyptians, who used them as money and put them in the tombs of kings ready for the afterlife. The Greeks and Romans revered leeks for their beneficial effect on the throat. Both onions and leeks are important in culinary and therapeutic traditions.

Benefits

Onions are better studied than leeks, and are notable for sulphur-containing compounds that give onions their strong smell and many of their beneficial effects. Leeks and onions both provide well-documented protection for the heart and blood vessels. Beyond that, because leeks are so similar in makeup to onions, they probably provide the same benefits, such as support for rheumatoid arthritis, atherosclerosis, type 2 diabetes and cancer prevention.

Onions and leeks also contain a flavonoid called quercetin, which has antibacterial properties that if simmered gently for soups, stocks and stews are not damaged or lost.

Ways to Eat

- Fry with your scrambled eggs.
- Sauté chopped onions and tomatoes in extra virgin olive oil, add oregano and lemon juice and serve with eggs or brunch.
- Use to make salsa.
- Eat onion soup or leek and sweet potato soup.
- Make gazpacho.
- Add to green, pasta, rice, bean, grain and mixed salads.
- Add chopped onion or leek to rice when cooking.
- Toss with balsamic vinegar and oil and roast until soft.
- Put on top of pizza.
- Bake into savoury quiches and layer into lasagne.
- Add small, halved or quartered onions to your roast.

How to Use

Peel onions before chopping. If the gas that comes from cutting onions really bothers your eyes – and puts you off eating them – wear goggles while prepping them.

Don't worry about onions that seem really hot when you are cutting them up, as the hotter the onion is when raw, the sweeter it is when it's cooked.

Top and tail leeks before chopping them and peel the outer layer if it's very tough.

Split Pea Soup

A classic recipe, this can be made with or without ham. Having grown up eating pea soup with ham, I was surprised at how deeply flavourful it is without, thanks to just the peas. But if you would like ham in this, add one organic 450g/1lb smoked ham hock or pork shoulder (with skin and bones) with the cooking peas and water, and omit the salt.

Serves: 4
Prep: 10 minutes, plus overnight soaking
Cook: 1hour 20 minutes

500g/1lb 2oz dried split peas
2 tbsp cider vinegar
1.6 litres/56fl oz/7 cups water
2 strips kombu, chopped (optional)
4 tbsp extra virgin olive oil
2 onions, chopped
2 leeks, halved lengthways and sliced
4 celery stalks, chopped, leaves and all
8 garlic cloves, roughly chopped
2 tsp savory or dried mixed Italian herbs
2 tsp sea salt or 2 tbsp miso

Put the peas, double the volume of warm water and vinegar in a medium saucepan and soak, covered, overnight. Rinse well, add the measured water and bring to the boil over a high heat. Boil hard for 10 minutes, skimming any scum. Reduce the heat to low, add the kombu, if using, and simmer, covered, for 2 hours.

Heat the oil in a large saucepan over a medium heat. Add the onions and leeks and sauté for 10 minutes until soft and beginning to brown. Add the celery, garlic (or add this towards the end of cooking if preferred, see page 94), savory or dried herbs, peas and cooking water and gently simmer, covered, for 1 hour until completely soft. Add the salt or dissolve the miso in a little of the soup liquid, add to the soup and mix well. You can part purée it if you want a creamier consistency.

Pumpkin/Squash

One of nature's great winter foods, squash and pumpkins vary in shape, colour, size and flavour, but are generally mild and sweet. A favourite of Native Americans, winter squash were brought back to Europe by Christopher Columbus and feature regularly in American dishes today. Squash are in season in October and November, but keep well through the winter, when they can be used for warming and hearty dishes.

Benefits

Winter squash is rich in beta-carotene, which our bodies use to make vitamin A. Vitamin A helps your immune system fight infections, helps you see in low lighting, and keeps the skin and linings of some body parts, like the nose, healthy. Squash is also amazing for phytonutrients and antioxidants and is a good source of vitamin C, dietary fibre, B vitamins and many more. The pectin in squash is anti-inflammatory.

Future research will probably confirm that pumpkin and squash protect against cardiovascular disease and cancer, and help to regulate blood sugar.

Ways to Eat

• Winter squashes make wonderful winter soups and stews.
• Steamed or roasted pumpkin/squash cubes can be added to salads.
• Baked squash can be stuffed with a mixture of veg and cheese, then baked again.
• Mash winter squash and mix with rice, onion and egg to make veggie patties.
• Toss cooked cubes into grain or lentil dishes.
• Add to savoury tarts.
• Make into risotto.
• Roast in the oven with lamb or chicken.
• Use grated squash in sweet, quick breads.
• Try steamed and mashed pumpkin for a filling pie.

How to Use

Skin: You don't need to peel the skins of most squash and pumpkins as they contain wonderful fibre and soften substantially during cooking.
Seeds: Separate the seeds from the pulp, spread on a baking tray and roast in a low oven at 50°C/120°F for 25–30 minutes to keep their healthy oils.
Steam: Cut into cubes and steam over simmering water until tender.
Roast: Cut into cubes or slices, toss with olive oil and sea salt and roast until tender.

Spiced Roasted Squash

This simple side dish will add North African flavours to your meal. Ras el hanout, available from major supermarkets, contains a beautiful mix of spices (ginger, paprika, cassia, coriander, cumin, turmeric, chilli, allspice, cardamom, nutmeg and rose petals) that complement the sweetness of squash or pumpkin.

Serves: 4
Prep: 5 minutes
Cook: 60 minutes

1½ tsp cumin seeds
1 butternut squash, deseeded and cut into slices (about 800g/1lb 2oz)
3 tbsp extra virgin olive oil
1 tbsp balsamic vinegar
1½ tsp ras el hanout
½ tsp fine sea salt

Preheat the oven to 200°C/400°F/gas mark 6.

Toast the cumin seeds in a dry small frying pan over a low heat for 2–3 minutes until fragrant.

Put the squash in a large roasting dish and mix with the olive oil, vinegar, toasted cumin seeds, ras el hanout and salt. Roast in the oven for 45–60 minutes until soft. Serve hot.

Green Beans

French beans, haricot vert, snap beans or green beans used to be called string beans because of a thin string that ran down the seam, but this has been bred out of them. If you've only ever eaten tinned green beans, then you're in for treat, because these fresh beans are a completely different animal. When lightly steamed, they have a wonderful texture and flavour eaten on their own or combined in salads.

Benefits

The most widely studied benefit of green beans is their antioxidant profile. They contain vitamin C and beta-carotene (in spite of their greenness), plus a combination of antioxidants that put them head and shoulders above other peas and beans. These antioxidants support the heart and combat inflammation. Also, green beans help with the underlying chronic internal inflammation present in type 2 diabetes. Studies show that the pod is the most beneficial, so don't think you're supposed to peel them and just eat the tiny beans.

Ways to Eat

• Use raw or lightly steamed as crudités for dipping.
• Put in sushi and nori hand rolls.
• Add to green, grain, pasta, bean and mixed salads.
• Steam and mix with mustard vinaigrette.
• Make a bean, sautéed garlic and pine nut salad.
• Mix with goat's cheese, sliced red onion and walnuts.
• Put in salad niçoise.
• Mix lightly toasted pecans with steamed beans and a Manuka honey dressing.
• Sauté 1 chopped onion in 2 tablespoons extra virgin olive oil for 10 minutes, then add 2 chopped tomatoes and ¼–½ teaspoon crushed chillies and cook for another 5 minutes, add 450g/1lb beans and 4 sliced garlic cloves and sauté for another 5 minutes.
• Put on pizza.

How to Use

Green beans are best barely cooked, lightly steamed over simmering water or sautéed for 5 minutes with a healthy oil. Then they retain their crunch, along with the nutrients that make them a valuable food.

Butter Sautéed Green Beans

Simple and classic, this side dish is still a winner. You can find many tasty variations of bean salads, hot and cold, but this option always delights. I use butter here, but of course you can substitute other oils. By toasting the flaked almonds lightly, you retain their precious oils.

Serves: 4
Prep: 5 minutes
Cook: 5 minutes

25g/1oz/⅓ cup flaked almonds, soaked if time (see page 169)
2 tbsp butter
450g/1lb green beans, ends trimmed
⅛ tsp fine sea salt

Heat the butter in a large frying pan over a medium heat. When it is sizzling, add the green beans, sprinkle on the salt, stir, cover, and cook for 5 minutes. Remove from the heat, put on a serving plate and top with the almonds. Serve warm.

Broccoli

Broccoli, a member of the cabbage family and closely related to cauliflower, was first cultivated in Italy. *Broccolo* in Italian means 'cabbage sprout' and it was developed from a wild cabbage. The Italians then brought it to America. You may think of broccoli as one of those everyday vegetables that you should swap for something more exciting. Well, think again.

Benefits

Broccoli is so incredibly good for you that it's impossible to fit its attributes into one little paragraph. Broccoli improves detoxification and reduces oxidation and inflammation. Because it does these three things in unison, broccoli is seen as unique in being anti-cancer. In fact, there are around 300 studies on broccoli and cancer.

Broccoli also improves eye health, skin and digestion and the metabolism of vitamin D, and is being studied for its cardiovascular support. It is high in antioxidants, fibre, vitamin C, vitamin K, folate, manganese, iron and potassium, and contains more protein than most vegetables.

Ways to Eat

- Include with crudités for hummus and other dips.
- Make broccoli soup, then add rocket (arugula) or watercress and whizz until smooth.
- Chop finely and add raw to salads.
- Mix into grain salads.
- Steam and toss with walnut oil and a little salt.
- Steam cubed potatoes and sweet potatoes until almost soft, then add chopped broccoli and steam for another 5 minutes. Add a healthy oil, herbs and salt and mash.
- Sauté broccoli with toasted sesame oil, tamari, grated ginger, chopped garlic and salt just until tender, then add sesame seeds or furikake.
- Include in stir-fries.
- Serve raw or steamed and enjoy with tahini dip (see page 196).
- Make broccoli pesto and use instead of tomato sauce on pizzas.
- Add to pasta mixes.
- Put in cheese soufflés.
- Spiralise the stems.

How to Use

Look for firm, crisp broccoli with no yellowing or flowering. When it is really fresh, it snaps when split apart. Broccoli is best chopped into florets and steamed over simmering water for 5–7 minutes until just tender. The amount of steam time depends on how small you've cut the florets, so check after 5 minutes. Remove from the heat and leave it to cool, so it doesn't keep cooking to sogginess. You can eat the stem, although you may need to peel or cut off the tough skin before slicing into discs. Eat the tender broccoli leaves, as well, raw or lightly steamed.

Broccoli Flatbread Pizza

I've made these without sauce to save time, because it takes time to make the flatbreads. However, once the flatbreads are cooked, you simply assemble and bake. You can use tomato sauce as a base, or for a dairy-free version, skip the cheese and use Parmesan-free pesto. You can also, of course, add any traditional pizza toppings you like.

Serves: 4
Prep: 30 minutes, plus overnight soaking
Cook: 7–8 minutes per pizza

480g/1lb 1oz/4 cups chickpea (gram) flour, plus extra for dusting
½ tsp fine sea salt
570ml/20fl oz/2⅓ cups water
3–4 tbsp extra virgin olive oil
4 tbsp yogurt, kefir or lemon juice
300g/10½oz tenderstem broccoli (broccolini), cut into small florets
100g/3½oz/1 cup walnuts, soaked if time (see page 169)
150g/5½oz Gorgonzola cheese, chunked

Optional ingredients to mix into flatbreads for pizza or flatbreads in general:
2 tbsp fresh herbs like parsley, oregano, rosemary or thyme
1 tsp spices like chilli powder, ground cumin, cumin seeds, ground coriander, paprika, ground turmeric, fennel seeds, za'atar (see page 49) and/or 2 garlic cloves, minced

Put the flour and salt in a medium bowl and mix well. Add the water, 2 tablespoons of the oil and the yogurt, kefir or lemon juice, and whisk until combined with no lumps. Leave to soak, covered, for 8 hours or overnight.

Sprinkle a baking sheet with chickpea flour. Heat 2 teaspoons of the oil in large frying pan over a medium heat. Pour 1 cup of the pizza batter into the pan. It should sizzle gently. Fry for 2–3 minutes until it lifts easily and is lightly browned. Flip over onto the other side and cook for 2–3 minutes until lightly browned. Put the flatbread on the floured baking sheet and repeat until you have 4 flatbreads, adding oil as needed.

Preheat the oven to 230°C/450°F/gas mark 8. Top each flatbread with broccoli and walnuts, then add the Gorgonzola, dividing up the toppings between the four flatbreads. Bake for 7–8 minutes until the cheese has melted and the broccoli and walnuts are just beginning to brown.

Cauliflower

Cauliflower belongs to the Brassica family along with cabbage, spring greens, kale, Brussels sprouts and broccoli. Although cauliflower and broccoli are closely related, people in the West eat more broccoli and people in the East eat more cauliflower. In fact, China produces almost three-quarters of the world's cauliflower. But with cauliflower's versatility, presence in raw diets and nutritional benefits, this could shift.

Benefits

Because of the phytonutrients in cauliflower called glucosinolates, cauliflower and other cruciferous vegetables support cardiovascular, digestive, immune, inflammatory and detox systems. Cauliflower is one of the best vegetable sources of vitamin C. It has many nutrients when eaten raw and cooked, so suits all kinds of dishes.

Ways to Eat

- Make cauliflower soup with or without Cheddar cheese.
- Add it raw, steamed, sautéed, grilled or roasted to every kind of salad.
- Use in stir-fries with ginger, garlic and toasted sesame oil.
- Steam lightly and toss in a vinaigrette.
- Make cauliflower rice, mix with finely chopped veg and a nice dressing and eat in rolled-up lettuce leaves.
- Include in vegetable and meat stews and soups.
- Steam, sauté or roast and mix with ground or chopped turmeric.
- Roast with chicken or lamb.
- Cut into slices and roast with capers, extra virgin olive oil and salt.
- Use in curries.
- Chop and steam with sweet potatoes for mashed goodness.
- Try on pizza.
- Add to tacos.
- Look up amazing things to do with raw cauliflower instead of grains.
- Create cauli fritters.
- Try cauliflower 'pastry' or pizza 'dough'.

How to Use

Like all vegetables, cauliflower should be steamed for about 5 minutes until just tender – never boiled. Include the stem and leaves, too.

Cauli Bites

These are like the American tater tots (or potato croquettes) and work well for lunch or as part of a dinner. When you scoop them onto the baking tray, they can seem a bit wet to hold together very well (unless you squeeze the cauliflower out thoroughly), but they're fine once baked. If you want them firmer, you can add a tablespoon of linseed (flaxseed) and let them set for 5–10 minutes.

Makes: 40
Prep: 30 minutes
Bake: 30 minutes

600g/1lb 5oz cauliflower florets (from about
    1 cauliflower), finely chopped or pulsed in a
    blender until small and some water squeezed out
1 small leek, quartered lengthways and chopped
25g/1oz kale, finely chopped
50g/1¾oz Cheddar cheese, grated
25g/1oz Parmesan cheese, grated
2 eggs, beaten with a fork
6 tbsp chopped parsley
1 tbsp extra virgin olive oil, plus oil for greasing
½ tsp fine sea salt

Preheat the oven to 180°C/350°F/gas mark 4.

Put all the ingredients in a large bowl and mix well.

Use a large melon baller or a cookie scoop equivalent to 1½ tablespoons to take a scoopful of mixture, pressing the mixture into the scoop, then place it carefully on a lightly oiled baking tray. Bake for 15 minutes until lightly browned.

Brussels Sprouts

Brussels sprouts are thought to have originated in Belgium in the 1500s and are part of the Brassica family. They are much maligned because they are often overcooked, but they are delicious sliced raw on salads, roasted with other veggies and mixed with great ingredients like miso.

Benefits

Brussels sprouts are excellent for vitamins C and K, and a good source of a long list of other vitamins and minerals. Brussels are top of the list for their glucosinolate content, which are important phytonutrients for cancer protection. Cooking Brussels sprouts helps their fibre bind with bile acids in the digestive tract.

Ways to Eat

- Make into soups.
- Thinly slice and add raw to pasta, rice, bean, grain, green and mixed salads.
- Steam and toss with ground ginger, ground cumin, ground coriander and chilli powder.
- Roast with cauliflower and eat as a side or mix with pasta.
- Put in a large baking dish, toss with shallots cut to the same size, add oil and salt and roast in the oven until tender.
- Thinly slice and use on pizza.
- Halve and steam with cubed sweet potatoes, potatoes, onion and garlic, then mash with healthy oil and salt.

How to Use

Brussels are great eaten raw, lightly steamed or roasted. Simply trim the end and peel any damaged leaves. To ensure they cook evenly, halve any large ones from top to bottom. Cook until just tender.

Brussels & Steak Stir-fry

Not just for Christmas, Brussels sprouts can be enjoyed from August into the winter. Stir-fried beef strips, which are from eye round or top round cuts, are fine to use here, or you could use more expensive and tender sirloin tips. Served with wholegrain rice – remember the many different types – and a fresh salad, this makes a great dinner.

Serves: 4
Prep: 20 minutes
Cook: 10–11 minutes

4 tbsp plain or toasted sesame oil
450g/1lb Brussels sprouts, halved
2 garlic cloves, sliced
2 tbsp chopped ginger
1 jalapeño pepper, sliced thinly into rings
2 tbsp soy sauce or tamari
1 tbsp brown rice vinegar or cider vinegar
225g/½lb steak, sliced thinly against the grain
1 carrot, grated
1 courgette (zucchini), grated
4 spring onions (scallions), sliced
freshly ground black pepper, to taste
cooked wholegrain rice, to serve

Put the oil in a wok or large frying pan and heat over a medium–high heat. Add the Brussels, cover and cook for 5–6 minutes, stirring occasionally, until slightly browned. Reduce the heat to medium, add the garlic, ginger and jalapeño, and fry for 2 minutes. Increase the heat to high, then add the soy sauce or tamari, vinegar and steak and cook for 3–4 minutes, stirring, until cooked.

Remove from the heat and add the carrot, courgette and spring onions and mix well. Add black pepper and serve hot over a whole grain like brown rice, wild rice, barley or another of your choosing.

Celeriac

A rising star in the root vegetable world, celeriac is a knobbly, celery-flavoured root that is great mashed, added to soups and stews and used for gratin. It is also known as knob celery, celery root or turnip-rooted celery.

Benefits

Celeriac is a good source of essential minerals, vitamins, plant nutrients and fibre. It is high in iron, which is always good for anaemic and pregnant women, reduces acidity in the body, which is good for bones, and it is high in vitamin C, which is good for the immune system. It helps produce bile, needed for digestion, and helps with overall colon health. Celeriac's high vitamin K content aids brain health. Celeriac soup is prescribed by Gerson Therapy (a natural treatment for degenerative diseases), and is said to be an effective kidney cleanse.

Ways to Eat

- Make root vegetable soup.
- Grate raw into all kinds of salads.
- Make slaw with kohlrabi and apple.
- Use for mash.
- Add to roasted vegetables or roast on its own with garlic, thyme or rosemary and healthy oil.
- Slice thinly, toss with extra virgin olive oil and salt, and roast until crispy.
- Include in savoury tarts or layer into frittatas.
- Grate and bake into savoury pancakes and savoury muffins.

How to Use

Celeriac is one vegetable that needs peeling because the skin is just too tough and dirty to eat.

Celeriac Slaw

A great take on coleslaw, this side dish turns a pretty pink when you mix all the root veg together. You can swap the sunflower seeds for poppy seeds or add chopped, fresh coriander (cilantro) for variety. When you're looking for another vegetable to add to the table, this is easy, raw and delicious.

Serves: 4
Prep: 15 minutes

1 celeriac, peeled and grated
1 carrot, grated
1 small beetroot (beet), grated
5 tbsp lemon juice
4 tbsp extra virgin olive oil
3 tbsp mayonnaise
2 tsp Dijon mustard
1 tsp sunflower seeds, soaked if time (see page 183)
$\frac{1}{8}$ tsp fine sea salt

Put all the ingredients in a large bowl and mix well.

Celery

Celery and celeriac are from the same plant, but are not interchangeable in cooking. Celery is often used to start classic stocks like *odori*, the foundation of most Tuscan soups, which is a combination of celery, red onion, carrots and parsley. The holy trinity of Cajun and Creole food is onion, celery and red pepper, and many countries have a stock base that starts with a veg mix including celery.

Benefits

Celery is best known for its anti-inflammatory, digestive tract and stomach benefits. In folk medicine, celery was historically used to combat hypertension, and recent research shows interesting connections between nutrients in celery and a decreased risk of cardiovascular inflammation and a reduction in blood pressure. Celery is also full of fibre.

The Organic Advantage

The Environmental Working Group in Washington DC, a non-profit, non-partisan organisation, has celery on its top 11 foods to eat organically. In fact, celery is the worst-affected vegetable according to their research, because it is so porous and retains the poisonous chemicals it is sprayed with. Buy organic celery for clean and free-from (pesticides) veg.

Ways to Eat

- Include with crudités for dipping in hummus, guacamole, salsa and other dips.
- Use as a basis for cooking calssic stocks.
- Fill with almond butter or other healthy nut butter for a snack.
- Make soup.
- Add chopped to egg mayo, tuna mayo, crab salad and chicken salad.
- Spread with cream cheese or ricotta.
- Use in stir-fries.

How to Use

Eat celery leaves, too!

Eat raw, or steam or roast until just tender.

Celery Za'atar Tabbouleh

I don't make tabbouleh with bulgur because it's just another form of wheat, which I think is well avoided. I usually make tabbouleh with quinoa, but sometimes I leave the grain out altogether, so we can just eat a big pile of parsley and celery. This is a great green side dish.

Serves: 4
Prep: 15 minutes

For the za'atar:
1 tbsp each ground sumac, dried thyme and sesame seeds

300g/10½oz flat-leaf parsley, chopped
5 inner celery stalks with leaves, chopped
2 tomatoes, chopped
4 tbsp extra virgin olive oil
4 tbsp lemon juice
¼ tsp fine sea salt

Put the ingredients for the za'atar in a small jar and shake, or grind using a pestle and mortar (for variation, add oregano or marjoram and little sea salt).

Put the parsley, celery, tomatoes, oil, lemon juice and salt in a large bowl, add the za'atar and mix until combined.

Jerusalem Artichokes

Also known as sunchokes, Jerusalem artichokes are in the same family as sunflowers, globe artichoke and lettuces. Native to the Eastern United States and Mexico, they have no connection with Jerusalem. Americans called them girasole, which is Italian for sunflower and maybe this Chinese whispered into Jerusalem.

Benefits

Jerusalem artichokes have lots going on for them, but what's most interesting is that the majority of the carbohydrates are in the form of inulin. Inulin is not broken down in the digestive tract, but arrives undigested in the large intestine. It is ideal food for good bacteria like bifidobacteria and lactobacilli, so it helps them proliferate.

Sunchokes are a good source of minerals, in particular copper, phosphorus, potassium and iron. Copper helps reduce the effects of ageing, such as age spots, wrinkles and kidney problems. Phosphorus helps create DNA and strong bones and teeth. Potassium helps lower blood pressure, protects the heart and reduces the risk of stroke. Iron is essential for muscle health and to prevent anaemia.

Ways to Eat

• Simmer into soup.
• Slice or shave paper-thin into salads.
• Make into mash.
• Roast like potatoes with meats.
• Use to replace potatoes.

How to Use

Leave the skin on to eat the whole food and get the benefit of the fibre. You can eat them raw or steam, sauté, bake or roast until just tender.

Miso Mustard Steak with Pan-fried Artichokes

This very umami recipe combines shiitake and steak with mustard and miso – both strong flavours, but excellent with the steak here. With the artichokes as a starch, it works well with some veggies or a mixed salad.

Serves: 4
Prep: 35 minutes
Cook: 15–20 minutes

4 tbsp healthy oil
3 garlic cloves, minced
450g/1lb Jerusalem artichokes, unpeeled and sliced
250g/9oz shiitake mushrooms, sliced
200g/7oz button mushrooms, sliced
½ tsp fine sea salt, plus extra to season
6 tbsp chopped parsley
1 tbsp white miso
1 tbsp Dijon mustard
4 sirloin steaks
freshly ground black pepper

Heat 2 tablespoons of the oil in a frying pan over a medium heat. Add the garlic, Jerusalem artichokes, shiitake mushrooms, button mushrooms, salt and some black pepper and sauté for 10–15 minutes until the artichokes are soft and the mushrooms have cooked dry (so that they no longer leach moisture). Remove from the heat, add the parsley and mix well.

Put the miso and mustard in a small bowl and mix well until there are no lumps.

Heat the remaining oil in a large frying pan over a medium–high heat. Season the steaks with salt and pepper and cook for 2–3 minutes on each side for medium rare. Remove from the heat and brush the tops with a thin coating of the miso mustard. Serve with the pan-fried artichokes and mushrooms.

Globe Artichokes

Artichokes are a type of milk thistle and are the buds of very large purple flowers. Ancient Greeks and Romans celebrated artichokes for medicinal and health-giving qualities. Abundant in the spring, they are seen as a natural liver cleanser after the heavy foods of winter.

Benefits

Although they take a bit of work to get into, artichokes carry nutrition that's worth the effort, because as well as being packed with antioxidants, they are a good source of folate, fibre and vitamins C and K. Folate is a group of water-soluble B vitamins naturally found in food; folic acid is a synthetic compound used in food fortification and supplements. Adequate levels of folate are important during pre-conception and early pregnancy. Vitamin K is for bones and the brain.

Artichokes are used in traditional medicine to combat water retention and support the liver. This may be because of their phytonutrients, which have diuretic properties and improve the flow of bile.

Ways to Eat

- Whizz into bean dips.
- Use for soup.
- Add to sweet potato, egg and tuna mayo or salad.
- Add to green, pasta or grain salads.
- Put in quiches, frittatas and savoury tarts.
- Prepare garlic bread and top with artichoke hearts before baking.
- Use for bruschetta.
- Include in omelettes.
- Layer on fish or chicken with fresh spinach, Parmesan, garlic and lemon, and bake in the oven.
- Bake with chicken.
- Put on pizza – artichoke and spinach or artichoke and pancetta are perfect together.
- Whenever you see fried artichoke hearts in a restaurant, order them.
- Layer into lasagne with sliced garlic and capers.
- For young, new season artichokes, slice the raw hearts very thinly and toss with shaved Parmesan, extra virgin olive oil and sea salt.

How to Use

You can grill, roast or bake frozen hearts after thawing (cook until just tender). Or prepare whole artichokes as below.

Steamed Globe Artichokes with Mustard Vinaigrette

Here is the simplest way to enjoy artichokes. Just steam over simmering water and enjoy the leaves and heart dipped in vinaigrette or melted butter. Or cook a big batch and add the chopped hearts to salads. You can also make a mixture of grated Parmesan, parsley, garlic, butter and breadcrumbs to stuff between each leaf before steaming. Then pull a leaf and scrape the filling and soft part of the leaf into your mouth.

Serves: 4
Prep: 5 minutes
Cook: 20–30 minutes

4 globe artichokes, stalks trimmed
4 spring onions (scallions), thinly sliced
1 garlic clove, pressed
1 tbsp Dijon mustard
2 tbsp extra virgin olive oil
1 tbsp cider vinegar
¼ tsp fine sea salt

Steam the artichokes over simmering water until the leaves come away easily. Remove from the heat and leave to cool. In a jar or small bowl, mix the spring onions, garlic, mustard, olive oil, vinegar and salt until combined. Dip the warm leaves into the vinaigrette, scraping the soft edible part into your mouth with your teeth, then remove the hairy choke and share out the heart.

Seed Sprouts

Sprouting profoundly transforms seeds or beans. Unless you grow your own food and are lucky enough to pick fruit off the tree and veg off the vine to munch on, sprouts are one of the few living foods you will eat. Once vegetables and fruits are picked, their nutritive value starts to decrease. But seed and bean sprouts like adzuki bean, alfalfa, broccoli, China Rose, lentils, mung, radish and sunflower, are living and growing.

Benefits

Because sprouts are still growing in the pot or bag in which you buy them, they are teeming with enzymes and loaded with vitamin C. The Chinese, in their wisdom, carried mung beans on long ocean voyages hundreds of years ago and sprouted them to avoid scurvy. Sprouts are highly digestible because sprouting is like pre-digesting – enzymes are produced which help us break down food. The phytic acid is largely dissolved along with indigestible sugars in beans that cause wind. Germinating or sprouting seeds creates a huge increase in carotene. It also increases the B vitamins, particularly vitamin B2, B5 and B6. If you can't buy sprouts locally, you can grow your own with a sprouting jar or sprouting kit.

A word of warning about alfalfa sprouts – because they contain an amino acid called L-canavanine, alfalfa sprouts can increase inflammation in people with Lupus and people with similar auto-immune diseases by stimulating the immune system and should therefore be avoided.

Ways to Eat

- Put on soups before serving.
- Add to every kind of salad you eat – raw or cooked.
- Make a salad of grated carrot, beetroot (beet) and courgette (zucchini), add sprouts and mix with vinaigrette.
- Take wholegrain toasts or crackers and layer avocado slices, hummus and sprouts.
- Stuff into sandwiches, pitta pockets and wraps.
- Add to stir-fries after cooking.

How to Use

Use sprouts within their sell-by date and if they smell bad, are shrinking instead of growing or are slimy, throw them out.

To help you eat lots of seed sprouts, the base recipe opposite is really simple so that you can remember it without having to continually look it up. You just need to soak equal parts of seeds to water with a pinch of salt – it really is that simple.

BASE RECIPE
Soaked & Sprouted Seeds

You can use this general method for other recipes in the book that call for soaked seeds. Simply stop at the end of the first step, or carry on if you want the seeds to sprout.

Step 1: Soak 70g/2½oz/½ cup/8 tbsp seeds in 120ml/4fl oz/½ cup/8 tbsp water with a pinch of salt in a sprouting jar or jar or bowl for 8 hours or overnight. Rinse until the water runs clear and drain, either through the sprouting lid or a colander. You can use these as soaked seeds or keep going for sprouts.

Step 2: For the next 2–3 days, rinse and drain the seeds at least twice a day and leave them in a sprouting jar or a regular jar with mesh over it. They should be well drained and have air circulating. Keep sprouts in the fridge and use within 2–3 days to avoid mould.

Egg Foo Yung

Although sprout lovers may consider beansprouts boring, they are the most widely available if you don't have a good health-food store nearby. Seed and beansprouts, best eaten raw, are easy to use in salads, sandwiches and burgers. This recipe cooks them a bit, but beansprouts are sturdy. This recipe works for breakfast, lunch or dinner.

Serves: 4
Prep: 10 minutes
Cook: 12 minutes

8 eggs, beaten with a fork
¾ tsp fine sea salt
1 onion, chopped
400g/14oz/4 cups beansprouts
25g/1oz/2 tbsp butter or healthy oil
soy sauce or tamari, to serve

Beat the eggs and salt together until combined. Mix in the onion and beansprouts.

Heat the butter or oil in a large frying pan over a medium-high heat. Pour the mixture into pools, about ½ cup each, to form patties about 10cm/4 inches wide. Cook for 3 minutes until browned and until you can flip them over, then brown on the other side. Or fill the bottom of the pan, cook for 12 minutes covered, loosen the sides, slide onto a serving plate and cut into triangles. Serve with soy sauce or tamari.

Peas

Peas are one of the first food crops cultivated by humans many thousands of years ago and today are grown nearly everywhere in the world and eaten fresh or cooked from dry. They are useful in organic agriculture as a nitrogen-fixing crop.

Benefits

There is a lack of studies that directly link peas to improved health, but they contain a wonderful range of nutrients with generally proven health benefits. Peas have a brilliant combination of protein and fibre, which slows down digestion and helps regulate blood sugar levels. They are absolutely packed with an amazing list of antioxidant and anti-inflammatory nutrients, which together lower the risk of heart disease, type 2 diabetes and arthritis. Excessive inflammation and oxidative stress together are risk factors in the development of cancers.

Ways to Eat

- For a great spread or dip, blend frozen thawed or fresh peas, grated Parmesan, fresh mint, lemon juice, garlic, salt and oil until combined.
- Make pea soup.
- Add to green, pasta, rice, bean, grain and mixed salads.
- Include in lunchboxes and picnics.
- Stir into mash.
- Make pea and lemon risotto.
- Add to stir-fries and omelettes.
- Mix with cooked chicken, flaked almonds, chopped red onion or spring onion (scallion) and mayonnaise or plain Greek yogurt.

How to Use

Just defrost. You don't need to cook or heat fresh or frozen peas.

Pea Dumplings

Here's a lovely, fun meal to make for adults and kids. Who doesn't love wrapped and steamed parcels of tasty vegetables? The ginger makes it spicy, so you can omit or increase depending on your personal taste. And for a fish or meat variation, add in pan-fried seafood or strips of chicken, pork or beef. Serve with wholegrain rice or similar.

Makes 14
Prep: 30 minutes
Cook: 15 minutes

14 Savoy cabbage leaves
75g/2¾oz shiitake mushrooms, chopped
75g/2¾oz red or green cabbage, grated
75g/2¾oz carrot, grated
150g/5½oz/1 cup peas
40g/1½oz/½ cup (about 5) spring onions (scallions), sliced
2 tsp chopped or grated ginger (optional)
2 garlic cloves, crushed
2 tbsp toasted sesame oil or extra virgin olive oil
2 tsp soy sauce or tamari

Cut the tough part of the rib out of the cabbage leaves. Steam the leaves over simmering water for 2–3 minutes until just soft.

Put the shiitake mushrooms, cabbage, carrot, peas, spring onions, ginger, if using, garlic, oil and soy sauce or tamari in a large bowl and mix well.

Put 2 tablespoons of the mixture into each cabbage leaf. Fold the sides in, then tightly roll up and wrap the filling. Put in a steamer basket, seam-side down, and steam for 10–12 minutes until hot all the way through.

Sweet Potato

Found in Central and South America, this incredibly healthy tuber is sometimes referred to as yams in America. Sweet potatoes are in the morning glory family, however, and are not the same as African yams, which are related to palms and grasses. Because of their natural sweetness, sweet potatoes are used in both savoury and sweet dishes. And if you eat sweet potatoes with healthy oil, you increase the absorption of the wonderful beta-carotene.

Benefits

Sweet potatoes get an extra star for being among the healthiest vegetables you can eat. They rank highly because of their fibre, complex carbohydrates, protein, natural sugars, vitamin C, iron and calcium. With their lovely orange colour, sweet potatoes are also one of the best sources of beta-carotene. Among the many benefits that they offer, sweet potatoes stand out for their antioxidant and anti-inflammatory value. Even though they are sweet, sweet potatoes have so much fibre that they help regulate blood sugar levels.

The Organic Advantage

Sweet potatoes are another high pesticide residue crop in England and are worth seeking out organically.

Ways to Eat

- Add some steamed and mashed to your pancakes.
- Create dips with sweet potato, yogurt and cumin or curry powder.
- Use in soups with spices like curry and ginger.
- Use instead of potatoes.
- Julienne and steam, sauté or roast with other veggies.
- Make sweet potato miso mash.
- Bake and enjoy hot with dinner.
- Make sweet potato fries by slicing into wedges, tossing with healthy oil, salt and herbs if you like, and roasting at 200°C/400°F/gas mark 6 for 30 minutes until crisp.
- Use in frittatas.
- Chop and steam with spinach or kale and use with mozzarella for quesadillas.
- Steam small chunks and add to burritos.
- Add to lamb stew.
- Roast with chicken.
- Use for pie instead of pumpkin.
- Steam and mash with banana, chopped walnuts and cinnamon for dessert, topped with plain Greek yogurt if you like.
- Make baked goods like sweet potato cookies, scones and cakes.

How to Use

Leave the skin on your sweet potatoes, peeling or cutting out any blemishes as necessary. Sometimes, you might want to peel sweet potatoes for sweet potato brownies or scones because the skin on the chunks of sweet potato makes it hard to cut the baked treat.

Sweet Potato Super Mash

This 'super mash' is a variation on colcannon, an Irish mash that combines potatoes with cabbage. You can add in grated carrot or beetroot (beet), combine broccoli with the kale, sprinkle with soaked seeds or vary in so many other ways. If you omit the cheese, add a little more salt. It's a great side dish or can be turned into a meal with some fish or meat.

Serves: 4
Prep: 25 minutes
Cook: 30 minutes

6 tbsp healthy oil
1 large onion, chopped
500g/1lb 2oz potatoes, unpeeled and chopped
500g/1lb 2oz sweet potatoes, unpeeled and chopped
2 turnips, unpeeled and chopped
360ml/12fl oz/1½ cups water or stock
225g/8oz kale or spinach, roughly chopped
1½ tbsp red rice miso or other type (or 1½ tsp fine sea salt)
125g/4½oz/1 cup grated Cheddar cheese, optional
2–4 spring onions (scallions), sliced into rings

Heat the oil in a large saucepan over a medium heat. Add the onion and sauté for 10 minutes until soft and beginning to brown. Add the potatoes, sweet potatoes, turnips and water or stock and simmer for 15 minutes until almost soft. Add the kale or spinach and simmer for 5 minutes. Roughly mash the mixture, then dissolve the miso in little hot water, add the cheese, if using, and mix well. Serve and garnish with spring onions.

Sweet Potato Scones

Steamed, mashed sweet potato plus wholegrain spelt flour form the basis of these healthy scones. Devour them warm from the oven for breakfast or afternoon tea. For a dairy-free version, use 50g/1¾oz extra virgin olive oil instead of the butter and vinegar and water instead of the yogurt, and simply toss it in with a fork.

Makes: 12
Prep: 25 minutes, plus 10 minutes steaming
Bake: 10–12 minutes

150g/5½oz sweet potato, peeled and chopped into chunks
240g/8½oz/2 cups wholegrain spelt flour, plus extra for dusting
1½ tsp bicarbonate of soda (baking soda)
¼ tsp fine sea salt
60g/2¼oz cold butter, cubed
1 egg, beaten with a fork
3–6 tbsp plain yogurt (or 1 tbsp vinegar and 2–5 tbsp water)

Steam the sweet potato over simmering water until completely soft. Remove from the heat, mash, transfer to a bowl and put in the fridge to cool for 15 minutes. Preheat the oven to 180°C/350°F/gas mark 4.

In a large bowl, mix the flour, bicarbonate of soda (baking soda) and salt. Rub in the butter until it resembles coarse breadcrumbs. Add 3 tablespoons of the yogurt to the sweet potato to cool it further and mix in the egg. Add to the flour mixture and toss with a fork.

Gather the dough into a ball, adding extra yogurt, a tablespoon at a time, if the mixture is too dry. On lightly floured greaseproof paper, roll out the dough to a 14 x 21cm/5½ x 8¼ inch rectangle, 2cm/¾ inch high. Cut into six 7cm/2¾ inch squares and then cut in half so you have 12 triangles. Or use a 5cm/2 inch pastry cutter to cut circles, re-rolling dough remnants until finished.

Place on a baking sheet and bake for 10–12 minutes until lightly browned. Serve warm with butter.

Salad Leaves

Lettuce is a leaf vegetable cultivated long ago by ancient Egyptians and revered by Greeks and Romans not only as a food, but also as a therapeutic medicine. Today, leaves like chicory (endive), lamb's lettuce, rocket (arugula) and Romaine add colour, crunch, flavour, freshness, variety and vitamins to meals and snacks throughout the day.

Benefits

Generally these salad leaves contain a wealth of nutrients and flavour. They have a high water content, vitamin C and K, fibre, beta-carotene and folate. You can vary salad mixes with soaked seeds, nuts, sprouts, avocado, olives and wonderful dressings with super ingredients like oils, lemon/lime, miso, ginger and tahini, and you can create a new dish every day. Avocado eaten with salad leaves increases the uptake of carotenoids.

The Organic Advantage

Non-organic lettuce can be sprayed up to 100 times. Choose organic lettuce, which is free of pesticide, herbicide and fungicide residues.

Ways to Eat

- Include in smoothies to add nutrients and water.
- Use Romaine and chicory (endive) to scoop hummus and other dips.
- Make green and mixed salads.
- Stir chopped or shredded crisp lettuce into soup when serving, for flavour and texture.
- Add to sandwiches and wraps.
- Swap Romaine and chicory (endive) for grain-based wraps, tortillas, pitta and spring rolls.
- Lightly grill radicchio, little gem and hearts of Romaine and serve as a side dish with olive oil and salt or a blue cheese dressing.
- Shred or chop and use instead of rice for dhal, curry or bean dishes.
- Add to spring roll fillings.

How to Use

Salad leaves should be washed and spun or towelled dry. If your organic leaves contain bugs and slugs, dilute 2 teaspoons bicarbonate of soda (baking soda), fine sea salt or vinegar in a large bowl of water and put the salad in for 5 minutes.

It's nice to tear or cut salad leaves into bite-sized pieces. This means you can make salad in a smaller bowl as it takes up less space, it is easier plated for the same reason and it is easier to eat.

Chicory Salad

This wonderful salad combines the crunch of chicory with the creaminess of Gorgonzola and the unctuousness of walnuts. The dressing works perfectly and the dish looks stunning with the mix of red and green leaves.

Serves: 4
Prep: 20 minutes

6 tbsp extra virgin olive oil
3 tbsp lemon juice
1 tbsp Dijon mustard
¼ tsp fine sea salt
3 green chicory (endive), chopped
3 red chicory (endive), chopped
100g/3½oz Gorgonzola picante, chopped
50g/1¾oz/½ cup walnuts, soaked if time (see page 169), roughly chopped

Put the oil, lemon juice, mustard and salt in a small jar and shake vigorously until combined. Put the chicory, Gorgonzola and walnuts in a medium bowl. Pour the dressing over the salad and mix well.

Okra

Okra is a flowering plant known in parts of the world as ladies' fingers or *bhindi*. We eat the seed pods, which are used in dishes from the Caribbean to China to Louisiana. Okra is a ridged, green, slightly fuzzy pod that contains rows of edible seeds. It is great for thickening soups and gumbo.

Benefits

Okra is filled with vitamins, minerals, organic compounds and mucilaginous fibre and improves digestive health, helps vision, protects the heart, boosts skin health, lowers blood pressure, prevents certain cancers, supports cardiovascular health, assists the immune system and strengthens bones. The high levels of beta-carotene and antioxidants are what help protect the skin and improve vision, and the potassium supports high blood pressure and the heart. Okra will significantly increase your fibre intake. Mucilaginous fibre moves food through your digestive tract by adding bulk, meaning less bloating, cramping, constipation and wind.

Ways to Eat

- Sauté okra in extra virgin olive oil with ground coriander, paprika or cayenne and celery seeds.
- Or sauté okra in extra virgin olive oil with garlic, thyme, fresh basil and crushed chillies.
- Add to veggie and seafood skewers to cook on a barbecue.
- Toss in extra virgin olive oil, balsamic vinegar, salt and pepper and grill. Serve with Yogurt Dip (see page 228).
- Make okra gumbo.
- Eat bhindi bhaji (okra curry) in a good Indian restaurant or find a good recipe to make at home.

How to Use

Trim and slice okra to release the goo that will thicken gumbo, soups and stews beautifully. To avoid the goo in stir-fries and other more delicate dishes, use okra whole, trimming the stem end as little as possible.

Cook for the shortest time until the okra is just tender.

Crispy Okra

The polenta (cornmeal) coating makes these okra nice and crispy, while cayenne pepper adds a simple uplifting spiciness. Serve this as a side dish (see photograph on page 115) when you want a more unusual vegetable. This dish works on its own, but with the chipotle mayo, it's fabulous.

Serves: 4
Prep: 5 minutes
Cook: 12 minutes per batch

75g/2¾oz/½ cup polenta (cornmeal)
¼–½ tsp cayenne pepper, to taste
1 tsp fine sea salt
175g/6oz okra, untrimmed
2 egg whites (add the yolks to Turmeric Scramble, see page 105)
4 tbsp extra virgin olive oil
chipotle mayo, to serve (see page 125, optional)

In a small baking dish, mix the polenta, cayenne pepper and salt and pour onto a plate. Dip each piece of okra in the egg white, wipe off any excess and lay in the polenta mix. Roll in the mixture without touching them or just hold the little stem, sprinkling polenta on if necessary. Put them on a plate.

Heat 2 tablespoons of the oil in a large frying pan over a medium heat. Add the dipped okra in batches and gently fry for 12 minutes, turning a few times so that they are browned on a few sides. Add more oil to the pan as necessary.

Mushrooms

Although usually considered a vegetable, mushrooms are not a plant and do not need soil or sun to grow. They are a fungus, a living organism without roots, leaves, flowers or seeds and grow on decaying matter like leaves or trees or fallen logs. Mushrooms are very nutritious and support many systems in the body.

Benefits

Mushrooms contain phytonutrients (plant nutrients) that are different from vegetables and support our immune systems and reduce inflammation. They also contain selenium, which is missing from many fruits and veggies. Because mushrooms have a strong defence against bacterial attack, they are an effective antibiotic for us. Button mushrooms, crimini and Portobello stand head to head with other more exotic mushrooms in terms of their nutritional profile.

The Organic Advantage

Non-organically grown mushrooms carry a risk of pesticides, heavy metals and other contaminating products used in conventional farming.

Ways to Eat

- Sauté with healthy oil, chopped garlic and salt, then toss with fresh parsley as a side dish or topping for toast.
- Sauté with healthy oil and balsamic vinegar and use for bruschetta.
- Combine roasted or grilled mushrooms with bitter greens.
- Bake with Brussels sprouts and eggs.
- Stuff with delicious fillings and bake.
- Grill mushroom and pesto paninis.
- Use in quiches and frittatas.
- Add to omelettes.
- Make mushroon soup.
- Slice raw and add to salads.
- Make mushroom risotto.
- Replace the meat in a cheeseburger with a large grilled Portobello mushroom.
- Throw into stir-fries.
- Top pizza with mushroom slices.
- Include with kebabs.
- Find an orzo (barley) and mushroom recipe.
- Make pasta dishes and combine with other ingredients.
- Layer into lasagne.
- Simmer mushrooms and sweet potato or mushrooms and beef to make a stew.

How to Use

Slice off the bottom of the mushroom stem and brush any dirt off with a brush or towel. Don't wash them as they absorb water and become soggy.

To retain the maximum nutrient value, it is best if you sauté mushrooms for 7 minutes in healthy oil over a fairly high heat.

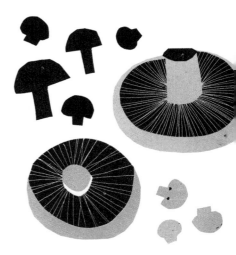

Mushroom Sloppy Joes

Sloppy Joes, unknown in England, are popular across America. The story goes that a long time ago, Joe, a cook in Iowa, added tomato sauce to his 'loose meat' or grilled mince sandwich, to be eaten with a knife and fork. These types of sandwiches, made with beef mince (ground beef), remain a staple in the US Midwest. When done with mushrooms instead of meat, it's a great veggie version of the old classic.

Serves: 4
Prep: 5 minutes
Cook: 25–30 minutes

4 tbsp extra virgin olive oil
400g/14oz button mushrooms, brushed clean and
    chopped
½ tsp fine sea salt
400g/14oz ripe tomatoes, chopped
1 red (bell) pepper, chopped
1 large onion, chopped
5 garlic cloves, minced
125ml/4fl oz/½ cup water or stock
¼ tsp chilli powder or more to taste
pinch of cayenne pepper
1 tbsp Worcestershire sauce
toasted wholegrain buns or bread, to serve

Heat the oil in a large frying pan over a medium heat. Add the mushrooms and salt and sauté for 7 minutes until the liquid is gone and the mushrooms are beginning to brown.

Add the tomatoes, red pepper, onion, garlic, water or stock, chilli and cayenne pepper, and cook over a medium–high heat for 15 minutes, stirring occasionally, until the vegetables have softened and the mixture is thick. Add the Worcestershire sauce and mix until combined.

Spoon generously onto toasted buns or bread to serve.

Shiitake

Shiitake, or Japanese forest mushrooms, are one of the most flavoursome mushrooms around. Shiitake are either grown on logs or sawdust, but most sold in supermarkets grown on sawdust are uniform, pale and cone-shaped and do not contain the quantity of polysaccharides that make natural shiitake so sought-after. A box of natural shiitake normally has a mix of different sizes, shapes and shades, with short stems.

Benefits

Almost a meat substitute, shiitake contain 18 amino acids, including all eight of the essential amino acids in the ratio considered ideal for protein. And they contain many enzymes and vitamins not normally found in plants. Research carried out in Japan since the 1930s celebrates shiitake's ability to build and stimulate the immune system because of its complex carbohydrates called polysaccharides. Shiitake are rich in a very absorbable form of iron and are also rich in B vitamins, including B12, which are not available from vegetables, but created by bacteria and fungi.

Ways to Eat

- Enjoy with eggs.
- Use in mushroom soup and miso soup.
- Fry in healthy oil and add to green, pasta, rice, bean, grain and mixed salads.
- Add to stir-fries.
- Include with noodles and fried rice.
- Brush with healthy oil and grill for 3–4 minutes.
- Sauté with onions and garlic, add chopped parsley and serve with meats or toast.
- Put on pizza.
- Use in quiches and frittatas.
- Sauté with leafy greens.
- Include in kebabs.
- Stir into risotto.

How to Use

Brush dirt off with a soft brush or paper towel. Remove the stems, which are tough and save/freeze for stocks and soups.

Simmer in a few tablespoons of broth for up to 7 minutes to preserve their goodness and release their wonderful flavour.

Dried shiitake do not have the same texture as fresh, but are perfect for soups, stews, gravies and baked dishes. Soak dried shiitake in boiled water for at least an hour. Discard the stems, which are very tough, and use the soaking water for stock.

Shiitake Spring Rolls

Here's another great meal where you can put all of the ingredients on the table and have everyone create their own. Spring roll wrappers are not the healthiest option, but you can use lettuce or cabbage leaves if you prefer. For a variation of this recipe, slice some carrots, courgette (zucchini), peppers and leeks into julienne strips, and stir-fry with green beans, garlic, ginger and shoyu.

Serves: 4
Prep: 40 minutes
Cook: 15 minutes

4 tbsp extra virgin olive oil
300g/10½oz peeled king prawns (shrimp), halved (or use strips of meat or chicken)
2 tsp lemon juice
300g/10½oz shiitake, brushed clean, stems removed and sliced
⅜ tsp fine sea salt
250g/9oz buckwheat or other wholegrain noodles
4 tbsp toasted sesame oil
2 tsp furikake (optional)
100g/3½oz green beans, steamed for 3 minutes
2 carrots, julienned
1 avocado, peeled, stoned (pitted) and julienned
1 cucumber, julienned
1 beetroot (beet), julienned
1 courgette (zucchini), julienned
1 red or yellow (bell) pepper, julienned
30g/1oz any sprouts (broccoli, China Rose, radish, fenugreek or other)
2 packs of spring roll wrappers or heart of Romaine leaves
organic hot and sweet sauce, to serve

Put 1 tablespoon of the oil in a medium frying pan and heat over a medium–high heat. Add the prawns, lemon juice and ⅛ teaspoon of the salt and sauté for 4–5 minutes until no longer translucent. Remove from the pan and put in a small bowl.

Add the remaining oil to the pan and when hot, add the shiitake and remaining salt and sauté for 7 minutes until beginning to brown. Remove from the heat and put in a small bowl.

Cook the noodles according to the package instructions, ensuring that you keep the water at a rolling boil as you add the noodles gradually so they don't clump. Immediately after cooking, rinse the starch off the noodles to prevent them from sticking. Put the noodles in a medium bowl and toss with the sesame oil and furikake, if using.

Put the beans, carrots, avocado, cucumber, beetroot, courgette, pepper and sprouts each in a separate small bowl and put all bowls on the table. Put a large bowl filled with hot water on the table in which to soften the spring rolls. Lay a softened spring roll on a plate and in a strip at the bottom edge of the plate, add noodles and other ingredients you want. Then fold the edges in and roll from the filled lower edge up until you have a parcel. Alternatively, fill a Romaine leaf with filling, fold the edges in and enjoy.

Leafy Greens

Often those old sayings are true and 'eat your greens' is certainly one of them. Leafy greens are bursting with vitamins, minerals, fibre and plant substances that protect you from diseases. They range in flavour from sweet to earthy to peppery to bitter. They are easy to buy, easy to use and completely versatile. You can always make a meal when you have greens in the fridge or garden.

Benefits

There are too many good things to say about leafy greens! All cruciferous veggies deliver a wide spectrum of nutrients that benefit a broad variety of systems in the body. A few highlights of leafy greens is that they lower the risk of cancer, cardiovascular disease and type 2 diabetes. They are also good for bone health, immune function, eye health and combatting inflammation.

The Organic Advantage

When grown conventionally, leafy greens often have high concentrations of organophosphate insecticides, which are very toxic to our nervous system. Buy organic to avoid this risk.

Ways to Eat

- Cook with eggs.
- Add to soups and stews at the end of cooking.
- Steam and add to every kind of salad.
- Steam and chop and include in sushi and nori handrolls.
- Add to frittata.
- Put on top of pizza.
- Sauté with extra virgin olive oil, chopped or pressed garlic, lemon juice, sea salt and pepper.
- Combine with sweet potato at the end of steaming to include in healthy mash.
- Sauté with mushrooms.
- Layer into lasagne.
- Thinly slice and add to stir-fries.
- Include in risotto.
- Stuff into pasta with goat's cheese or ricotta.
- Use with enchiladas.

- **Beet Greens:** less bitter than other greens, they need much more rinsing before cooking
- **Broccoli Rabe/Rapini:** nicely bitter greens. These need a little more cooking to reduce their bitterness. Or blanch briefly in boiling water.
- **Brussels Tops:** cut off the tough skin, roughly chop and sauté with butter.
- **Cabbage:** ferment into sauerkraut, grate into coleslaw, fill and steam or steam and use as wraps.
- **Collard Greens:** mild flavoured, collard greens are used like other greens and also as wraps.
- **Dandelion Greens:** yes, go and pick them outside – rinse well – and add raw to salads or cook like other leafy greens.
- **Kale:** best cooked (see page 31).
- **Mustard Greens:** with a spicy mustard flavour, these are great with fresh lemon juice.

- **Turnip Greens:** these bitter greens need less cooking than other greens and are traditionally eaten with pork in the Southern US.
- **Spinach:** best cooked.
- **Swiss Chard:** like spinach, red or green chard is best cooked.

How to Use

To wash greens, swish them around in a sink or large bowl full of water and repeat until the water is clear. If you are using organic greens containing bugs, add a tablespoon of bicarbonate of soda (baking soda), fine sea salt or vinegar and leave the greens to sit for 5 minutes to get rid of them.

Steam or sauté for 8–10 minutes until just soft.

Super Greens Sauté

Use any combination of greens for this supercharged side dish. You could almost eat a different version of this sauté every day by just swapping in different greens, using a different oil, changing the spice, switching miso with tamari and alternating or omitting the seeds.

Serves: 4
Prep: 5–10 minutes
Cook: 6 minutes

3 tbsp coconut oil
1 tbsp freshly grated turmeric or 1 tsp ground turmeric
200g/7oz mixed greens, roughly chopped
½ tbsp miso, dissolved in 1 tbsp water
3 tbsp sunflower seeds, soaked if time (see page 183)

Heat the coconut oil in a large frying pan over a medium heat. Add the turmeric and sauté for 1 minute until fragrant. Add the greens and sauté for about 5 minutes until just cooked. Remove from the heat, add the miso and sunflower seeds and mix until combined.

Ricotta & Spinach Gnocchi

If you like, you can boil these in the traditional way. Put them in boiling water, wait until they float, cook for another 2 minutes, drain and then brown them off in the frying pan with the sage. But I find it much quicker and easier to just cook and brown them as below.

Serves: 4
Prep: 30 minutes
Cook: 8–10 minutes per batch

175g/1lb 7oz fresh spinach
250g/9oz ricotta cheese, drained
80g/3oz/1 cup grated Parmesan cheese
60g/2oz/½ cup wholegrain flour, plus flour for dusting
2 eggs, beaten with a fork
½ tsp ground nutmeg
½ tsp fine sea salt
2 tbsp extra virgin oil
12 sage leaves

Put the spinach in a bowl, pour boiling water over it and let it sit for 2 minutes. Drain, squeeze out the liquid and chop.

In a medium bowl, mix the chopped spinach, ricotta, Parmesan, beaten eggs, nutmeg and salt until a sticky dough forms.

Put greaseproof paper on the worktop or table and dust with flour. Roll ovals or balls of dough in your hands and then in the flour until coated. In a large frying pan, heat the olive oil over a medium heat. Fill the pan with gnocchi, flatten the balls into puck shapes and fry gently for 4–5 minutes each side. Add the sage leaves at the end to cook for 2–3 minutes until crisp.

Fruit

Avocado

Avocados are rather interesting. They are a fruit and they are composed of great fat, two words which we don't usually think of in combination. In fact, this beautiful fruit is one of the fattiest plant foods you can eat. And it carries with it almost every vitamin and mineral recommended for daily intake, except vitamin B12.

Benefits

Most of the fat in avocados is oleic acid or omega-9, which is very beneficial for the heart. An avocado contains more potassium than a banana and 20 different vitamins and minerals. Potassium supports healthy blood pressure levels, which also supports the heart. Avocados also contain about 7 per cent fibre by weight.

Avocados are almost a perfect food. They benefit the heart, joints, hair, skin, eyes, blood pressure and diabetes. When you eat them with salad leaves or leafy greens that are low in fat but high in carotenoids, avocados help with the absorption of vitamin A.

Ways to Eat

- Use in smoothies instead of yogurt for added creaminess and good fats.
- Make guacamole – classic style or souped-up with turmeric.
- Add to salads and sandwiches.
- Blend with oil and vinegar for creamy dressings.
- Put with mozzarella and tomato.
- Add to gazpacho or other cold soup.
- Top soups with chopped avocado.
- Purée it, mix with soured cream and put on baked potatoes.
- Fill the seed hole with tuna or crab mayonnaise or with balsamic vinegar and healthy oil, or with oil and vinegar or lemon juice.
- Cut in half, crack an egg into each seed hole, sprinkle with hot sauce and bake at 220°C/425°F/gas mark 7 for 12 minutes.
- Swap for mayonnaise in chicken salad or egg mayonnaise.
- Replace the butter in mashed potatoes with mashed avocado.
- Dip slices in beaten egg, roll in cooked quinoa and bake at 200°C/ 400°F/gas mark 6 until crisp.
- Chop and put in quesadillas.
- Mash and feed to babies.
- Replace butter in cake with avocado using a one-to-one ratio.
- Try dairy-free avocado cheesecake.
- Make raw dairy-free icing: blend 1 avocado with 3–4 tbsp each of raw cacao powder and maple syrup.

How to Use

Cut the avocado in half from end to end, twist and separate the halves, then gently knife the stone and remove. Cut each half into thirds or quarters and peel like a banana to retain the dark flesh under the skin that is particularly rich in antioxidants.

To get the optimum nutrition from avocados, it is best to enjoy them raw to preserve their great fat content.

Guacamole

Firmish avocados are ideal in salads and on sandwiches, but when they get soft, it's got to be guacamole. Great as a starter, side or snack, guacamole is a crowd-pleaser. You can serve with thin wholegrain toast, crackers, organic tortillas or crudités. You may want to double this recipe!

Serves: 4
Prep: 15 minutes

2 ripe avocados, peeled, stoned (pitted) and mashed
1 ripe tomato, finely chopped
2 tbsp finely chopped spring onions (scallions)
2 tbsp chopped coriander (cilantro)
2 tbsp chopped parsley
1½ tbsp lime juice
1 small garlic clove, crushed
½ tsp ground cumin
½ tsp hot sauce
½ tsp fine sea salt
crudités, crackers, thin wholegrain toast or organic tortillas, to serve

Put all the ingredients in a bowl and mix until combined.

Avocado Goddess Sandwich

Goddess Dressing originates from a hotel in San Francisco that made it to honour George Arliss who was opening in a play called 'The Green Goddess' in the early 1920s. Various versions of the dressing have been created since then with soured cream, tahini or mashed avocado. We love it with grilled halloumi, but smoked salmon makes a delicious dairy-free version.

Serves: 4
Prep: 30 minutes
Cook: 6 minutes

250g/8¾oz halloumi, sliced, or 100–150g/3½–5⁄4oz smoked salmon
8 sourdough bread slices, toasted
mayonnaise, for spreading
8 lettuce leaves, washed and spun dry
2 avocados, peeled, stoned (pitted) and sliced
2 tomatoes, sliced

For the dressing:
4 tbsp well-mixed tahini
4 tbsp extra virgin olive oil or toasted sesame oil
4 tbsp chopped parsley
2 tbsp lemon juice
1 tbsp chopped spring onions (scallions)
1 tbsp water
¼ tsp fine sea salt
pinch of cayenne pepper, optional

To make the dressing, put all the ingredients in a small blender or food processor and whizz for 30 seconds until smooth and combined.

Heat a frying pan over a medium–low heat and dry-fry the halloumi for 3 minutes on each side until brown. Remove from the heat. Meanwhile, chop the veg and assemble the sandwich. Spread 2 teaspoons Goddess Dressing on 4 sourdough slices. Spread mayo on the other sourdough slices. Layer two lettuce leaves, half an avocado, half a tomato and a quarter of the fried halloumi on the mayo-spread slices and top with the dressing-spread slices to make a sandwich.

Apples

An apple a day keeps the doctor away because it has many important health benefits. It's easy to take apples for granted because they are in plentiful supply and seem so ordinary. But they are well worth including regularly in your diet, and there are so many different varieties that you are bound to find one that suits your palate – whether sweet and juicy or crisp and tart.

Benefits

There is much research proving that apples provide cardiovascular and antioxidant benefits because of their pectin or water-soluble fibre and their unusual mix of polyphenols (compounds found in plants that have antioxidant properties). Recent research has focused on this unique balance of polyphenols in apples, some of which are more concentrated in the skin than the pulp. These studies have linked eating apples with a lower risk of asthma and a lower risk of lung cancer. Apples also help regulate blood sugar.

Scientists are looking at the positive effect of apples on the balance of bacteria in the digestive tract, as well, which is so important to overall health.

The Organic Advantage

A favourite with children, apples are also one of the top ten most highly sprayed food crops. Buy organic and eat whole apples without the worry of agricultural residues.

Ways to Eat

- Grate, chop or slice into parfaits, Bircher muesli, porridge (oatmeal), smoothies and smoothie bowls.
- Slice and spread with almond butter or other healthy nut butter.
- Mix with pear.
- Cut or slice, toss with lemon juice and ground cinnamon and take to the beach, on picnics or on hikes.
- Find a great raw apple pie recipe using ingredients like nuts, seeds, dates and spices.
- Blend with ground cinnamon to make raw apple sauce.

How to Use

Like all fruits and berries, apples are best eaten raw if you want all of their goodness. Eat them with their skin intact, even if a recipe calls for peeling, as the skin of the apple is unusually rich in nutrients.

Apple & Ginger Thickie

As well as simply munching on an apple a day, which I'm a firm advocate of, smoothies are a great way to enjoy apples. This simple mix is already good for you, but of course you can add many other ingredients or super powders to smoothies and smoothie bowls to boost their nutritional punch.

Serves: 2
Prep: 10 minutes, plus overnight soaking

300ml/10fl oz/1¼ cups water
50g/1¾oz/½ cup oats
2 tbsp lemon juice
2 tbsp pecans or walnuts
1 tbsp chia seeds
4 apples, cored and roughly chopped
1½–2 tbsp finely chopped ginger root

Put the water, oats, lemon juice, nuts and chia seeds in a blender and leave to soak, covered, overnight. The next morning, add the apple and ginger, and blend until smooth. Serve straight away.

Olives

Olives are drupes, or fruits with a pit or stone, and have been cultivated for possibly up to 8,000 years with some trees living up to 2,000 years. Olives need to be cured or pickled to get rid of their bitterness before they are eaten. Green olives are unripe olives; black ones are ripe olives. Traditionally, green are for eating and black are for cooking.

Benefits

About 80 per cent of the calories in olives comes from fat. Almost three-quarters of this fat is oleic acid, a monounsaturated oil linked to a reduced risk of cardiovascular diseases and high blood pressure. Olives' phytonutrient content is staggering.

They offer a wide range of antioxidant and anti-inflammatory nutrients, some of which are only found in olives. There are about 25 of these different nutrients, which benefit not only our cardiovascular system, but also our respiratory, nervous, musculoskeletal, immune, inflammatory and digestive systems. These nutrients also reduce our risk of cancer.

Ways to Eat

• Put out in bowls before or with meals.
• Stuff with cream cheese, Gorgonzola or walnut pieces for a snack or starter.
• Finely chop with capers, parsley and garlic, add extra virgin olive oil and lemon juice (or pulse in a blender) for a tapenade to enjoy on wholegrain crackers or toast.
• Blend green or black olives into hummus.
• Add to green, pasta, rice, bean, grain or mixed salads.
• Make Greek salad with chopped tomatoes, Kalamata olives, cubed feta, thinly sliced red onion, extra virgin olive oil and oregano.
• Add to garlic bread (see page 94) with some grated cheese.
• Add to ratatouille.
• Use as a pizza topping and add to red pasta sauce.
• Roast with chicken, lemon and rosemary.
• Make tuna pasta with olives and artichokes.
• Mix with chopped tomatoes, spinach and capers and bake with fish or chicken.
• Add with rosemary to your bread dough for olive bread.

How to Use

Some olives are heavily salted, so look for olives that are lower in salt. Rinsing with water can help.

Avoid tinned or jarred olives with flavour enhancers – olives are delicious on their own.

Olives marry very well with capers, anchovies, fresh or sun-dried tomatoes, artichokes, feta and garlic.

Leek, Tomato & Olive Salad

This dish always surprises and delights those who are not sure about eating a pile of leeks. It has a wonderful combination of flavours with the vinegar, Dijon mustard, leeks, tomatoes and olives, and is perfect as a starter or side dish. Ensure that the leeks are steamed to complete softness so that they cut easily and are not tough to eat.

Serves: 4
Prep: 20 minutes
Cook: 12–15 minutes

350g/12oz leeks, trimmed and quartered lengthwise
1 small shallot, minced
3 tbsp extra virgin olive oil
2 tsp red wine vinegar or cider vinegar
1½ tsp Dijon mustard
¼ tsp fine sea salt
100g/3½oz/½ cup cherry tomatoes, quartered
  lengthways
50g/1¾oz/⅓ cup pitted Kalamata or Niçoise olives,
  sliced in half lengthways
2 tbsp chopped parsley

Steam the leeks over a large pan of boiling water for 12–15 minutes until completely soft. Remove from the heat, drain and blot dry with paper towels.

In a small bowl, mix the shallot, oil, vinegar, mustard and salt until combined. Take a long serving platter and spread a tablespoon of dressing on it. Put the leeks on the platter and pour the dressing evenly across the leeks.

When you are ready to serve, sprinkle the leeks with the tomatoes, olives and parsley. Serve warm, at room temperature or chilled.

Tomatoes

Like aubergine (eggplant), peppers and potatoes, tomatoes are members of the nightshade family. Thought of as a vegetable, a tomato is not only a fruit, but is actually a berry because it has only one ovary. But because tomatoes work well with other savoury ingredients, tomatoes are usually classed with vegetables. They are an incredibly important ingredient in many cultures and cuisines.

Benefits

The ordinary tomato holds a wealth of nutrients, but their true fame lies in the organic compound lycopene that they have in abundance. Lycopene – which comes from cooked tomatoes – protects the body against cancer-causing free radicals.

Tomatoes are also high in vitamins A, C and K, as well as having notable amounts of B6, thiamin and folate. One tomato will meet 40 percent of your vitamin C requirement for a day. They are also good for fibre and contain protein.

The Organic Advantage

Tomatoes are one of the most highly sprayed vegetable crops in the UK and should be purchased organically. Grow some in a pot outside or on a balcony if you have a sunny spot.

Ways to Eat

- Cut cherry tomatoes in half and use as hummus scoops.
- Make fresh or cooked salsa.
- Make bruschetta.
- Enjoy slices on toast with mayo.
- Make gazpacho.
- Eat tomato soup – as it is or over wholegrain rice.
- Add to soups, stews and casseroles.
- Eat Caprese salad made from tomatoes, mozzarella, extra virgin olive oil, balsamic vinegar and salt (and avocado and basil, if you like).
- Make tomato-based salads like tabbouleh (parsley and bulgur salad), panzanella (Italian bread salad) and fattoush (Levantine bread salad) or just toss with cut cucumber and avocado with some mayo or vinaigrette.
- Include in sandwiches and wraps.
- Put tomatoes in cheese on toast or grilled cheese sandwiches.
- Create pasta sauces with simmered tomatoes.
- Cook tomatoes with beans and spices and serve over rice.
- Use tomato purée (paste) – one of the best sources of lycopene there is.
- Halve them, brush with oil and salt and grill.
- Stuff and eat raw or baked.

How to Use

Often tomatoes are blanched and peeled to remove the skins, but if you chop or finely chop them, the skin is not a problem. I believe in eating the whole food whenever possible, and also, tomato skins contain much of the beneficial carotenoids and flavonols, so you'll get the maximum nutrition by eating the skin and all.

When cutting tomatoes, even if your knives are incredibly sharp, it is easier to use a serrated knife.

Tinned tomatoes have a higher risk of leaching BPA (bisphenol A) – an industrial chemical used to coat the inside of metal products – because of their acidity. Chop or purée them yourself or look for chopped tomatoes or passata in glass jars.

Don't refrigerate tomatoes because they develop an unpleasant sponginess.

Slow-roasted Tomato Bruschetta

Bruschetta is a great way to enjoy tomatoes. Slow-roasting deepens the tomato flavour, but you can skip the roasting if you want, for a quick and tasty lunch or a starter for dinner. Baking the oiled bread gives a crispness that is different to simply toasting it.

Serves: 4
Prep: 10 minutes
Cook: 55–60 minutes (or 10–15 minutes if not roasting tomatoes)

450g/1lb (about 6 tomatoes), halved
4 tbsp extra virgin olive oil, plus oil for greasing
4 wholegrain bread slices
1 garlic clove, peeled and halved
2 tbsp chopped basil leaves
½ tbsp balsamic vinegar
⅛ tsp fine sea salt

Preheat the oven to 200°C/400°F/gas mark 6. Grease a baking dish, put the tomatoes in it, skin-side up, and bake for 45 minutes until browned and soft.

Put the bread on a baking tray and use a pastry brush to apply oil to one side. Bake the bread for 10–15 minutes until crisp. Rub the cut end of the garlic on each slice of bread.

Roughly chop the tomatoes and add the rest of the oil, basil, vinegar and salt and toss until combined. Spread evenly on the bread and serve.

Lemons & Limes

Lemons were historically vital in keeping scurvy at bay on long sea journeys. Today they are considered valuable for many reasons and are a must-have in the kitchen. As well as being delightful squeezed into water for a refreshing drink on a hot day, there is a very long list of cooking and baking uses for lemons and limes, and they are also useful around the home to freshen and cleanse.

Benefits

Although people consider lemon and lime to be acidic, their effect on the body is to alkalize. Lemon and lime juice is used to treat kidney stones, reduce stroke and lower body temperature. They are high in vitamin C and a list of other vitamins and minerals that is surprisingly long for a fruit so universally appealing. The pectin in lemons and limes is good for colon health and is antibacterial. Lemons and limes also stop coughs and are soothing for sore throats.

The Organic Advantage

If you're zesting lemons and limes (which you should because the zest is excellent added to baking and cooking), avoid the wax and the chemical residues on the outer skin by only buying organic.

Ways to Eat

- Add to smoothies.
- Start your day with half a lemon or lime squeezed into warm water, for a gentle morning cleanse.
- Squeeze on your pancakes.
- Use in dressings as a change from vinegar.
- Mash with avocado, hot sauce and tomatoes for guacamole.
- Squeeze the juice from lemon or lime wedges onto fish and seafood.
- Sprinkle the juice on grilled meats and vegetables.
- Mix juice with pasta and grain dishes to lift the flavour.
- Make lemonade and limeade.
- Create a risotto with lemon or lime and zest.
- Use the zest in fishcakes (see page 127) or sweet cakes.
- Make lemon meringue or Key lime pie.
- Try Coconut Lime Squares (see page 178).

How to Use

Like figs, lemons and limes should be picked at the peak of ripeness, as they don't ripen once they're off the tree. They should be stored at room temperature.

If you have lemons or limes that are starting to get old, zest them (avoiding the bitter white pith underneath), then pack the zest in a teaspoon or tablespoon measure, put in the freezer to harden, pop them out and freeze in non-PVC clingfilm (plastic wrap). Juice ageing lemons or limes, freeze the juice in ice-cube trays and store in non-PVC ziplock bags to use in refreshing drinks and lemony recipes.

Lemon Pudding Cake

This delightful and refreshing dessert separates into two layers as it bakes, with cake on top and pudding underneath. Leftovers aren't great as they get a bit watery, but I always make a double batch, particularly for guests, and it always disappears.

Serves: 4
Prep: 20 minutes
Bake: 30 minutes

3 lemons
125ml/4fl oz/½ cup rice milk
125ml/4fl oz/½ cup yogurt
3 large eggs, separated
60g/2¼oz/4 tbsp butter, melted, plus butter for greasing
135g/4¾oz ⅔ cup organic sugar
30g/1oz/¼ cup wholegrain spelt or gluten-free flour
¼ tsp fine sea salt

Preheat the oven to 180°C/350°F/gas mark 4. Grease a 20cm/8 inch square baking dish.

Grate 1 tablespoon of zest and squeeze ⅓ cup of juice from the lemons. In a large bowl, beat the rice milk, yogurt, egg yolks, butter, zest and juice and half the sugar. Beat in the flour and salt until blended.

In a small bowl, beat the egg whites until foamy. Slowly beat in the remaining sugar until soft peaks form. With a large spoon, fold the egg whites into the lemon mixture until just combined. Pour into the prepared baking dish.

Place the baking dish in a 31 x 23cm/13 x 9 inch baking dish and put in the oven. Pour boiling water into the larger baking dish to come half way up the sides.

Bake for 30 minutes until the top is golden and cake is set. Remove from the oven and cool on a wire rack for 10 minutes. Serve warm.

Goji Berries

Goji berries, also called wolfberries, are small, bright and orangey red, and come from a shrub native to China. Used in Chinese medicine for 6,000 years, they are eaten in Asia to promote long life. Gojis are said to boost brain and immune function, and protect against cancer and heart disease, but there has been very little research done, so there is no scientific proof yet.

Benefits

The studies that have been undertaken on goji berries point to their high level of antioxidants, which neutralise the effects of free radicals and protect our cells. Goji berries also contain taurine, an amino sulfonic acid that strongly supports longevity. Taurine is also noteworthy in its protection of the eyes. Other nutrients in goji berries include vitamin E, beta-carotene, some B vitamins and fibre.

Ways to Eat

• Include in breakfast parfaits and chia pots.
• Add to smoothies and smoothie bowls.
• Mix into fruit salads.
• Use in trail mix.
• Include in raw bars and energy balls.

How to Use

Soak goji berries for 10 minutes or overnight to plump, soften and release their sweetness. Eat them raw for maximum benefit.

Goji Omega Mix Porridge

For a warming porridge with the benefit of gojis, the creaminess of almond butter and a good balance of essential fats, try this. One measure of sesame, sunflower and pumpkin seeds combined with two of linseeds (flaxseeds) gives a good amount of omega-6 and omega-3 balanced together. Soaking the goji berries brings out their natural sweetness.

Serves: 2
Prep: 10 minutes, plus overnight soaking
Cook: 5 minutes

100g/3½oz/1 cup rough oats
455ml/16fl oz/2 cups warm water
1 tbsp yogurt, kefir or lemon juice
4 tbsp goji berries
1 tbsp sesame seeds
1 tbsp sunflower seeds
1 tbsp pumpkin seeds
120ml/4fl oz/½ cup water
pinch of fine sea salt
2 tbsp milled linseeds (flaxseeds)
1–2 tbsp almond butter
fresh berries or chopped fruit, to serve (optional)

Put the oats, warm water and yogurt, kefir or lemon juice in a small saucepan and leave to soak, covered, overnight. Put the goji berries, sesame seeds, sunflower seeds and pumpkin seeds in a small bowl or jar with the water and salt, and leave to soak overnight.

Bring the oat mixture to a simmer over a low heat, stirring occasionally, for 5 minutes until creamy. Remove from the heat, add the goji seed mix, linseeds and almond butter, and mix well. Serve as is or with fresh berries or chopped fruit.

Berries

What's not to love about berries? Acai berries (see page 206), blackcurrants, blueberries, bilberries, blackberries, black raspberries, cranberries, goji berries (see opposite), gooseberries, mulberries, raspberries, redcurrants, strawberries and more, are usually small, juicy, brightly coloured sweet or sour, delicious fruits. Technically, they are a fruit produced from the ovary of a single flower.

Benefits
It's the high levels of phytochemicals that make berries special and valuable. The concentration of these naturally occurring nutrients helps prevent cell damage. They also contain compounds called anthocyanidins, a type of flavonoid that is almost unique to them, that keep you mentally sharp. And they help manage diabetes because of their fibre.

The Organic Advantage
All berries are fairly heavily sprayed because they are so delicate. Strawberries in particular top the UK and US lists of most heavily sprayed fruits and are always on the 'buy organic' list.

Ways to Eat
- Add to breakfast foods like yogurt, porridge (oatmeal), Bircher muesli, chia pots, smoothies, smoothie bowls or breakfast parfaits.
- Sprinkle on top of pancakes instead of sugar.
- Create light and fresh desserts with layered berries, yogurt, nuts and raw cacao nibs.
- Make frozen yogurt, nice cream and lollies.
- Use on top of no-bake cheesecakes.

How to Use
For maximum nutritional benefit, eat berries raw.

Even when they're not in season, you can buy frozen berries, which retain their goodness. They can get mushy and lose liquid, so use them in appropriate recipes.

Strawberry Shortcake

Simple, low-sugar cake like this with strawberries and whipped cream is the American answer to the British scone. I normally have a rule of never adding sugar to fruit when making desserts, but adding sugar to strawberries in this recipe draws out their juices so you have juicy strawberries to pour onto the cake.

Makes: a 20cm/8 inch cake
Prep: 15 minutes
Bake: 20–25 minutes

For the strawberries:
450g/1 lb/4½ cups strawberries, hulled and chopped
1 tbsp organic sugar

For the shortcake:
240g/8½oz/2 cups wholegrain spelt or other flour
3 tbsp organic sugar
1 tsp baking powder
1 tsp bicarbonate of soda (baking soda)
½ tsp fine sea salt
185ml/6½fl oz/¾ cup full-fat Greek yogurt
185ml/6½fl oz/¾ cup non-dairy milk

For the whipped cream (optional):
360ml/12fl oz/1½ cups double cream
1 tbsp organic sugar
1½ tsp vanilla extract

Preheat the oven to 200°C/400°F/gas mark 6. Grease a 20cm/8 inch square baking tin.

Mix the strawberries with the sugar and refrigerate for 30 minutes until the juices develop.

Mix together the flour, sugar, baking powder, bicarbonate of soda (baking soda) and salt in a medium bowl.

Add the yogurt and milk and mix until just combined. Put the mixture in the prepared baking tin and smooth the top. Bake for 25 minutes until golden. Cool on a wire rack for 10 minutes, then remove from the tin.

To make the whipped cream, use a hand-held mixer or electric mixer to beat the cream, sugar and vanilla for 1½–2 minutes until soft peaks form.

Cut the cake into 6 pieces and split each piece in half horizontally. Spoon some of the strawberries with their juice onto each shortcake bottom. Top with a generous dollop of whipped cream, if using, then the shortcake top. Spoon more strawberries over the top and serve.

Pomegranate Seeds

Classed as a berry, pomegranate's ruby red, jewel-like seeds are a Middle Eastern fruit. They are said to be one of the healthiest fruits on earth and have been used for medicinal purposes for thousands of years. Eating the 600 seeds inside an average pomegranate will give you about 40 per cent of your recommended daily intake of vitamin C.

Benefits

Pomegranates contain two unique, potent plant compounds called punicalagins and punicic acid, which make them powerfully anti-inflammatory, antibacterial and antifungal. They are also rich in vitamins, minerals and fibre. Regular consumption of pomegranate juice has been shown to lower blood pressure as quickly as within two weeks, but more research is needed in this area.

Ways to Eat

- Include in smoothies.
- Sprinkle on breakfast foods like porridge (oatmeal), Bircher muesli, chia pots, smoothie bowls and yogurt.
- Layer into breakfast parfaits.
- Serve with olives as a pre-dinner nibble.
- Add to wholegrain bruschetta with olive tapenade or goat's cheese.
- Add to fruit salads.
- Put on frozen yogurt or ice cream.
- Put on cheesecake.

How to Use

Choose pomegranates that are large and heavy, as these will be the ripest. Peel away the tough skin and white pith, and eat the seeds raw.

Pomegranate Salad

Pomegranate seeds thrown into a salad add a tart, sweet crunch amidst savoury flavours and zingy dressing. Great as part of a meal or a starter for dinner, this salad also includes other great ingredients that aren't featured in this book, like broad (fava) beans, fennel and mint.

Serves: 4
Prep: 30 minutes
Cook: 5 minutes

200g/7oz broad (fava) beans, fresh (about 850g/1lb 14oz in pods) or frozen, podded
150g/5½oz pomegranate seeds
100g/3½oz watercress, roughly chopped
1 fennel bulb, cored, quartered and thinly sliced
4 tbsp pumpkin seeds, soaked if time (see page 183)
2 tbsp chopped mint
4 tbsp chopped parsley

For the dressing:
zest and juice of 1 lemon – you will need 1 tsp zest and 2–3 tbsp juice, depending on taste
3 tbsp extra virgin olive oil
1 tbsp Dijon mustard

Steam the beans for 3–5 minutes. Remove from the heat, drain, cool with cold water and peel. In a large bowl, put the beans, pomegranate seeds, watercress, fennel, seeds, mint and parsley. Mix well.

In a small jar, add the lemon zest and juice, olive oil and mustard and shake until combined. Pour the dressing on the salad and toss until well mixed.

Figs

Figs are an ancient fruit, mentioned in the Bible and other ancient texts. They are inverted flowers with the opening at the bottom of each fig. Fresh figs are delicate, highly perishable and don't ripen once picked. Because of this, they are more commonly known as a dried fruit. If you are lucky enough to have a Ficus tree that gets enough sun to produce ripe figs, you can enjoy black, green, purple or pink-coloured delights.

Benefits

Figs are one of the best fruits for fibre, which is essential for digestion and elimination of waste. Fruit fibre reduces the risk of postmenopausal breast cancer in women. Figs are also a good source of potassium, which helps control blood pressure. They are also good for manganese, a trace mineral that is important for bone health.

The Organic Advantage

Conventionally grown figs are usually treated with sulphites to keep them from spoiling. Buy organic fresh and dried figs to avoid sulphur dioxide.

Ways to Eat

Dried Figs:
- Soak and add to yogurt, breakfast parfaits, smoothies and smoothie bowls.
- Add chopped figs to soaking porridge (oatmeal), Bircher muesli or chia pots.
- Bake into muffins, flapjacks and quick breads.
- Mix into fruit salads.
- Look up Indian dried fig dessert recipes.
- Soak and use in raw bars and balls.

Fresh Figs:
- Cook into pancakes.
- Slice with pears and serve as a fruity starter.
- Use on pizza with Gorgonzola cheese.
- Put on bruschetta with goat's cheese and pecans.
- Make fig tart.
- Serve with cheese and walnuts.
- Roast and serve with ice-cream or panna cotta.
- Dip in melted chocolate.

How to Use

Once picked, figs are fragile and don't ripen. Choose ripe figs that are soft to the touch and beginning to crack on the bottom.

Remove any stem, then eat the whole thing raw; they don't need to be peeled.

Fig Squares

If you have a fig tree, these are a must-try, but happily, they're great with dried figs, too. You can let the flour soak by making the pastry the night before or by doing it in the morning and then waiting until the afternoon to assemble the squares. Good-quality vanilla makes a big difference.

Makes: about 12 squares
Prep: 20 minutes, plus soaking and resting time
Cook: 20 minutes
Bake: 30 minutes

450g/1lb fresh figs or 225g/8oz dried figs, finely chopped
120ml/4fl oz/½ cup water for fresh figs or 240ml/8fl
    oz/1 cup for dried figs
240g/8½oz/2 cups wholegrain spelt flour
½ tsp fine sea salt
125g/4½oz butter, diced, or healthy oil, plus extra
    for greasing
1 egg, beaten with a fork
2 tbsp plain yogurt, kefir or lemon juice
2 tsp vanilla essence
3–4 tbsp cold water

If using dried figs, put the figs and water in a medium saucepan for 30 minutes to soak.

In a small bowl, mix the flour and salt. Add the butter and rub with your fingers until it is the consistency of coarse breadcrumbs.

Put the egg, yogurt and vanilla in a medium bowl and whisk until combined. Add the egg mixture to the flour mixture and mix with a fork. Add water, a tablespoon at a time, until the mixture easily comes together. Gather into a ball, wrap in clingfilm (plastic wrap) and refrigerate for 30 minutes.

Meanwhile, cook the figs over a low heat, stirring occasionally for 20 minutes until syrupy. Leave to cool.

Preheat the oven to 180°C/350°F/gas mark 4. Grease a 20 x 33cm/8 x 13 inch or similar baking dish. On floured greaseproof paper, roll out half the dough to the inner dimensions of the baking dish. Place the dough in the dish and spoon the fig mixture on the top, using the back of the spoon to even it out.

On floured greaseproof paper, roll out the other half of the dough to the same dimensions. Put the pastry on top of the fig spread, press gently and bake for 30 minutes until lightly browned. Leave to cool in the baking dish on a wire rack. Cut into squares and serve warm or at room temperature.

Stone Fruit

Stone fruits like apricots, cherries, lychees, nectarines, peaches and plums are members of the rose family. They are the flavours of summer, bursting with goodness and delicious eaten off the tree, freshly bought. If you want something sweet, reach for a piece of fruit.

Benefits

Stone fruits, packed with nutrients and fibre, support healthy digestion, boost your immunity, strengthen bones and teeth, create beautiful skin, improve vision and promote healthy nerves and muscles.
Many people eat foods that are overly processed or overcooked, compromising the value of the raw materials. Eating fresh raw fruits gives you a gift direct from nature that is bursting with minerals, vitamins and plant nutrients in a perfect package.

Ways to Eat

- Create beautiful fruit salads with lemon juice, spices like cinnamon, shredded coconut and soaked seeds and nuts.
- Use to top porridge (oatmeal), Bircher muesli, pancakes, waffles and French toast.
- Add to yogurt, breakfast parfaits, chia pots, smoothies and smoothie bowls.
- Make rainbow fruit kebabs.
- Use in raw energy or protein balls or bars.

How to Use

Stone fruits, like all fruits and berries, should be eaten raw to obtain all of the nutrients. Some vitamins, minerals and phytonutrients can be destroyed or lost during cooking.

Raw Stone Fruit Pie

Lovely flavours in the crust combine with gorgeous stone fruits, while linseeds (flaxseeds) add healthy oils and hold the chopped fruits together. Aim for about 600g/1lb 5oz chopped stone fruits in whatever combination you like. If you prefer, you can use traditional wholegrain pastry (see page 228) and bake it blind before filling it.

Makes: a 20cm/8 inch pie
Prep: 25 minutes

65g/2⅓oz/1 cup sprouted buckwheat (see page 149), drained and patted dry
40g/1½oz/½ cup shredded coconut
50g/1¾oz/½ cup walnuts, soaked if time (see page 169)
80g/2¾oz/½ cup pitted dates
1 tbsp melted coconut oil
1 tsp ground cinnamon
¼ tsp ground allspice
⅛ tsp ground nutmeg
¼ tsp fine sea salt
1 peach, stoned (pitted) and chopped
1 nectarine, stoned (pitted) and chopped
3 apricots, stoned (pitted) and chopped
2 plums, stoned (pitted) and chopped
200g/7oz/1 cup pitted cherries, halved
2 tbsp milled linseeds (flaxseeds)
1 tbsp lemon juice

Put the buckwheat, coconut, walnuts, dates, coconut oil, cinnamon, allspice, nutmeg and salt in a food processor or blender and blend for up to 1 minute until like coarse breadcrumbs. Spread and press into a 20cm/8 inch pie dish.

Put the peach, nectarine, apricots, plums, cherries, linseeds and lemon juice in a bowl and mix well. Put the fruit in the raw crust. Refrigerate or let sit for 30 minutes before serving.

Herbs
& Spices

Garlic

Treasured as a culinary ingredient and valued for its therapeutic qualities, garlic is part of the Allium or Lily family and related to onions, leeks and spring onions. Allium vegetables are rich in sulphur-containing compounds, which create the strong smell and the health benefits.

Benefits

People have written volumes about the health attributes of garlic. The most impressive benefits come from garlic's unusual set of sulphur-containing compounds, which provide protection against both inflammation and oxidative stress. This means blood cell and vessel protection, making garlic very good for your heart, circulation, blood pressure, joints and immune system. Garlic is also antibacterial, antiviral and anti-cancer.

Ways to Eat

- Purée with cooked beans, extra virgin olive oil and spices for different dips.
- Make aioli, a garlic mayonnaise.
- Mix crushed garlic into Greek yogurt and add finely chopped or grated cucumber for tzatziki.
- Crush raw into salads or dressing.
- Rub garlic on wholegrain toast as a base for bruschetta.
- Make garlic bread by spreading oil or butter on wholegrain bread, adding chopped or crushed garlic and salt, then baking until crisp.
- Steam cut potatoes or sweet potatoes and garlic cloves until soft, then mash with the steam water or stock, healthy oil, salt or miso for garlicky mash.
- Use a head or three of garlic instead of a few cloves, especially when roasting garlic.
- Add garlic slices to your pizza toppings.
- Create marinades for meats, fish and tofu with crushed garlic, healthy oils, ginger and lemon.
- Roast garlic alongside vegetables, meats and fish.
- Sauté slices of garlic alongside any vegetables.

How to Use

To harness the power of garlic, it is best eaten raw. Remove any green sprouts running up the centre of the clove because these are difficult to digest. Ideally, you crush or press garlic, which stimulates the conversion of alliin to allicin, which is the key ingredient providing the health benefits of garlic.

If you don't want raw garlic, then add towards the end of cooking.

There are two different effects from garlic: if you chop it, the flavour stays contained in the individual pieces, so that you occasionally get a taste of garlic when you bite it. If you crush it, you break all of the cells and the garlic flavour permeates the entire dish.

Garlic Salad Dressing

In a small jar, mix 2 tablespoons extra virgin olive oil (or other oil, like walnut), 1 tablespoon vinegar of choice and 1 crushed garlic clove. Shake. Increase in the same proportions for large green, mixed or pasta salads.

Roasted Cauliflower & Garlic

If you're trying to find a way to eat more cauliflower – or get your kids to eat more – this is it. With only four ingredients, this recipe is incredibly easy. You can use it as a simple side dish or add different herbs and other vegetables to turn it into something more complex.

Serves: 4
Prep: 15 minutes
Cook: 25–30 minutes

1 large cauliflower (about 750g/1lb 10oz)
2 heads of garlic
4 tbsp extra virgin olive oil
1 tsp fine sea salt

Preheat the oven to 200°C/400°F/gas mark 6. Remove the leaves from the cauliflower and roughly chop the nice ones. Cut the cauliflower in half from top to bottom, then lay on the flat side and slice into 1cm/½ inch slices. Break the slices up and put in a large bowl.

Separate the garlic cloves and peel. Slice any large cloves in half horizontally. Add the garlic, oil and salt to the bowl and toss well. Tip everything out into a large baking dish and bake for 25–30 minutes until al dente but beginning to brown.

Sumac

Sumac is a tangy, lemony spice that comes from the berries of flowering plants that grow in temperate and subtropical regions from North America to East Asia. The spice is often used in Mediterranean and Middle Eastern cooking, valued for its sourness and astringency. Native Americans used sumac in their tobacco and made a drink with it like lemonade.

Benefits

Sumac has a healing reputation that stretches round the globe. It is known as antifungal, anti-inflammatory, antimicrobial, anti-ageing and full of antioxidants. The National Institutes of Health & Ageing rank it the number one food for neutralising free radicals through antioxidant levels.

Ways to Eat

• Add to smoothies to liven them up.
• Mix into hummus and bean dips.
• Include in eggs and egg salad.
• Make your own za'atar (see page 49) and coat hard-boiled eggs or have on toasted wholegrain bread drizzled with extra virgin olive oil.
• Add ¼–½ teaspoon to dressings to add zing to your salads.
• Shake onto sandwiches.
• Add to stews and soups.
• Mix into healthy mash.
• Sprinkle onto steamed, stir-fried or roasted veggies.
• Use in meat marinades and rubs.
• Marinate pork ribs in orange juice, olive oil, honey, garlic, sumac and fine sea salt.
• Sprinkle on seafood and fish.
• Toss with popcorn.
• Add to pizza dough or put on pizza.

How to Use

Use as a ground spice.

Sumac Meatloaf

This is a sumac version of my family's meatloaf, which we used to love with mashed potatoes. Turn it out onto a serving plate and serve slices of meatloaf with Sweet Potato Super Mash (see page 56) and a green side.

Makes: a 23 x 12.5cm/9 x 5 inch loaf
Prep: 20 minutes
Bake: 50–60 minutes

2 tbsp extra virgin olive oil or other healthy oil, plus extra for greasing
2 onions, chopped
900g/2lb beef mince (ground beef)
2 garlic cloves, chopped
1 green (bell) pepper, chopped
35g/1¼oz/generous ⅓ cup fresh wholegrain or gluten-free breadcrumbs, or cooked quinoa
125ml/4fl oz/½ cup water or stock
4 tbsp chopped parsley
1 egg, beaten with a fork
1 tbsp ground sumac
1 tsp chopped thyme
2 tsp fine sea salt
freshly ground black pepper

Preheat the oven to 180°C/350°F/gas mark 4 and grease a 23 x 12.5cm/ 9 x 5 inch loaf tin.

Heat the oil in a medium frying pan over a medium heat. Add the onions and sauté for 10 minutes, stirring occasionally. Put the rest of the ingredients in a large bowl. Add the cooked onions and mix well, using your hands if necessary. Form the mixture into a loaf, put in the prepared loaf tin and bake for 50–60 minutes until cooked through and brown on top. Serve with Sweet Potato Super Mash (see page 56).

Chilli

Chilli peppers are part of the Capsicum family, of which there are hundreds of varieties, ranging from your everyday green pepper to habaneros. In Europe and South America, chilli peppers have been cultivated for over 7,000 years. Apparently, Christopher Columbus, while sailing the oceans blue, found them in the Caribbean Islands and brought them back to replace black pepper, which was an expensive Asian import. Ground chilli peppers make chilli powder, used to season a whole range of foods, and are respected for their medicinal qualities.

Benefits

Chillies give natural pain relief because of the active component capsaicin, which has positive effects on arthritis, nerve damage and psoriasis. Chilli can also help clear mucus congestion in the nose and lungs. Because red chilli peppers help the body to dissolve fibrin, which helps the body form blood clots, cultures where hot peppers are used freely have lower incidences of heart attack and stroke. Chillies can also help prevent ulcers because they can kill bacteria, and they also help reduce high levels of insulin in the blood, a problem with type 2 diabetes.

Ways to Eat

- Put a pinch in your smoothies and smoothie bowls.
- Purée chilli peppers or powder in bean and other dips.
- Stir into soups and stews.
- Add to green, pasta, rice, bean, grain and mixed salads.
- Include in egg, chicken, sweet potato salads.
- Make chilli con carne (or non carne) and curries.
- Add to coatings for fish and chicken.
- Mix with vegetables that you are sautéing, grilling or roasting.
- Put a tiny bowl of chilli powder on the table so your family can choose to add it to their food.
- Steam or sauté collard greens, spinach, kale or mustard greens and add chilli and freshly squeezed lemon juice.
- Mix a little chopped or ground chilli to Greek yogurt and serve with meats and vegetables.
- Use harissa, a spicy, aromatic chilli paste used in North Africa and the Middle East as a condiment.

How to Use

While working with fresh chilli peppers, don't put your fingers in your eyes and wash your hands afterwards with soap and water.

Add chilli powder incrementally to a recipe, as powders will vary in potency. Old chilli powder loses heat.

Chilli Chicken

This dish has a depth of flavour that belies the brief time it takes to make it and is visually beautiful, as well. Serve with wholegrain rice for the gorgeous sauce. If you don't want the chicken skin, remove it, and then add the chicken after you mix the other ingredients in the pan. Push the chicken into the sauce and then cook.

Serves: 4
Prep: 10 minutes
Cook: 50 minutes

2 tsp cumin seeds
4 tbsp extra virgin olive oil
4 chicken breasts or thighs
200g/7oz spinach
2 tomatoes, chopped
1½ tsp ground chilli powder
1½ tsp fine sea salt
2 garlic cloves, chopped
cooked wholegrain rice, to serve

In a large frying pan, dry-fry the cumin seeds over a medium heat for 3–5 minutes until toasted, then transfer to a bowl while you cook the chicken.

Add 2 tablespoons of the oil to the hot pan and fry the chicken, skin-side down, for 3–5 minutes until the skin is brown, then remove from the pan and set aside.

Reduce the heat to low and add the remaining oil to the pan. Add the spinach, tomatoes, chilli powder, salt and toasted cumin seeds and mix well. Transfer the chicken back to the pan (push the pieces down into the sauce) and cook, covered, for 25 minutes. Add the garlic and cook for 10 minutes until the chicken is cooked through. Serve the chilli chicken with the cooked rice.

Parsley

Probably the world's favourite herb, parsley used to be an innocuous garnish that was generally left on the plate. Today it is celebrated as a nutrient-dense and flavourful addition worth noticing. Parsley is easy to grow in a pot inside or outside, and has such a fresh taste that it can be added to just about anything.

Benefits

Parsley contains a huge amount of vitamin C and is a good source of vitamin K. It is also a good source of folate, which is one of the most important B vitamins. It contains powerful volatile oils and is rich in antioxidants. Packed with nutrients, parsley supports the immune system, joints, digestion, bones, blood pressure and diabetes.

Ways to Eat

- Include it in your green drinks, smoothies and smoothie bowls.
- Use instead of basil for pesto (see right).
- Blend into hummus.
- Sprinkle generously on soups before serving.
- Mix into salad dressings.
- Add to green, pasta, rice, bean, grain and mixed salads.
- Make tabbouleh.
- Try it in egg mayonnaise and potato salad.
- Add to sandwiches.
- Sauté mushrooms with garlic, salt and oil, then add parsley.
- Combine with crushed garlic, lemon zest, oil and breadcrumbs to top fish for grilling.
- Put in fishcake mixture.
- Keep persillade – a mix of chopped parsley and garlic – handy to put on roasted meats, fish and vegetables.
- Add lemon zest to your persillade to make gremolata.

How to Use

Think of parsley as a vegetable, instead of a garnish.

Curly parsley can be a little bitter, but it is easy to chop and holds its shape nicely. Flat-leaf parsley is good for cooking as it has a stronger flavour and holds up better when heated.

Chop up the stems and use them with the leaves or chop and freeze them and to add to soups and stews.

Parsley Pesto

It's very easy to buy large bags of organic parsley and have pesto ready in minutes, so move over basil! This has a beautiful, appealing colour and that wonderful parsley freshness. You can use it on pasta, spread it on toast or dip crudités or wholegrain crackers into it.

Serves: 4
Prep: 10 minutes

50g/1¾oz/generous ⅓ cup pine nuts
80g/3oz/2 cups chopped flat-leaf parsley
3 garlic cloves
¼ tsp fine sea salt
125ml/4fl oz/½ cup extra virgin olive oil

Toast the pine nuts lightly under a hot grill or in a dry hot frying pan for 3 minutes until turning golden.

Put the parsley, garlic, toasted pine nuts, salt and extra virgin olive oil in a food processor or blender and blend for 30–45 seconds until combined and smooth.

Ginger

Ginger, closely related to turmeric, cardamom and galangal, is a pretty flowering plant from China. It is the rhizome or underground part of the stem that is used as a food and for healing. In cooking, ginger adds a stimulating, lively edge. In baking, it's divine.

Benefits

Ginger has been called a medicinal marvel and is renowned for its ability to soothe the intestinal tract and remove wind from the digestive system. The powerful compound in ginger is called gingerol, which is a strong anti-inflammatory and antioxidant. People find relief from arthritic pain after eating even a relatively small amount cooked in their food. Ginger is also famous for relieving seasickness, morning sickness and menstrual cramping. It supports the heart and brain, too.

Ways to Eat

- Use in smoothies and smoothie bowls.
- Mix 1 teaspoon minced ginger to your pancakes.
- Serve pickled ginger with sushi.
- Add to soups for spice and warmth.
- Add zing to stir-fries.
- As soon as rice has cooked, stir in chopped ginger, garlic, coriander (cilantro) and extra virgin olive oil.
- Include in curries and exciting sauces.
- Marinate tofu, fish or chicken in a mix of chopped ginger, garlic and soy sauce or tamari.
- Bake gingerbread people and ginger cookies, flapjacks and cakes.
- Make apricot and ginger chia jam.
- Try ginger cheesecake.
- Make ginger tea (see right).

How to Use

Fresh, young ginger doesn't need to be peeled, but we rarely see this in the West. Peel the tough skin from the ginger, then grate, chop or slice and use.

If you feel a cold coming on or just want a stimulating and refreshing hot drink, make a ginger tea. Simply peel and slice 20–40g/ ¾–1½oz fresh ginger and place in a mug. Pour in boiling water, leave to steep for a few minutes, then enjoy. (You can eat the ginger after you've enjoyed the tea.)

Cajun Ginger Fried Rice

This rice, veg and prawn dish has great combined flavours of ginger, soy and garlic with a kick from the Tabasco and a nice crunchiness from the beansprouts. It's quick to prepare for you and your family, but interesting enough to serve to guests.

Serves: 4
Prep: 20 minutes, plus overnight soaking
Cook: 45 minutes

1½ tbsp soy sauce or tamari
2 large garlic cloves, minced
2 tbsp finely chopped ginger
3 tsp Tabasco or hot sauce
450g/1lb raw prawns (shrimp), peeled and deveined
3 eggs, beaten with a fork
1 tsp sea salt
3 tbsp sesame oil
2 tsp toasted sesame oil, plus extra to serve
1 onion, quartered and thinly sliced
180g/6¼oz/1 cup red rice, soaked and cooked
   (see page 143)
100g/3½oz/1 cup grated carrot
240g/9oz/2 cups frozen peas
200g/7oz/2 cups beansprouts
toasted sesame seeds, to serve

In a small bowl, combine the soy sauce or tamari, garlic, ginger and 1 teaspoon of the Tabasco or hot sauce. Stir in the prawns and set aside.

In another small bowl, beat the eggs with ½ teaspoon salt and 1 teaspoon Tabasco.

Heat 1 tbsp of the sesame oil in a large frying pan over a medium-high heat. Add the eggs and sauté for 1 minute until just firm. Remove from the pan into a small bowl.

Add the remaining sesame oil, the toasted sesame oil and the remaining Tabasco or hot sauce to the pan and when hot, add the onion and sauté for 5 minutes until soft. Add the prawn mixture and cook for 3–5 minutes until just cooked. Add the rice, carrot, peas and remaining salt and sauté until warmed through. Add the beansprouts and egg and mix well.

Remove from the heat and serve hot with extra toasted sesame oil and toasted sesame seeds.

Turmeric

Turmeric comes from the root of the *Curcuma longa* plant of the ginger family and has a tough brown skin and a deep orange flesh. It has long been used as a powerful anti-inflammatory in both the Chinese and Indian systems of medicine and has been used throughout history as a condiment, healing remedy and textile dye. It has a peppery, warm and bitter flavour and a mild fragrance slightly reminiscent of orange and ginger.

Benefits

There are many great things about turmeric. One is that you only need to eat a very small amount – even less than a daily tiny pinch – to enjoy some benefits after a matter of months. Two is that it is a source of curcumin, which has powerful anti-inflammatory and antioxidant properties. And another is that using turmeric in a marinade for grilled meats negates the health risk associated with heterocyclic amines (HCAs).

But, of course, that's not all. New research on turmeric is studying the theory that it improves arthritis, blood sugar balance, cognitive function, kidney function and some digestive disorders. Old research studied its ability to detox the body, reduce the risk of cancer and its anti-inflammatory attributes.

Ways to Eat

- Use a couple of pinches in your green smoothies and smoothie bowls.
- Mix into savoury porridge (oatmeal) with cream or butter.
- Sprinkle onto avocado or mash into guacamole.
- If you add it to soups, you get the goodness, but not too much flavour.
- Use in salads, salad dressing, miso dressing and tahini dressing.
- Add to eggs and egg salad.
- Include in bean dishes where you season with cumin.
- Mix with steamed, sautéed or roasted cauliflower.
- Sauté or roast vegetables in healthy oil with garlic, turmeric and sea salt.
- Make colourful, healthier mashed potatoes or sweet potatoes with it.
- Use in lentil dishes.
- Stir into rice or pasta for a beautiful colour and flavour.
- Make curry with turmeric, black pepper and other warming spices.

How to Use

Black pepper enhances the body's absorption of curcumin in turmeric, so eat them in combination.

You can now find fresh turmeric rhizomes in more shops, which you can scrub and grate. You don't have to peel it, but you can if you prefer.

1 tbsp fresh, grated turmeric = 1 tsp ground turmeric

Turmeric's gorgeous colour will stain your clothes, so be careful when cooking and eating it! To reduce the risk of stain, quickly wash with soap and water, then wash properly as soon as possible.

Turmeric Tonic

When you feel a cold coming on, mix 1½ tablespoons Manuka honey with ½ tablespoon ground turmeric and take 1 teaspoonful every 2 hours.

Turmeric Tea

Bring a cup of water to the boil in a small saucepan. Add ¼ teaspoon ground or ¾ teaspoon freshly grated turmeric and simmer for 10 minutes. Drink as is or add Manuka honey and/or lemon.

Turmeric Latte

For a coffee alternative and for turmeric that is very bioavailable, warm a cupful of your favourite non-dairy milk in a small saucepan, add 1 tablespoon freshly grated or 1 teaspoon ground turmeric, 1 tablespoon coconut oil, 1 teaspoon ground cinnamon and a pinch of black pepper and simmer gently for 10 minutes. For variation, add 1 tablespoon freshly grated or ground ginger.

Turmeric Scramble

Scrambled eggs are great. Stir in some mustard or sprinkle on Tabasco, and they're even better. And here is a fabulous twist on scrambled eggs that is quick, easy, nutritious and delectable. Kale adds lovely colour and nutrients, and if you include some Redbor and Red Russian kale you'll have red as well as green.

Serves: 4
Prep: 15 minutes
Cook: 10 minutes

4 tbsp extra virgin olive oil
3 tbsp freshly grated turmeric or 1 tbsp ground turmeric
50g/1¾oz chopped kale
10 eggs, beaten with a fork
½ tsp fine sea salt
freshly ground black pepper, to taste
3–4 tbsp thinly sliced spring onions (scallions)
6 tbsp chopped parsley
wholegrain pitta bread or flatbread, to serve (optional)

Heat the oil in a medium frying pan over a medium heat. Add the turmeric and sauté for 1 minute until fragrant. Add the kale and sauté for 3 minutes, then add the eggs and sprinkle the salt and pepper. Sauté for another 3–5 minutes until the eggs are just cooked, then turn off the heat and add the spring onions and parsley. Mix well.

Serve hot on a plate, stuff into a pitta pocket or spread a portion one-third of the way from the bottom of a flatbread and roll tightly.

Paprika

The fourth most popular spice in the world, paprika is used for colour and flavour. It can be sweet, smoky or spicy depending on which *Capsicum annuum* peppers are used, and how they are dried and prepared. Look for hot and sweet paprika from Spain or Hungary, which is from toasted and blended peppers; this creates paprika that is rich and sweet, but can vary in heat and pungency.

Benefits

Capsaicin, the ingredient that makes chilli peppers hot, relaxes blood vessels and relieves pain. Just 1 teaspoon of paprika contains 37 per cent of your daily recommended intake of beta-carotene. Paprika is also packed with essential vitamins and minerals that support the heart, eyes, skin, cuts, wound healing, hair growth and digestion; it also reduces inflammation, promotes sleep and prevents anaemia.

E. coli and Salmonella poisoning is from eating food contaminated with bacteria. Paprika contains a protein that inhibits the growth of bacteria, so cooking with paprika will reduce this risk.

Ways to Eat

- Sprinkle into scrambled eggs.
- Sprinkle very generously on hummus.
- Add to barbecue sauce, salsa and ketchup.
- Use in egg dishes like frittata and quiche.
- Toss with sautéed, grilled or roasted vegetables.
- Add to beef burgers, chicken burgers and fishcakes.
- Use in chilli con carne and chilli non carne.
- Rub into fish, chicken and meat before roasting or grilling.
- Make Hungarian stews, such as Goulash, which is based on paprika.
- Include in curries and dhal.
- Add to meatloaf or meatballs.
- Stir into risotto.
- Use in pork dishes.

How to Use

Paprika burns easily, so heat it gently, adding it to food that is cooking, not into hot oil.

Some ground paprika doesn't specify what kind it is. Look for paprika that says:
Sweet: this is less hot
Smoked: smoky and hot
Hot: you guessed it

Paprika Mushroom Soup

This soup has wonderful, pungent flavours. Use Hungarian paprika, which is spicy, if you like hot food, or use sweet paprika, which adds flavour, but less heat. This is a quick recipe with a surprising depth of flavour. You can make it dairy-free if you omit the yogurt.

Serves: 4
Prep: 10 minutes
Cook: 30 minutes

60g/2¼oz/4 tbsp butter or healthy oil
2 onions, chopped
350g/12oz button mushrooms, sliced
2 tsp dried dill
½ tsp–1 tbsp Hungarian or sweet paprika
3 tbsp wholegrain flour
720ml/26fl oz/3 cups water
1 tbsp soy sauce or tamari
1 tsp fine sea salt
240ml/8fl oz/½ cup Greek yogurt (optional)
30g/1oz/½ cup parsley, chopped, to serve
1 tbsp lemon juice
freshly ground black pepper

Heat 2 tablespoons of the butter in a large frying pan over a medium heat. Add the onions and sauté for 10 minutes until soft and beginning to brown. Add the mushrooms, dill and paprika and sauté for 8 minutes until beginning to brown.

Meanwhile, heat the remaining butter in a large saucepan over a medium–high heat. Stir in the flour and cook, stirring, for 3 minutes until beginning to brown. Add 240ml/8fl oz/1 cup of the water and cook, stirring frequently over a low heat for 10 minutes until thick.

Stir in the mushroom mixture, remaining water, soy sauce and salt, and simmer gently, covered, for 10 minutes. Just before serving, add the yogurt, if using, parsley, lemon juice and black pepper.

Cinnamon

Cinnamon is an old and valued spice and medicine that comes from the inner bark of the Cinnamomum tree. A time-honoured ingredient, cinnamon was considered rare and valuable in Ancient Egyptian times; it was a gift suitable for a king. There are two varieties of cinnamon – Chinese (or Cassia) and Ceylon. Look for Ceylon cinnamon, dubbed 'true' cinnamon – it is sweeter, more delicate and pricier, so it is not what is generally sold as ground cinnamon.

Benefits

Cinnamon's reputation for healing is attributed to three compounds in the tree bark's oil. These components are used to stop unwanted clumping of blood platelets or clotting, and also make it an effective anti-inflammatory. Cinnamon is considered to be a useful anti-microbial food, combatting fungus and bacteria. It is also high in antioxidants, heart supportive, good for blood pressure, helps balance blood sugar levels and is beneficial for brain function.

Ways to Eat

- If you're having Manuka honey on toast, then sprinkle generously with cinnamon.
- Use with yogurt, Bircher muesli, chia pots, smoothies, smoothie bowls, breakfast parfaits or porridge (oatmeal).
- Add to simmering beans.
- Include in rice or lamb dishes with raisins and other vegetables.
- Put in curries.
- Cook lamb shawarma.
- Steam apples, mash, add cinnamon and eat for a treat or serve with pork dishes.
- Sprinkle generously on apple slices tossed with lemon juice.
- Add to chocolate chip cookies for a wonderful flavour combination.
- Mix into muffins and carrot cake.
- Make pumpkin pie.
- Use for apple or blueberry pie.
- Make spice cookies.
- Seek out cinnamon ice cream.
- For a warming winter drink, heat your favourite nut milk and add ½–1 teaspoon ground cinnamon.

How to Use

Although cinnamon bark lasts longer, ground cinnamon has a stronger flavour.

Cinnamon Cake

This cake is ridiculously quick to make, plus healthy and delicious. With wholegrain spelt flour, the cake is wheat-, egg- and dairy-free.

Makes: a 20cm/8 inch square/round tin or 12 regular
    cupcakes
Prep: 10 minutes
Bake: 35 minutes

360g/12¾oz/3 cups wholegrain spelt or other flour
180g/6¼oz/scant 1 cup organic sugar
4 tbsp ground cinnamon
2 tsp bicarbonate of soda (baking soda)
½ tsp fine sea salt
500ml/17fl oz/2 cups water
125ml/4fl oz/½ cup extra virgin olive oil, plus oil
    for greasing
2 tbsp cider vinegar
2 tsp vanilla extract

Preheat the oven to 180°C/350°F/gas mark 4. Grease and line a 20cm/8 inch baking tin with greaseproof paper.

In a large bowl, mix the flour, sugar, cinnamon, bicarbonate of soda (baking soda) and salt. In a measuring jug, mix the water, oil, vinegar and vanilla. Add the wet ingredients to the dry and whisk quickly and briefly with a wire whisk until just combined.

Pour into the prepared tin and bake for 35 minutes until the cake comes away slightly from the sides. (If making cupcakes, pour into a 12-mould cupcake tin and bake for 20 minutes.) Remove from the oven and cool on a wire rack for 15 minutes, then turn out of the tin and cool right-side-up on a wire rack.

Radish

Like our 'apple a day' and the Japanese 'an umeboshi a day' sayings, there is apparently a Chinese proverb that goes, 'Eating pungent radish and drinking hot tea, let the starved doctors beg on their knees', showing their respect for this root veg. Another member of the *Brassica* family, radish have long been considered a healthy and sustaining food. They range from mild to very hot, like daikon to wasabi.

Benefits

If you suffer from asthma or frequent colds and coughs, including radish is a great idea because it has anti-congestive properties that help fight allergies of the respiratory system, protect the respiratory linings from infections and clear the mucus in your throat. Radish also improves immunity to keep colds and coughs away.

Radish is a strong cleanser, supporting your liver and stomach and because it is a natural diuretic, it keeps your kidneys healthy by eliminating toxins. Radish is antibacterial, fighting bacteria in the mouth, and anti-inflammatory, helping with arthritis.

Ways to Eat

Horseradish
- Mix with eggs instead of hot sauce.
- Add a little to dips and spreads, from guacamole to hummus to fish patés.
- Include in egg salad and potato salad.
- Have with sushi instead of wasabi.
- Take toasted wholegrain bread, add a piece of pan-fried fish, lettuce, tomato, onion, mayo, ketchup and horseradish for the best fish sandwich.

- Enjoy with roast beef.
- Instead of tartare sauce for fish, mix horseradish and ketchup.

Daikon/Mouli/Mooli
- Think of them as crudités.
- Slice or grate and add to salads.
- Add to soups, stews, pasta dishes and salads.
- Use in any way you would use a carrot.
- Slice, toss with oil and salt, and bake until crunchy.
- Roast with other veggies.

Black Radish
- Grate into salads.
- Fry thick slices in healthy oil with a little salt.
- Peel, steam, mash and mix with healthy oil and salt or miso.
- Roast wedges with chicken.

Wasabi
- Make a salad dressing with toasted sesame oil, vinegar, soy sauce or tamari, wasabi, minced ginger and crushed garlic.
- Mix into mayo.
- Add to your barbecue sauce.
- Eat with sushi and sashimi.
- Mash avocado with a little soy sauce or tamari and wasabi.
- Mix a little into noodle dishes with soy sauce or tamari.

- Mix wasabi to taste with sesame oil and tamari, mix with vegetables or brush on fish or chicken and roast.
- Add a little to coleslaw, egg salad, chicken salads and other salads where a little mustardy heat will improve the flavour.
- Use with roast beef and steak.

How to Use

Daikon – the half nearer the leaves is always sweeter, making it better for eating grated and raw, while the other half is better for cooking. Tender greens on tops of the radish can be enjoyed as leafy greens.

Wasabi Salmon or Chicken

This simple dish is another great recipe for your fish and chicken repertoire. When you want something a little different, use this marinade to liven up your main course. Serve for dinner with a colourful grain or pasta dish and veggies or a salad.

Serves: 4
Prep: 15 minutes
Cook: 6–10 minutes

1 tbsp soy sauce or tamari
1 tbsp cider vinegar
2 tbsp toasted sesame oil
1–2 tsp wasabi powder (for mild to medium heat)
4 salmon or chicken fillets

Put the soy sauce or tamari, vinegar, 1 tablespoon of the sesame oil and the wasabi in a dish just large enough for the fillets and mix until the wasabi is dissolved and evenly distributed. Place the salmon or chicken in the dish for 5 minutes, then turn over to marinate for 5 minutes on the other side.

Heat the remaining oil in a large frying pan over a medium–high heat. Put the salmon or chicken, skin-side up in the pan and fry for 3–5 minutes until browned. Turn the heat off until the sizzling stops, then turn the salmon or chicken over. Turn the heat up to medium–high again and cook for 3–5 minutes until browned on the other side and slightly raw in the middle for salmon or however you prefer it. (The salmon will continue to cook once you remove it from the pan.)

Wasabi Peas

These hot peas are great as an afternoon snack or to take on picnics. Adjust the wasabi for a weaker or stronger taste depending on your personal preference. You can also vary the recipe by adding a tablespoon of nutritious, delicious tahini.

Preheat the oven to 180°C/350°F/gas mark 4. Put 500g/1lb 2oz fresh or defrosted frozen peas and 1 tablespoon extra virgin olive oil in a medium bowl and mix well.

In a small cup or bowl, mix 1 tablespoon brown rice vinegar or cider vinegar and 2–3 teaspoons wasabi powder, to taste. Mix with the peas, spread on a baking sheet and bake for 25–30 minutes until crunchy. Toss the peas with ¼ teaspoon fine sea salt and serve.

Quick Daikon Salad

With a rotary grater, this gorgeously coloured, fresh, raw salad is ready in just a few minutes. It's a great addition to any meal where you want that one extra side dish, and it is satisfyingly crunchy as well as very pretty.

Serves: 4
Prep: 10–15 minutes

2 carrots, grated
1 beetroot (beet), grated
1 daikon, grated
2 tbsp extra virgin olive oil
1 tbsp brown rice vinegar
¼ tsp fine sea salt

Put all the ingredients in a medium bowl and mix well.

Dairy, Meat & Fish

Butter

Ah, butter. Butter is beautiful. Butter is made from churning cream. From cooking to baking, butter is an amazing ingredient. Think of American-style blueberry pancakes with butter, vegetables sautéed in butter, butter sauces, lobster dipped in butter, fresh bread with butter, pastry, cakes and buttercream frosting. The list is endless.

Benefits

Fats are a concentrated source of energy and provide building blocks for cell membranes and hormones. When we eat fats with food, they make us feel satisfied, slow down the absorption of nutrients and convert beta-carotene to vitamin A. Butter is rich in the fat-soluble vitamins A, E and K2 and is also a great source of conjugated linoleic acid that supports metabolism and is anti-cancer.

Not pure fat, butter is around 16–17 per cent water, with milk solids accounting for another 3–4 per cent. So butter is about 80 per cent fat, which is important to know when you're substituting oil for butter.

The Organic Advantage

Organic, grass-fed animals produce milk with higher nutritional levels. Turn that into butter and it's better.

Ways to Eat

- Try butter in porridge (oatmeal) – it is delicious and helps absorb the fat-soluble minerals in the oats.
- Put on pancakes and waffles.
- Spread on toast or oatcakes, then spread almond butter on top.
- Blend flavoured compound butters, like herb and garlic or walnut and raisin.
- Make garlic butter (see right) and spread it on wholegrain bread to make healthier garlic bread.
- Bake butter cookies and pound cake.
- Make wholegrain butter pastry (see page 228).
- Try ghee, a form of clarified butter, which has a high smoke point.

Parsley Butter Steak

This super-quick and simple recipe is an amazing topping for grilled or fried steak. For such a simple addition, it really transforms the meat. You can also spread the parsley butter on thick slices of wholegrain bread and bake into garlic bread. Or brush onto prawns (shrimp) and then grill.

Serves: 4
Prep: 5 minutes
Cook: 12 minutes

45g/1½oz/3 tbsp butter
3 large garlic cloves, pressed
2 tsp finely chopped fresh parsley
healthy oil, to grease the pan
4 steaks (weighing about 680g/1½lb in total)
fine sea salt and freshly ground pepper, to taste

In a small saucepan over a medium heat, melt the butter. Add the garlic and heat to a medium–high heat, bringing the mixture almost to the boil. Remove from the heat and leave to cool.

Heat a large frying pan with a little oil over a medium-high heat. Add the steaks, season with salt and pepper, and fry for 4–5 minutes on each side until browned and cooked how you prefer. Remove from the heat. Add the parsley to the butter mixture and mix well. Plate the steaks and spoon the butter mixture over the top.

Eggs

Eggs are truly a wonder of nature. The humble egg is so versatile, so nutritious, so perfect, so inexpensive. An egg is low in calories, high in protein, simple to prepare (young kids can make scrambled eggs) and are part of so many dishes. From a simple fried egg to the magic of meringue, eggs give endless possibilities in the kitchen.

Benefits

Because an egg holds everything to make the bird, it is nutritionally rich. It has the complete and perfect amino acid profile, brain nutrients, linoleic acid, two excellent antioxidants (lutein and zeaxanthin), plus small amounts of almost every vitamin and mineral required by the human body. It's no wonder that eggs are called nature's multivitamin.

The Organic Advantage

Like many things, not all eggs are created equal. People buy free range in the misunderstanding that the chickens are all roaming around a field or in the woods. The reality is that most 'free range' birds spend most of their lives inside dirty sheds with thousands of other birds.

Organically reared hens offer the highest potential standards of animal welfare. They have less crowded living conditions, better-quality feed and enjoy more access to the outdoors. And the result is that organic eggs are higher in omega-3 fatty acids, free of antibiotic residues and contain no arsenic (added to factory-farmed chicken-feed to prevent infections and promote growth).

How to Use

The list of uses for eggs in breakfasts, salads, quiches, frittatas, soufflés and baked goods goes on and on, so instead, here are some egg facts you may not know.

Not a great raw food, eggs are best cooked, which neutralises the protective anti-nutritional proteins and makes the protein more digestible.

Bake with room temperature eggs to prevent the butter from hardening. When adding eggs to beaten butter and sugar, to prevent curdling, add one at a time and beat on low until incorporated, then turn up the speed and beat for 5 minutes.

Beat egg whites in a bowl that is free from detergent, egg yolk and fat or oil.

The green-grey colour that you sometimes see on the yolk of a hard-boiled egg is simply the combination of iron and sulphur. The longer you cook/overcook an egg, the more likely this is to happen.

To prevent your scrambled, fried or over-easy eggs from sticking in the frying pan, heat the butter until the water in the butter sizzles away. The fat in the butter then completely coats the pan so the eggs don't stick. Or use olive oil.

You need to put some welly into beating eggs by hand that are then added to other ingredients, the frying pan or pancake batter and so on. You should beat with a fork until there are no strings apparent and the yolk and white are combined.

Never add salt to the simmering water when poaching eggs as it causes the eggs to break up.

Avocado & Poached Egg on Toast

For another colourful, nicely balanced breakfast or brunch, start with wholegrain or gluten-free toast, then spread avocado mashed with chilli or turmeric and salt on top, then top with a poached egg. Or try peas mashed with a little extra virgin olive oil, lemon zest and mint leaves on toast, with an egg on top.

Open Omelette

It's great to have a few simple, nutritious meals like this up your sleeve for time-pressured weeknights. Chop lots of different vegetables, put them in bowls on the counter and let your children or partner choose which toppings they'd like. You can try different herbs, Cheddar or feta cheese, (bell) pepper, tomatoes or sundried tomatoes, courgette (zucchini), kale, broccoli and more.

Serves: 1
Prep: 10 minutes
Cook: 3–5 minutes

15g/½oz/1 tbsp butter
1 small onion, chopped
1 small garlic clove, chopped
2 shiitake mushrooms, sliced
¼ tsp dried tarragon
2 eggs, beaten with a fork
⅛ tsp fine sea salt
15g/½oz fresh spinach, roughly chopped
30g/1oz artichoke hearts, sliced
30g/1oz olives, halved

Heat the butter in a small frying pan over a medium heat until it has sizzled. Scatter the onion, garlic, mushrooms and tarragon evenly across the pan. Cook for 10 minutes until soft and beginning to brown, then pour the egg across the veg and sprinkle on the salt.

Cook for 3–5 minutes until the egg is just firm, then turn over onto a plate and top with the spinach, artichokes and olives.

Meat (Organic)

The basic premise of organic farming is that healthy soil creates healthy vegetables and healthy animals for a healthy you. Organic farming prohibits or restricts the use of antibiotics, insecticides and hormone and other veterinary treatments that can be used in non-organic, grass-fed systems.

Benefits

Organic animals are kept healthy with natural methods such as access to the outdoors, clean housing, rotational grazing, not overcrowding and a healthy diet. Organic livestock are given high-quality feed that is non-GMO, grain-based, includes organic and does not routinely include antibiotics. The quality of meat is directly influenced by these systems.

It has been proven that eating organic meat will increase your intake of essential omega-3 fats, polyunsaturated fatty acids and iron – and will reduce your intake of unwanted heavy metals. Organic meat contains 50 per cent more beneficial omega-3 fatty acids than conventionally produced equivalents. It also has slightly lower concentrations of two saturated fats that are linked to heart disease.

The Organic Advantage

Eating high-quality organic meat occasionally is better than eating conventional meat regularly. Organic systems also protect the environment and create biodiversity

Meatballs

Meatballs can be made in a big batch and frozen for convenience. You can make large meatballs and cook them in homemade spaghetti sauce for an hour, then enjoy with pasta or slice them in half for meatball sandwiches.

Makes: 40 meatballs
Prep: 30 minutes
Cook: 22–25 minutes

2 tbsp extra virgin olive oil
2 onions, finely chopped
60ml/2fl oz/¼ cup water
15g/½oz/¼ cup grated Parmesan cheese
2 tbsp chopped parsley
1 egg, beaten with a fork
5 garlic cloves, chopped
¼ tsp dried chilli flakes
1½ tsp fine sea salt
¼ tsp ground black pepper
50g/1¾oz/½ cup fresh wholegrain breadcrumbs
900g/2lb organic beef mince (ground beef)
wholegrain flour, for coating

Preheat the oven to 180°C/350°F/gas mark 4. Heat the oil in a frying pan over a medium heat. Add the onions and sauté for 10 minutes. Remove from the heat, add the water and stir to release anything stuck to pan. Let the pan cool slightly.

Add the Parmesan, parsley, egg, garlic, chilli flakes, salt and pepper and mix until combined. Add the breadcrumbs and mix through. Add the meat and mix until combined. Shape into balls the size of golf balls and roll in the flour.

Place the meatballs on a large baking dish or tray and bake for 12 minutes until cooked through, then grill under a hot grill for 2–3 minutes until brown.

Bone Broth

Bone broths made from meat, chicken and fish are not new, but the same great stocks that our mothers and grandmothers made as the basis for soups and stews. It is not an old wives' tale that chicken soup is good for colds because these nourishing broths provide a wealth of nutrition. The simple idea is a long cooking time to extract gelatine and other important minerals from the bones.

Benefits

Broths contain nutrients from bones, marrow, cartilage and the electrolytes of vegetables. During the cooking, vinegar added to the broth helps draw out calcium, magnesium, potassium and other minerals from the bones. Amino acids in broth boost immunity and fight inflammation. Bone broth in general relieves symptoms of colds and flu, strengthens bones and teeth, builds muscle, improves your mood and probably re-hydrates better than water because of the electrolytes. Eating good (organic) gelatine helps with digestion, intestinal disorders and much more.

The Organic Advantage

If you're going to be cooking bones, marrow and cartilage down for hours to provide a nourishing broth, you really want to ensure that it is the best quality. Organic is a must.

Ways to Eat

- Use instead of water or stock when making soups and stews.
- Freeze in small pots to defrost and use whenever you need water for cooking.
- Replace water used to cook rice and grains.
- Use in mashed potatoes.
- Make gravy and sauce.
- Use for refried beans (unless you're having veggie friends over).
- Use for homemade red sauce.

How to Use

Freeze in ice-cube trays and store in a container for when you need smaller quantities.

Chicken Broth

The basis for chicken soup, homemade chicken broth is rich in folklore as a flu remedy. Modern research has proven it helps prevent and treat infectious diseases. You really should buy organic, and once you've enjoyed your roast chicken and used the carcass for broth, you'll have got your money's worth.

Makes: 3.5 litres/6 pints/14 cups
Prep: 10 minutes
Cook: 4+ hours

1 organic chicken carcass
2 onions, chopped
2 carrots, chopped
2 celery sticks, chopped
4 garlic cloves, roughly chopped
4 litres/7 pints/16⅔ cups water or enough to cover
3 tbsp cider vinegar
4 parsley sprigs
4 rosemary sprigs
2 bay leaves
2 tsp freshly grated or ground turmeric

Put the chicken carcass in a large saucepan and add the onions, carrots, celery, garlic, water and vinegar and bring to the boil over a high heat. Boil for 10 minutes and skim the scum that rises to the surface. Reduce the heat to low, add the parsley, rosemary, bay leaves and turmeric and simmer, covered, for 4 hours or more – the longer it cooks, the more nutrients are released from the bones.

Remove any chicken pieces with a slotted spoon and leave to cool. Strain the stock into a large bowl and refrigerate until the fat has congealed at the top. Skim this off and pour the stock into convenient-sized containers. For freezing, chill completely first in the fridge, then remove any fat from the surface. Leave room for the liquid to expand as it freezes and then freeze for up to 3 months.

Note: To cool the broth quickly and prevent bad bacteria from forming, put the pan or bowl in the sink and fill the sink with cold water and ice. You can give it up to 2 hours to cool down, and then refrigerate.

Fish Broth

The best fish for fish bone stock are sole and turbot, but other non-oily fish are fine. Avoid oily fish as the unsaturated oil becomes rancid with the long cooking time. The vinegar helps release minerals such as calcium, magnesium and potassium into the broth. Then use broth instead of water, bouillon or stock when making soups and stews.

Makes: 3.5 litres/6 pints/14 cups
Prep: 10 minutes
Cook: 4+ hours

2 tbsp healthy oil
1 onion, chopped
1 carrot, chopped
1 celery stick, chopped
3–4 fish carcasses, stripped of flesh, but heads remaining
4 litres/7 pints/16⅔ cups water or enough to cover
60ml/2fl oz/¼ cup cider vinegar
2 garlic cloves, roughly chopped
2 parsley sprigs
2 thyme sprigs
2 bay leaves

In a large saucepan, heat the oil over a low heat and add the onion, carrot and celery. Cook for 30–40 minutes until they are soft. Add the fish, water and vinegar and bring to the boil over a high heat. Boil for 10 minutes and skim off any scum that rises to the surface. Add the garlic, parsley, thyme and bay leaves, reduce the heat to low, cover, and simmer for 4 hours or more.

Remove from the heat and leave to cool. Remove the fish carcasses and strain the liquid through a fine colander into convenient-sized containers. For freezing, chill completely first in the fridge, then remove any fat from the surface. Leave room for the liquid to expand as it freezes and then freeze for up to 3 months.

Note: To cool the broth quickly and prevent bad bacteria from forming, put the pan or bowl in the sink and fill the sink with cold water and ice. You can give it up to 2 hours to cool down, and then refrigerate.

Oily Fish

Oily fish such as anchovies, carp, eel, herring, jack, mackerel, pilchards, salmon, sardines, sprats, trout, fresh tuna and whitebait contain oil throughout their bodies, as opposed to white fish, whose oil is in the liver, which we don't eat. They are an excellent source of omega-3 fatty acids.

Benefits

Scientists found that oily fish, as well as being a good source of protein, vitamin D, B vitamins and selenium, is a rich source of omega-3 – the oil that you want to eat a lot of because it feeds your body and brain. High levels of omega-3 in oily fish help against cardiovascular disease, prostate cancer, loss of vision associated with ageing, and dementia.

Because pollutants like PCBs (polychlorinated biphenyl) and dioxins concentrate in the fat of fish, it is best to eat the smaller fish that are low on the food chain. Fish from the Pacific Ocean are less polluted than from the Atlantic. Always buy wild fish.

Canned tuna doesn't count as a good oily fish because the canning process reduces the amount of long-chain omega-3 fatty acids.

How to Use

Poaching or cooking using lower temperatures is the best way to eat oily fish and is least likely to destroy essential fats.

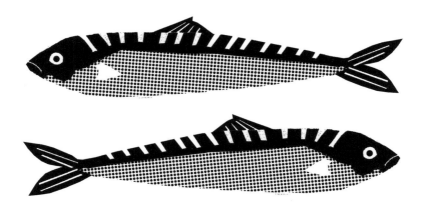

Salmon Tacos

This is a brilliant way to eat fish. You can make these as spicy as you like with the chipotle mayo and if you have any left over, keep it in the fridge to spice up sandwiches, wraps or burgers.

Serves: 4
Prep: 25 minutes
Cook: 15–18 minutes

16 corn tortillas (or use Romaine lettuce leaves)
shredded red cabbage or shredded Romaine

For the sweetcorn salad:
450g/16oz fresh or frozen sweetcorn
1 orange (bell) pepper, deseeded and finely chopped
1 red onion, finely chopped
10g/¼oz/½ cup chopped coriander (cilantro)
½ tsp dried cumin
4 tbsp extra virgin olive oil
2 tbsp lemon juice
½ tsp fine sea salt

For the chipotle mayo:
125ml/4fl oz/½ cup mayo
1–2 chipotles in adobo sauce
1 tbsp lemon juice

For the fish:
4 x 125g/4½oz salmon fillets,
2 tbsp extra virgin olive oil

Preheat the grill to high. Put the sweetcorn on a baking tray and grill for 12–14 minutes until browned. In a large bowl, put the sweetcorn, pepper, onion, coriander, cumin, oil, lemon juice and salt and toss well. In a small bowl, mix the mayo ingredients.

Heat the oil in large frying pan over a low heat. Fry the salmon for 3–5 minutes on each side, depending on thickness, until cooked through. Flake onto a plate for serving. Place a warm tortilla on a plate. Spread on some chipotle mayo, then add some fish, sweetcorn salad and shredded cabbage or lettuce.

Sardines

A brilliant fast food, sardines are inexpensive, easy to use and tasty. They are named for the Italian island Sardinia, where large schools of them once swam. You can eat tinned sardines straight from the tin or buy fresh sardines to cook.

Benefits
This superfish is loaded with protein and essential omega-3 fats. They are one of the best sources of B12 and are an excellent source of vitamin D. Rich in many nutrients, sardines are particularly good for both your heart and bones.

Sardines are an oily fish at the bottom of the fish food chain, and because they feed on plankton rather than other fish, don't bio-accumulate heavy metals like mercury, which is found in other oily fish. Because of this, sardines are great for kids and pregnant women, and can be eaten frequently.

Ways to Eat
• Make sardine paté with a little thick plain Greek yogurt, chopped spring onion (scallion), some fresh coriander (cilantro), a pinch of salt and lemon juice.
• Take a wholegrain cracker, crispbread or rye toast, spread with mayo (or mash) and lay sardines on top.
• Swap for tuna in Niçoise Salad.
• Put on toast rubbed with garlic, drizzled with olive oil and add sliced red (bell) pepper for bruschetta.
• Mix with mayo and make a sandwich with lettuce, tomato and gherkins or pickles.
• Mash and mix into pasta with olives, capers, garlic and lemon.
• Use in fishcakes.
• Grill fresh sardines with fresh dill and lemon slices.
• Use like tuna.

How to Use
If you or your kids are a little squeamish about eating sardines, bones and all, buy the fresh, large sardines or buy the filleted ones in tins. You'll miss the benefit of some of the calcium, but if it gets you and your children eating more sardines, then it's worth it.

Sardine Fishcakes

People who don't like sardines can be tricked into eating them in these fishcakes, because the flavours from the sweet potato, coriander (cilantro) and lime are more dominant. Served with a vegetable side dish or salad, these make a lovely lunch or dinner. They are gluten- and grain-free.

Serves: 4
Prep: 30 minutes
Cook: 8 minutes per batch

400g/14oz unpeeled sweet potatoes, diced
200g/7oz/2 tins sardines, drained and mashed
2 large eggs, beaten with a fork
3 spring onions (scallions), sliced
4 tbsp chopped fresh coriander (cilantro) leaves
2 tbsp milled linseeds (flaxseeds)
2 tbsp Dijon mustard
1 tbsp grated lime zest
¾ tsp fine sea salt
2 tbsp extra virgin olive oil or other healthy oil
lime wedges, to serve

Steam the sweet potatoes over boiling water for 10 minutes until soft. Put in a large bowl and mash with a fork. Add the sardines, eggs, spring onions, coriander leaves, linseeds, Dijon mustard, lime zest and sea salt and mix well.

Heat 1 tablespoon of the oil in a large frying pan over a medium heat. Drop a large spoonful of the fishcake mixture into the pan and roughly shape into a circle. You should be able to fit 4 in the pan. Cook for 3–4 minutes until browned, turn over and cook for 3–4 minutes on the other side. Repeat with the remaining mix, adding more olive oil to the pan if it becomes dry. Serve with fresh lime wedges for squeezing over.

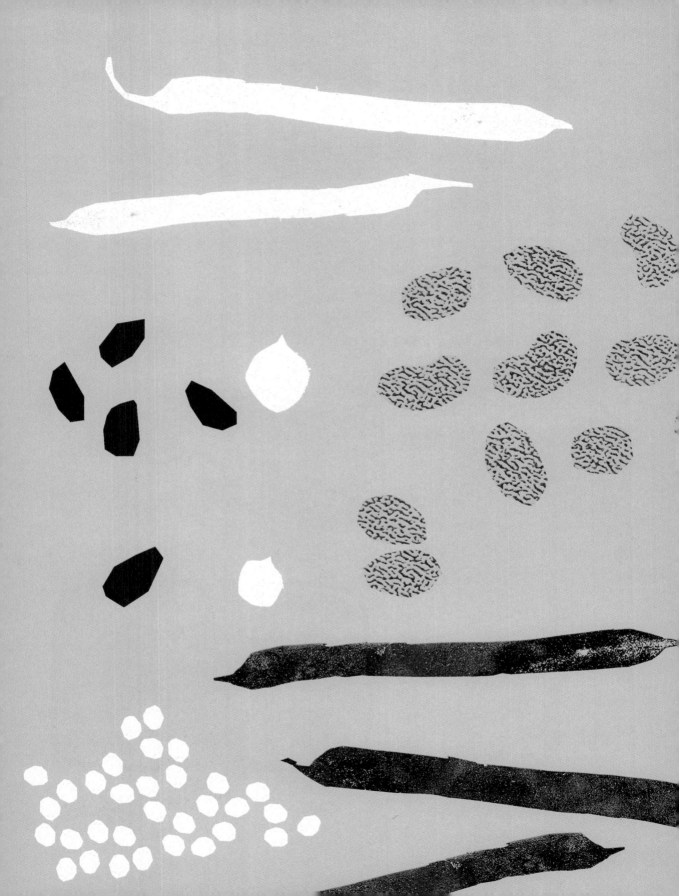

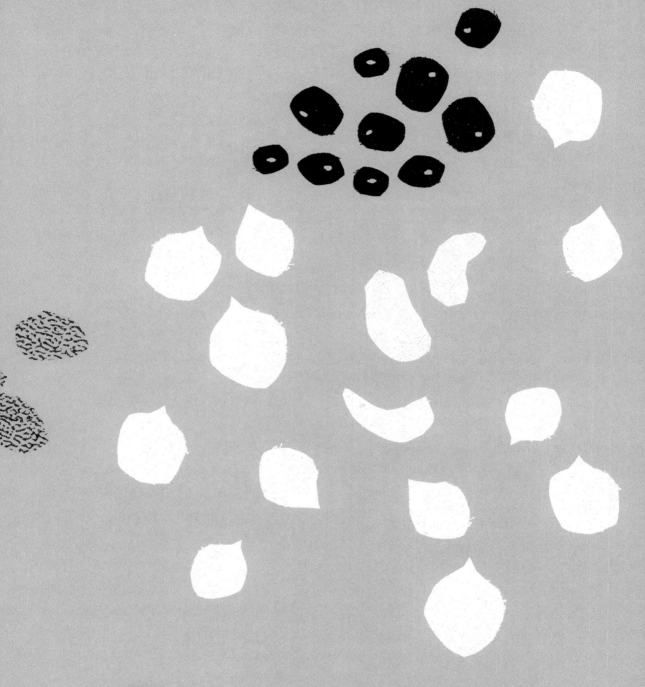

Beans

Beans

Beans are a cheap and versatile form of protein. They can be used in a range of dishes, from spreads to salads to stews. They suit every age and palate. They are great for diabetics and they are easy to prepare.

Benefits

As well as providing protein, beans are a complex carbohydrate with high fibre. The fibre in beans stabilizes blood sugar, prevents constipation and is heart healthy, satiating and filling.

Beans are packed full of antioxidants, vitamins and minerals. Their antioxidants plus fibre means that beans promote health and reduce the risk of chronic diseases – so enjoy the abundant colours and shapes of beans that nature provides.

Beans that are not considered healthy are groundnuts, because of aflatoxins, and soy beans, because of phytoestrogens.

Ways to Eat

- Blend into smoothies.
- Make bean dips and spreads.
- Make a layered dip with cooked beans, mashed avocado, chopped tomatoes and red onion, Greek yogurt and grated cheese.
- Toss with vinaigrette, avocado, red onion and tomatoes.
- Create hearty soups and stews.
- Find recipes for regional bean specialities.
- Make chilli con carne and chilli non carne (see page 157).
- Eat quesadillas – a flour or corn tortilla, spread with beans and cheese, then folded over or topped with another tortilla and grilled.
- Make burritos – a flour tortilla filled with beans, rice, vegetables and additions like cheese, then wrapped (see page 132).
- Enjoy enchiladas – a burrito-style meal but in a corn tortilla covered with chilli sauce and cheese, then heated in the oven.
- Try tacos – a crisp corn tortilla folded over, filled with beans, lettuce, tomatoes and cheese.
- Have nachos with beans.
- Add to salads and pasta dishes.
- Sprout (see page 53) and add to anything you like.
- Put on baked potatoes.
- Look up great bean burger recipes.
- Make your own baked beans.
- Make cassoulet.

How to Use

It's always best to prepare your own beans (see opposite), as they provide the best nutrition and reduce unwanted wind. Making your own beans isn't difficult, it just takes a lot of soaking and simmering time. (If you're in a hurry, tinned organic beans are a good second, but you should rinse tinned beans to reduce the salt.)

Cooking dried beans has a three-fold purpose. Soaking beans in acidulated water (a) breaks down the phytic acid and (b) neutralises growth inhibitors that stop the bean from sprouting at the wrong time, but are not good for our digestion/absorption. After soaking overnight, the beans are rinsed well, then boiled hard for 10 minutes while you skim the scum – or indigestible sugars – that create the wind that makes beans infamous. Then you simmer over a low heat with kombu, a sea vegetable, until the beans are tender. Skimming the scum and cooking with kombu (c) reduces the effect of the windy sugars.

Always add salt *after* the beans are cooked as it toughens their skins during cooking. Use 1 teaspoon fine sea salt (or 1 tablespoon miso, dissolved in a little warm water) for every 1 cup of uncooked beans.

BASE RECIPE

Soaked & Cooked Beans

This recipe works for all beans, such as adzuki, black beans, pinto beans and so on. The only variables might be the the cooking time (most beans need 2 hours but adzuki only need 1½) and the amount of fresh water needed (simply add boiling water if beans run dry while cooking). When you can easily squash a bean against the side of the saucepan with a fork, they are ready.

Serves: 4
Prep: 5 minutes, plus overnight soaking
Cook: 2 hours 10 minutes

200g/7oz/1 cup dried beans
1 tbsp cider vinegar or lemon juice
740ml/26fl oz/3 cups warm water
1 kombu strip, cut into small pieces
1 tsp fine sea salt or 1 tbsp miso

Put the beans and vinegar or lemon juice in a medium saucepan and cover with double the volume of warm water. Leave to soak, covered, at room temperature overnight.

Rinse the beans well, then add the water. Bring to the boil over a high heat and boil hard for 10 minutes, skimming the scum from the surface.

Reduce the heat to low, add the kombu and simmer, covered, for 2 hours (1½ hours for adzuki beans) until soft. Drain any remaining water and add the salt or dissolve the miso in a little warm water before adding to the beans.

Black Beans

Black beans are also known as black turtle beans or Cuban black beans. They are inexpensive to buy, easy to prepare, versatile to use and tasty to eat. In Brazil, where they value beans within their diets, they have a special bean category on their Food Pyramid.

Benefits

What's special about black beans is their high levels of antioxidants because of their concentration of anthocyanin, which are pigments that give black and blue fruits, berries and beans their colour and health benefits; the darker the bean, the higher the value of antioxidant.

Black beans are rich in protein, fibre, zinc, copper and molybdenum. Molybdenum, is a key, but lessknown mineral needed to form and activate enzymes for detoxification in the body. It is also associated with longevity. One of the general benefits of beans is that they all contain resistant starch, which arrives undigested in the large intestine where it helps the growth of good bacteria.

Ways to Eat

- Purée with oil, garlic and ground spices to make a dip.
- Mix with lime, coriander and a chopped avocado for a bean salad.
- Make Cuban black bean soup.
- Create black bean brownies.
- See more suggestions on page 130.

How to Use

Black beans marry really well with coriander (cilantro) or lime.

It's fine to buy tinned black beans occasionally for when you need beans quickly.

Black Bean Burritos

The beauty of these burritos is that they are a complete meal on their own, especially if you add further toppings such as avocado, red onion, cheese, tomatoes or Greek yogurt. For a gluten-free version, use corn tortillas.

Serves: 4
Prep: 20 minutes
Cook: 2 hours 30 minutes

200g/7oz/1 cup dried black beans, cooked (see page 131)
90g/3⅓oz/½ cup cooked wholegrain black or red rice (see page 143)
3 tbsp chopped coriander (cilantro)
1 courgette (zucchini), cut into strips
1 red (bell) pepper, deseeded and cut into strips
1 tbsp extra virgin olive oil
1 tsp dried oregano
1 tsp paprika
½ tsp ground cumin
½ tsp fine sea salt
¼–½ tsp chilli powder (optional)
1 garlic clove, crushed
8 wholegrain flour tortillas or 12 corn tortillas

Preheat the oven to 190°C/375°F/gas mark 5. In a medium bowl, put the beans, rice and coriander and mix well. Put the courgette and pepper in a small bowl, add the oil, oregano, paprika, cumin, salt and chilli powder, if using, and toss until combined. Put in a small oven dish and bake for 15–20 minutes until the vegetables are soft and beginning to brown. Remove from the heat and mix in the garlic.

Lay a tortilla flat on a plate. Put the rice and bean mixture in a line across the middle and add the roast vegetables and any other toppings you like. Fold the sides over the edge of the filling, then fold the bottom half just under the bottom line of the filling and roll. If you'd like it warm, fry the burritos in a pan, seam-side down. for 3–4 minutes on each side until lightly browned.

Chickpeas

Like all beans and legumes, chickpeas (also known as garbanzo beans) are a cheap source of protein, and eating some type of bean a few times a week or even every other day will increase your health. Chickpeas are famous for the part they play in Middle Eastern and Indian dishes like hummus, falafel and curries. Chickpeas are easily available dried and cooked.

Benefits

As well as a source of protein, chickpeas are a good source of manganese for bone development and wound healing, fibre for digestive support and folate for brain development. Because three-quarters of the fibre is insoluble and remains undigested until it reaches the end of the large intestine, it is very beneficial for your colon. The fibre combined with the protein is the perfect duo for regulating blood sugar levels, ensuring that food is digested slowly and passes through the digestive tract at the right speed. Chickpeas will support your heart and blood pressure, skin and hair and are anti-inflammatory.

Ways to Eat

- Buy good hummus or make your own (blend chickpeas, extra virgin olive oil, tahini, garlic, lemon juice and salt).
- Make chickpea flatbreads (see page 42).
- Add to soups whole or puréed.
- Find a great recipe for Italian *ceci* (chickpea) soup.
- Sprout (see page 134) and eat raw in green, mixed, pasta or grain salads.
- Sprinkle on salads.
- Cook Indian dishes like chana masala or chickpea dhal.
- Mix with penne, feta, extra virgin olive oil and oregano.
- Simmer with tomatoes and spices and serve over wholegrain rice.
- See more suggestions on page 130.

How to Use

It's always best to prepare your own chickpeas (see page 134), as they provide the best nutrition and reduce unwanted wind. Making your own chickpeas isn't difficult, it just takes a lot of soaking and simmering time. If you're in a hurry, tinned organic chickpeas are a good second, but you should rinse them to reduce the salt.

Some hummus enthusiasts expound the virtues of picking the skins off for a creamier hummus, but the fibre is good for you.

BASE RECIPE
Cooked Chickpeas

Put 200g/7oz/1 cup chickpeas (garbanzo beans) in a large saucepan and cover with double the volume of warm water. Add 1 tbsp apple cider vinegar and leave to soak, covered, for 8 hours or overnight.

Rinse well, add 700ml/24fl oz/2¾ cups fresh water, bring to the boil and boil hard for 10 minutes, skimming the scum that forms on the surface. Reduce the heat to low, add 1 kombu strip (you can either chop it finely with scissors or chop it afterwards when it is soft), and simmer, loosely covered, for 2 hours until soft.

Drain any remaining water and Add 1 tsp fine sea salt.

Chickpea Salad

This simple salad always delights. Once the beans are cooked, it is quick to prepare and makes a great starter or a light summer dinner. Serve with Chicory Salad (see page 58) and noodles tossed with toasted sesame oil and sesame seeds or furikake, a Japanese seasoning mix of black and white sesame seeds with bits of nori and shiro leaves.

Serves: 4
Prep: 15 minutes
Cook: 2 hours 10 minutes

270g/9½oz/1½ cups dried chickpeas (garbanzo beans), cooked (see above)
200g/7oz/2 cups finely chopped tomatoes
1 small red onion, finely chopped
6 tbsp chopped parsley
6 tbsp extra virgin olive oil
2 tbsp lemon juice
1 tbsp ground cumin
1 tsp ground coriander
1½ tsp fine sea salt
pinch of cayenne pepper

Mix all the ingredients together in a large bowl and serve.

BASE RECIPE
Sprouted Chickpeas

Put 100g/3½oz/½ cup chickpeas (garbanzo beans) in a large bowl and add double the volume of water. Soak for 24 hours.

Rinse and put in sprouting jars if you have them or in a medium bowl. Cover with water and rinse 2–3 times a day, drain in a colander and return to the bowl.

After 2–3 days, the chickpeas are ready to add to all kinds of salads.

Crunchy Spiced Chickpeas

This is probably the only bean recipe in this book where you don't want kombu in the final dish, so if you are cooking your own beans for this (see above), put the kombu in whole and remove it before making your spiced chickpeas. Make sure the chickpeas have a nice crunch before you take them out of the oven.

Makes: 425g/15oz/3 cups
Prep: 15 minutes
Cook: 35–40 minutes

200g/7oz/1 cup dried chickpeas (garbanzo beans), cooked (see above), or 425g/15oz/scant 3 cups cooked or tinned
2 tbsp extra virgin olive oil
1 tsp curry powder
1 tsp ground cumin
1 tsp fine sea sat

Preheat the oven to 200°C/400°F/gas mark 6. Drain the chickpeas and leave in a colander or spread on paper towels until dry.

In a medium bowl, mix the oil, curry powder, cumin and salt. Add the chickpeas and mix until combined. Spread on a large baking dish and bake for 35–40 minutes until lightly browned and crisp. Cool completely and eat the same day (or crisp in the oven briefly the following day).

Adzuki Beans

The adzuki bean is a small red-brown bean with a cream-coloured seam. These beans are widely used in Asian cooking and are prized in Japan as the king of beans. They have a nutty, ever so slightly sweet flavour, and are used in soups, but are particularly popular in Japan and China as a sweetened bean paste inside cakes, mochi (a Japanese rice cake) and other desserts.

Benefits

In Japan, adzuki beans are reputed for benefitting the liver and kidneys. In traditional Chinese medicine, they are valued for their healing properties for the kidneys, bladder and reproductive function. Macrobiotics say that adzukis are the most 'yang' or warming of beans and therefore good for strength.

In the West, we consider them nutritional powerhouses like other great beans: rich in protein, folate and fibre. They are known for antioxidant benefits, preventing diabetes, gastrointestinal support, assisting brain function, reducing the symptoms of PMS and contributing to strong bones and teeth.

Ways to Eat

- Purée with cumin, garlic, olive oil, lemon juice and sea salt to make a dip.
- Create beautifully coloured salads with a rainbow of veggies, leaves, seeds and more.
- Cook, season, add veggies and eat with different whole grains like rice, quinoa, barley and more.
- Find recipes for adzuki burgers.
- Try Japanese desserts with sweet adzuki bean paste.
- See more suggestions on page 130.

Adzuki Calamari Salad

This makes a lovely starter, or you could have it for lunch with good grains like wholegrain bread, rice or quinoa. The flavours of the grilled calamari combined with the slight heat of the onion, crunch of the pepper, freshness of the parsley and sweetness of the oranges works wonderfully. Swap scallops or shrimp for the calamari if you prefer.

Serves: 4
Prep: 20 minutes
Cook: 10–13 minutes

350g/12oz calamari, cut into rings
4 tbsp extra virgin olive oil
1¼ tsp fine sea salt
200g/7oz/1 cup adzuki beans, cooked (see page 131)
1 orange (bell) pepper, deseeded and cut into strips
1 small red onion, chopped
10 tbsp chopped parsley
3 oranges, 1½ juiced and 1½ peeled and roughly chopped

Heat the grill to high. Dry the calamari thoroughly on paper towels, then mix with 1 tablespoon of the oil and ¼ teaspoon of the salt. Put a single layer in a baking dish and grill for 10–13 minutes until tender and beginning to brown.

In a medium bowl, put the cooked adzuki beans, grilled calamari, remaining oil, the orange pepper, red onion, parsley, orange juice and pieces, and the remaining salt. Mix together well, then serve.

Lentils

Lentils are legumes, the seeds that grow in a pod. The lentil plant originally comes from Asia and North Africa where it is a staple part of many people's diets and a great, cheap source of protein. In their array of beautiful colours of yellow, red, green, brown and black, lentils have nurtured us for about 10,000 years.

Benefits

Lentils punch above their tiny weight because of their spectrum of minerals, B vitamins, fibre and protein. Not strongly flavoured, the beauty of lentils is that they absorb the herbs and spices with which they are cooked. They combine well with acid flavours like lemon juice and cheese or fermented foods like sauerkraut (see page 234) and kimchi (see page 236). Puy lentils, from the Le Puy region in France, are beautiful because they hold their shape. Split lentils, like yellow and red, cook down into a creamy purée, perfect for dhal.

Ways to Eat

• Simmer red lentils until tender and add cinnamon, dried fruits, nuts and something sweet if you like (coconut sugar, Manuka honey, brown rice syrup) for a protein-packed breakfast.
• Whizz them into dip or paté with crushed garlic, healthy oils, spices and salt instead of chickpeas (garbanzo beans).
• Cook them, dry them and bake them for tiny crunchy snacks.
• Make lentil soup, particularly Moroccan versions.
• Create lentil, vegetable and cheese salads with lemony dressings.
• Sprout them (see page 53).
• Mix with sweet potato, egg, onion, garlic and herbs to make veggie burgers.
• Add to quiche and savoury tarts and pies (see page 228).
• Try different kinds of dhal on wholegrain rice or served with wholegrain chapatis.
• Use in stuffing.

How to Use

The best way to cook lentils is to soak them for at least 8 hours in warm acidulated water. This enables you to digest them easily by neutralising the phytic acid and enzyme inhibitors (that stop them from sprouting at the wrong time) and the indigestible sugars that cause bloating and wind.

Always add salt after the lentils are cooked as it toughens their skins during cooking. Use 1 teaspoon fine sea salt for every 1 cup of uncooked lentils.

Black Lentil Dhal

Dhal is delicious, but Urad Dhal is divine. Traditional versions cook for a very long time in a beautiful clay pot, but this version is really worth making. Served over red Camargue rice or wholegrain rice, it's stunning and satisfying. Throw in a green salad for a complete meal.

Serves: 4
Prep: 30 minutes, plus overnight soaking
Cook: 1 hour 10 minutes

410g/14½oz/2 cups black lentils
2 tbsp cider vinegar or lemon juice
4 tbsp extra virgin olive oil
1 onion, chopped
960ml/32fl oz/4 cups water
4 very ripe tomatoes, chopped
2 bird's eye chillies, finely chopped
1½ tbsp finely chopped or grated ginger
½ cinnamon stick or ¼ tsp ground cinnamon
1 tsp ground cumin
1 tsp ground coriander
½ tsp ground turmeric
2 cardamom pods
4 garlic cloves, chopped
1½ tsp fine sea salt
2 tbsp lemon juice
wholegrain rice, to serve
2 tbsp plain yogurt per bowl, to serve (optional)
20g/¾oz chopped coriander (cilantro), to serve

Put the lentils and cider vinegar or lemon juice in a large saucepan and cover with double the volume of warm water. Leave to soak, covered, at room temperature overnight or for 8 hours.

Drain and rinse the lentils. Add the oil to a medium saucepan and heat over a medium heat. Add the onion and sauté for 10 minutes until beginning to brown. Add the measured water, lentils, tomatoes, chillies, ginger, cinnamon, cumin, ground coriander, turmeric and cardamom, bring to a simmer and cook over a low heat, covered, for 50 minutes.

Add the garlic and simmer for another 10 minutes until the lentils are soft. Add the salt and lemon juice. Serve over wholegrain rice with yogurt, if using, topped with chopped coriander.

Grains

Grains

Cereal grains and pseudocereals are the major source of carbohydrate for most people. Cereals, grown for their edible starchy seeds for eating or milling into flour, are part of the grass family. Pseudocereals are grown and used for the same purpose, but are not part of the grass family. Cereal grains include corn, barley, millet, oats, rice, sorghum, rye, spelt, teff, wild rice, wheat and others. Pseudocereals include amaranth, buckwheat and quinoa.

Benefits

Cereal grains have had a bad rap in the last few years. When eaten whole, in moderation and properly prepared, grains offer a wealth of goodness. The problem may be largely the consumption of too much white flour, too much wheat and too much fast-food grain.

A great whole food, grains are loaded with goodness. They are rich in protein, B vitamins, trace minerals, antioxidants, bran and fibre. The fibre in whole grains supports healthy digestion, promotes the growth of good bacteria in the colon and prevents constipation.

Whole grains reduce the risk of many chronic diseases, heart disease, high blood pressure, type 2 diabetes, obesity and some cancers.

Ways to Eat

- Eat whole grains and wholegrain flakes for breakfast with warming spices, soaked nuts and seeds, and super ingredients.
- Make wholegrain pancakes (see page 146) and waffles.
- Bread fish and chicken using wholegrain breadcrumbs.
- Use wholegrain pastas made from a variety of cereals.
- Try wholegrain Japanese noodles like buckwheat, barley, rice and more.
- Experiment with wholegrain rice of every type and colour.
- Add whole grains to soups and stews to thicken.
- Make pilaf with different whole grains.
- Eat wholegrain salads like tabbouleh.
- Make risottos with whole grains like barley, buckwheat, millet, quinoa and oats as well as rice.
- Swap white flour for wholegrain and sprouted wholegrain flours.
- Swap to wholegrain breakfast cereal, bread, pitta bread, crispbreads, cookies, crackers, biscuits, oatcakes, pasta and cereal bars.
- Eat soaked and cooked whole grains (see opposite) as a side dish.

How to Use

Grains are most nutritious and easiest to digest after soaking (see opposite). Although it is always best to eat whole grains, they need proper preparation so you can reap the full nutritional value and neutralise the phytic acid and enzyme inhibitors. Soaking also breaks down the gluten, or protein, in grains that is hard to digest and taxes our digestive system.

Reduce your consumption of wheat by substituting regular flour for ancient equivalents like spelt and Kamut or Khorasan. You can swap white flour for wholegrain spelt flour in any recipe, including in baking. Kamut flour is generally more expensive and has poorer quality gluten that is less elastic than spelt, but combined in equal measure with wholegrain spelt flour, Kamut creates pastry (see page 228) and pizza dough that are a delight to handle. Wholegrain Kamut flour is wonderful for making fresh pasta and in combination with rye for sourdough bread (see page 154).

BASE RECIPE
Soaked & Cooked Grains

Preparing grains properly means soaking them in warm acidulated water before you cook them. The ratio of grain to water depends on the type of grain and certain grains require more or less salt and cooking time. Use the individual quantities in the table below and then apply the following method for all (if using teff, whisk this into the water to distribute the grains).

Put the grain, warm water and 1 tablespoon plain yogurt or lemon juice in a saucepan and leave to soak, covered, for 8 hours or overnight at room temperature (24 hours for teff). Place the pan over a high heat, add the salt, bring to the boil, then reduce the heat to low and simmer, covered, for the correct time until tender.

BASE RECIPE
Toasted & Cooked Quinoa or Millet

Put 200g/7oz/1 cup quinoa or millet in a saucepan and toast over a medium–high heat, shaking the pan occasionally until the grain has browned slightly and begins to pop.

For quinoa, reduce the heat to low, carefully add 480ml/16fl oz/2 cups water and 1 teaspoon fine sea salt and simmer over a low heat for 20 minutes until tender.

For millet, add 480ml/16fl oz/2 cups water (carefully as it will splatter) and 1 teaspoon fine sea salt, and simmer, covered, for 25 minutes until tender. This will give you a dryish millet to use like rice or quinoa. For creamy porridge (oatmeal), increase the water to 720ml/24fl oz/3 cups and stir frequently.

Grain	Warm water	Fine sea salt	Cook
200g/7oz/1 cup quinoa	480ml/16fl oz/2 cups	1 tsp	15–20 mins
170g/7oz/1 cup buckwheat	600ml/20fl oz/2½ cups	½ tsp	15–20 mins
200g/7oz/1 cup millet	720ml/24fl oz/3 cups	1 tsp	15 mins
200g/6¾oz/1 cup rye	480ml/16fl oz/2 cups	½ tsp	45 mins
180g/6¼oz/1 cup barley	720ml/24fl oz/3 cups	½ tsp	45 mins
180g/6¼oz/1 cup spelt	480ml/16fl oz/2 cups	½ tsp	45 mins
200g/7oz/1 cup brown rice	540ml/18fl oz/2¼ cups	1 tsp	35 mins
150g/5½oz/1 cup wild rice	480ml/16fl oz/2 cups	1 tsp	40 mins
200g/7oz/1 cup teff	720ml/24fl oz/3 cups	½ tsp	15–20 mins

Oats

Before they were eaten as food, oats were used for medicinal purposes. Oats are a hearty cereal grain, able to withstand difficult soil conditions where other crops fail. Some say the strength of the oat is transferred to those who eat it. After harvesting and cleaning, oats are roasted and hulled, but the bran and germ are left intact, leaving them with great nutrients and fibre.

Benefits

For a long time, it was said that oats contain gluten. However, because they are often processed using the same farm equipment and in the same factory as gluten-containing grains, oats are often cross-contaminated. Oats do not contain gluten, but they do contain avenin, a protein similar to gluten, but tolerated by coeliacs.

Oats contain antioxidant compounds called avenanthramides, which are unique to them, and reduce the risk of cardiovascular disease, reduce inflammation and itching. Oats contain a specific type of fibre called beta-glucan, which enhances our immune system's ability to fight bacterial infections. Beta-glucan also produces much lower rises in blood sugar levels, making it a good way to start the day, and beta-glucan increases the growth of good bacteria in the digestive tract.

Ways to Eat

- Add leftover porridge (oatmeal) to smoothies.
- Mix leftover porridge (oatmeal) with an egg and a pinch of salt and fry as a big patty in healthy oil.
- Eat oatcakes with hummus; bean dip with grated carrot or beetroot (beet); salmon and cream cheese; butter; Cheddar; kimchi and prawns (shrimp); mashed avocado; sardines; a thin round slice of apple; pesto; mashed peas and crumbled feta; prosciutto or ham and mustard; almond butter and banana slices; egg, tuna or chicken mayo; grilled artichokes; olive tapenade and more.
- Eat savoury or fruit-sweetened porridge (oatmeal) at other times of the day.
- Bake oaty cookies.
- Add oats to pancakes (see page 146) and bread dough.
- Swap 10 per cent of your flour for oats in muffins and quick breads.
- Enjoy crumble.
- Make traybakes.

How to Use

Like every grain, oats are most nutritious and easiest to digest after soaking (see right).

BASE RECIPE
Soaked & Cooked Oatmeal

For each person, in a saucepan, put 45g/1½oz/½ cup medium oatmeal, 200ml/7fl oz/¾ cup water and ½ tbsp yogurt, kefir or lemon juice. Leave to soak, covered, at room temperature overnight. The next morning, add ⅛ tsp fine sea salt, bring to a simmer and cook for 5 minutes, stirring occasionally.

BASE RECIPE
Soaked & Cooked Porridge (Oatmeal)

For each person, in a saucepan put 45g/1½oz/½ cup porridge or rough oats, 240ml/8fl oz/1 cup warm water and ½ tbsp yogurt, kefir or lemon juice. Leave to soak, covered, at room temperature overnight. The next morning, add ⅛ tsp fine sea salt, bring to a simmer and cook for 5 minutes, stirring occasionally.

Savoury Oatmeal

Top this divine oatmeal with a fried or poached egg for protein. Or go the traditional porridge (oatmeal) route instead, omitting the spinach, avocado and tomato, and adding fresh or dried fruit, seeds, nuts and more.

Serves: 4
Prep: 10 minutes, plus overnight soaking
Cook: 5 minutes

180g/6¼oz/2 cups medium oatmeal
800ml/28fl oz/3½ cups warm water
2 tbsp plain yogurt, kefir or lemon juice
¾ tsp fine sea salt
60g/2oz spinach, roughly chopped
2 tomatoes, chopped
2 avocados, chopped
2 tbsp extra virgin olive oil
2 tsp ground cumin
1 tsp ground turmeric

Put the oatmeal, water, yogurt, kefir or lemon juice and salt in a medium saucepan, stir, and leave to soak, covered, at room temperature overnight.

Add the spinach, mix and bring to a simmer over a medium–high heat. Reduce the heat to low and simmer for 5 minutes, stirring often, until it has thickened, but is not stiff. Add the tomatos, avocados, oil, cumin and turmeric and serve.

Wholegrain Flour

Refined, white flour has the bran and germ removed; it is a simple carbohydrate with so little nutritional value that by law, synthetic vitamins must be added back in. In contrast, wholegrain flour includes the beauty and benefits of the whole grain with its germ and bran intact.

Benefits

In white flour, more than half of some of the B vitamins, vitamin E, folic acid, calcium, phosphorus, zinc, copper, iron and fibre are lost. The germ, included in wholegrain flour, is the embryo of the grain, and is packed with vitamins and minerals. Using wholegrain flour gives you all of the nutrients that nature provides. Not only does eating wholegrain products reduce the risk of type 2 diabetes, but it should also be a focus within the diet for diabetics.

The Organic Advantage

The highest concentration of agro-chemicals is found in the outer layer of the grain. Buy organic and avoid the worry and risk.

How to Use

For regular baking, I prefer wholegrain spelt flour, which you can simply substitute for white flour. Barley, Kamut, oat and rye flours also contain less gluten, so you can mix with other flours depending on the baked good. For gluten-free baking, avoid highly refined flours and look for wholegrain flours instead.

Soaking flour provides the best nutrition, but is not always easy to do. Use sprouted flours if you can and find recipes for soaking flour like in this pancake recipe (right) and the soaked pastry on page 228.

Overnight Wholegrain Pancakes

These American-style pancakes are great breakfast for kids, providing sustained energy. For a weekend treat, mix part of the batter on Friday night so the flour can soak and break down the phytic acid, and then on Saturday morning, finish the batter off and you're ready to roll.

Serves: 4
Prep: 10 minutes, plus overnight soaking
Cook: 8–12 minutes

100g/3½oz/1 cup rough oats (or millet, barley or buckwheat flakes)
120g/4¼oz/1 cup wholegrain spelt flour
240ml/8fl oz/1 cup warm water
2 tbsp plain yogurt, kefir or lemon juice
¼ tsp fine sea salt
1 tsp bicarbonate of soda (baking soda)
1 egg
50g/1¾oz/scant ½ cup blueberries
lemon and organic sugar or butter and maple syrup, to serve

Optional toppings:
fruit such as raspberries, blackberries or chopped strawberries, bananas, peaches or nectarines; soaked nuts such as pecans, walnuts, almonds or shredded coconut; seeds like milled linseeds or soaked sunflower seeds

Mix the oats or flakes, flour, water, yogurt, kefir or lemon juice and salt in a medium bowl. Leave to soak, covered, overnight at room temperature.

Add the bicarbonate of soda (baking soda) and mix well. Add the egg and mix well. Add the blueberries and/or nuts and/or seeds, if using, Heat a griddle pan (frying pan with oil) over a medium–low heat and cook for 2–3 minutes on each side until lightly browned. Serve in a stack with your favourite toppings – butter and a little sugar, maple syrup or lemon and sugar.

Buckwheat

Buckwheat is a pseudocereal. Although it is eaten like a cereal, it doesn't grow on grass and is a fruit seed like quinoa and amaranth. Buckwheat is an interesting triangular shape and is naturally gluten-free. It is sold raw or toasted, the latter of which is called 'kasha'. It is also ground into flour and can be used for pancakes, used in baking and made into noodles.

Benefits

Buckwheat is high in minerals and antioxidants. Eaten as a whole seed, it is a good source of fibre and helps moderate blood sugar levels. It is rich and well-balanced in amino acids, so is a good source of protein. Because it is lower in phytic acid than other grains, even without soaking, buckwheat offers better absorption of its minerals than other grains. Its manganese supports healthy metabolism and growth, its copper is an important trace element that may help the heart, its magnesium may lower the risk of type 2 diabetes and heart disease, its iron reduces the risk of anaemia and its phosphorus supports growth and maintenance of tissues in the body.

Ways to Eat

- Soak and cook buckwheat porridge (oatmeal).
- Make pancakes or waffles with buckwheat flour.
- Add to soups.
- Use sprouted buckwheat to make tabbouleh.
- Try buckwheat noodles instead of pasta.
- Use cooked buckwheat in place of rice or pasta.
- Make buckwheat salad with salad leaves or vegetables.
- Add to soups to thicken.
- Create buckwheat grain burgers with beans, egg and Cajun spices of cayenne, thyme, oregano, basil and parsley.
- Replace rice with buckwheat for risotto.
- Bake chocolate-chip cookies with buckwheat flour.

How to Use

Buy untoasted buckwheat so you can soak or sprout it. Like every grain, buckwheat is most nutritious and easiest to digest after soaking (see page 143).

BASE RECIPE
Sprouted Buckwheat

Prep: 2–3 days

Day 1:
Rinse 200g/7oz/1 cup buckwheat in a colander, then put in a sprouting jar, filling it with water. Leave to soak for 30 minutes. Drain the water, rinse 2–3 times and drain. For the first day, rinse and drain every hour or so until the water is clear.

Days 2–3:
Rinse and drain 3 times a day. Repeat if necessary on a third day until the sprouts are 1–2.5cm/½–1 inch in length. Rinse and drain well and keep in an airtight container in the fridge for up to 3 days.

Creamed Raw Buckwheat

Sprouted buckwheat mixed with fruits, seeds and yogurt is a great breakfast, but throwing it in the blender creates a creamy mix that's even better. You can experiment with different fruits, soaked nuts and seeds for varied flavour combinations and nutritional results.

Serves: 4
Prep: 15 minutes

200g/7oz/1 cup buckwheat, sprouted (sprouted weight should be about 450g/1lb)
360ml/11fl oz/1½ cups rice milk or other non-dairy milk
1 banana, sliced
100g/3½oz/1 cup strawberries, sliced
40g/1½oz/½ cup flaked almonds
yogurt and bee pollen, to serve (optional)

Put the sprouted buckwheat, rice milk and banana in a blender or food processor and blend until smooth. Pour into bowls and top with strawberries, almonds and hemp seeds. Add yogurt and bee pollen if desired.

Millet

Thought to have originated in Africa, millet has been consumed since prehistoric times and is mentioned in the Bible as an ingredient for unleavened bread. Millet is technically a seed, not a grain, and is gluten-free. It is often eaten as porridge (oatmeal), but is also good mixed into dishes like veggie burgers and salads.

Benefits

Millet is a good source of copper, manganese, phosphorus and magnesium. It is very high in silica, which helps keep bones flexible as we get older, and it is low in phytic acid. Millet has heart-protective properties, helps with the development and repair of body tissues, lowers the risk of type 2 diabetes, can help women avoid gallstones, protects against breast cancer and as a whole grain, can help reduce childhood asthma. Many studies show that eating whole grains like millet is linked to many health benefits.

Millet contains a goitrogen – a substance that disrupts the production of thyroid hormone – in the hull, so should be avoided by those with thyroid problems.

Ways to Eat

- Have millet porridge (oatmeal) with your favourite toppings for breakfast.
- Simmer with onion, garlic, water, cumin and curry powder for a spiced side dish.
- Put some soaked millet into soup to thicken.
- Create millet salads with beef, chicken or fish, lots of chopped vegetables and spices like toasted mustard and coriander seeds.
- Mix with chopped veg and spices and stuff into vegetables.
- Use instead of rice, quinoa or pasta.
- Swap millet flakes for porridge (rolled) oats in cookies, traybakes, quick breads and yeasted breads.

How to Use

Like every grain, millet is most nutritious and easiest to digest after soaking (see page 143).

Millet Bean Burgers

Burgers are all about the fixin's, so serve these with lettuce, tomato, gherkin and red onion on a wholegrain burger bun with mayonnaise, mustard and/or ketchup. Or keep them gluten-free and serve plated with sliced avocado. If you dust the uncooked burgers with buckwheat flour, they'll be crisper.

Serves: 4 (makes 10)
Prep: 25 minutes, plus overnight soaking
Cook: 10–12 minutes per batch

100g/3½oz/½ cup millet
350ml/12fl oz/1½ cups water
½ tbsp yogurt, kefir or lemon juice
200g/7oz/1 cup dried black beans or 440g/15½oz/
   2½ cups cooked black beans (see page 131)
1 tbsp cider vinegar
1 kombu strip (optional)
2 eggs, beaten with a fork
1 onion, chopped
1 small or ½ unpeeled beetroot (beet), grated
1 carrot, grated
4 tbsp chopped parsley
2 tbsp milled linseeds (flaxseeds)
2 garlic cloves, crushed
2 tbsp Dijon mustard
2 tsp balsamic vinegar
1½ tsp dried thyme
1¼ tsp fine sea salt
2 tsp extra virgin olive oil

Put the millet, water, yogurt, kefir or lemon juice and salt in a small saucepan and leave to soak, covered, for 8 hours or overnight. Put the black beans, double the amount of warm water and the vinegar in a medium saucepan and leave to soak, covered, overnight.

Bring the millet and water to the boil over a high heat. Reduce the heat to low and simmer for 15 minutes until soft. Drain the beans, add 1.2 litres/40fl oz/5 cups water and cook for 15 minutes until tender. Add the kombu, if using, reduce the heat to low and simmer the beans, covered, for 2 hours. Drain and mash the beans.

In a medium bowl, mix the millet, black beans, eggs, onion, beetroot, carrot, parsley, linseeds, garlic, mustard, balsamic vinegar, thyme and salt and mix well, ensuring you break up the clumps of cooked millet. Take 5 tablespoons of the mixture and form it into 8cm/3¼ inch patties – you can use a pastry cutter if you want perfect circles or just drop large spoonfuls into the pan. They are a bit wet, so you can form them on a plate and then slide into the frying pan.

Put the oil in a large frying pan (skillet) and heat over a medium heat. Put the burgers in the pan and fry for 5–6 minutes on each side until browned. Serve with lettuce, tomato, gherkins and red onion on a wholegrain burger bun with your choice of sauce, or serve bunless with sliced avocado.

Rye

Rye is a low-gluten grain, known for dense, dark, sour breads in Germany and Scandinavian countries. While growing, rye is tougher than other grains, and is able to thrive in hard soils and poor climates. It competes well with weeds and adds to soil fertility, so it is often used in crop rotation. Because it is low in gluten and lacks elasticity, it is ideal for making sourdough breads.

Benefits

Rye is a good source of fibre that is extraordinarily good at binding with water. This gives a feeling of being full and satisfied, making rye bread a much better choice than wheat. Rye is high in insoluble fibre, which can help prevent gallstones in women. Its richness in magnesium, which is involved in the body's use of glucose and insulin release, plus its high fibre, make rye a good option for those with type 2 diabetes. As a whole grain, rye has cardiovascular benefits for post-menopausal women and generally helps prevent high blood pressure and heart attacks.

Ways to Eat

- Have rye porridge (oatmeal) for breakfast.
- Use cooked rye grain in salads with other vegetables, fresh herbs, cheese, and lovely dressings.
- Substitute rye bread for sandwiches – it marries well with cheese, smoked salmon, egg, pastrami and mustards.
- Make rye bread.
- Swap up to a quarter of flour in baked goods for wholegrain rye flour.

How to Use

Like every grain, rye is most nutritious and easiest to digest after soaking (see page 143).

Rye Porridge

The nice thing about rye porridge is that it retains a slightly chewy texture, which makes a nice change. On its own, like many grains, this is a bit dull, but add dried cranberries, milled linseeds (flaxseeds), Greek yogurt and rice milk, and it's delicious. Add lovely toppings or mix-ins as you would with oat porridge.

Serves: 2
Prep: 5 minutes, plus overnight soaking
Cook: 10 minutes

120g/4¼oz/1 cup rye flakes
480ml/16fl oz/2 cups water
1 tablespoon plain yogurt, kefir or lemon juice
¼ teaspoon fine sea salt

Soak the rye flakes in the water and plain yogurt, kefir or lemon juice. Leave to soak, covered, at room temperature for 8 hours or overnight.

Add the salt and bring to a simmer. Cook over a low heat, for 10 minutes, stirring occasionally, until tender. Add toppings or mix-ins as desired.

Sourdough Wholegrain Rye Bread

It takes about a week to get your starter going for this recipe but making the bread is easy because you don't have to knead it. I always make two loaves because it is no extra work and you can slice and freeze one. This bread has a lovely texture and a delicate sourness. It is gorgeous toasted and marries well with nut butters or cheese.

Although this is not a heavy, dark rye loaf, you can lighten it in the second phase by using 500g/1lb 2oz/4 cups Kamut flour and 150g/5½oz/1¼ cups wholegrain rye (instead of 660g/1lb 7oz/2 cups wholegrain rye flour). For variation, you can add 2 tbsp of cracked linseeds (flaxseeds) or caraway seeds in Phase 2.

Makes: 2 loaves
Prep: 30 minutes, plus waiting time
Bake: 50 minutes

For the starter:
9 tbsp organic wholegrain rye flour
9 tbsp water, plus more if needed

Put 3 tablespoons each of the flour and water in a glass jar (I don't like plastic and it should not be metallic) and mix well. Lightly cover the mixture, but don't screw a lid on as the pressure can explode the jar. Leave the jar on the worktop.

Every day or so for a week, add another tablespoon of flour and water, stirring until combined – it should be the consistency of thick, Greek yogurt. By day 7, you should have a bubbling starter that smells pleasantly yeasty. If you live in the countryside it is easier and quicker because there are more natural yeasts in the air.

Phase 1:
100g/3½oz rye starter
300g/10½oz/2½ cups wholegrain rye flour
570ml/20fl oz/2½ cups warm water

In a large bowl, mix the starter, flour and water – a wire whisk works well. Leave covered with a towel or in a cold oven for several hours until it is really bubbling. I like to mix it in the evening and leave it until the next evening.

Phase 2:
10g/¼oz fine sea salt
200ml/7fl oz/scant 1 cup warm water
650g/1lb 7oz/5½ cups wholegrain rye flour
healthy oil, for greasing

Add the salt and water to the starter and mix well. Add the flour and mix with a wooden spoon. The dough should be stiff, but soft enough to incorporate all of the flour.

Grease two 23 x 11cm/9 x 4½ inch bread tins (if they are made of tin, line with greaseproof paper first) and divide the dough evenly between the two. Smooth the tops and let them rise in a cold oven until they are nearly at the top of the tin. Push the bread gently with your finger – if it springs back, it can rise some more. If it stays indented or moves back very slowly, it is ready for baking. I let mine rise overnight and bake them in the morning because a long fermentation increases the nutrients.

Preheat the oven to 230°C/450°F/gas mark 8. Bake the loaves for 15 minutes, then lower the temperature to 200°C/400°F/gas mark 6 and continue baking for 35 minutes.

Remove the loaves from the tins and cool on wire racks until completely cool. Rye bread will cut better if you wait a day, but if you are desperate and want it hot, eat it straight away, although it will stick to the bread knife. It will keep for at least a week without getting mouldy.

If two loaves are too much for you to eat in a week, simply wait until the next day, then slice the second loaf, put it in a plastic bag and freeze. It's the same effort to make two and you'll have one in the freezer for toasting.

Feed the depleted starter with about 4 tablespoons of flour and water, cover and put in the fridge until you want to make rye again. The day before, take it out and add another 5 tablespoons flour and water. Leave on the worktop until the next evening, then start again.

If the starter grows mould and doesn't smell good, throw it away and begin again.

Barley

Barley is one of the earliest cultivated grains and is one of the most widely eaten grains in the world. It is nutty with a pleasant, chewy texture. Barley is sold in two forms: pot and pearl. Pot barley, which has the bran and germ intact, with only the inedible outer shell removed, is a whole food and offers superior nutrition. Pearl barley has the outer husk and bran removed.

Benefits

Like other whole grains, barley is a good source of vitamins, minerals and fibre, but when compared to other grains, pot barley punches above its weight for high soluble and insoluble fibre and trace minerals. It is also a very good source of selenium, an important mineral, particularly for fighting cancer.

Barley and other whole grains are rich sources of magnesium, a mineral that acts as a co-factor for more than 300 enzymes, including enzymes involved in the body's use of glucose and insulin secretion.

Barley is a low-gluten grain, the gluten of which is good for making bread. Historically, it has been used for baking, particularly barley and rye in combination.

Ways to Eat

- Use barley flakes to make hot cereal for a change from porridge (oatmeal).
- Add to soups and stews.
- Mix with chopped vegetables and tahini or other dressings for cold salads.
- Make barley burgers or fritters.
- Cook in water or stock and use instead of rice for risotto or pilaf.
- Substitute some barley flour for other flour in baking for a sweet flavour.

How to Use

Like every grain, barley is most nutritious and easiest to digest after soaking (see page 143).

Barley & Black Bean Chilli

The cooking time might look lengthy here, but as long as you're at home, you can do other things while the beans and chilli are simmering away. Also, if you use cooked beans, you can reduce the cooking time to just over an hour. This is a satisfying chilli with rich flavours, perfect for cold nights. It is dairy-free, but marries well with yogurt or cheese. This makes a large quantity, but it is worth making for sharing or freezing.

Serves: 4
Prep: 25 minutes, plus overnight soaking
Cook: 2 hours 50 minutes

400/14oz/2 cups dried black beans or 1kg/2lb 4oz/
    4 cups cooked black beans
2 tbsp cider vinegar
1 kombu strip, finely chopped (optional)
200g/7oz/1 cup uncooked pot barley
1 tbsp yogurt, kefir or lemon juice
2 litres/3½ pints/8 cups water or stock
4 tbsp extra virgin olive oil
2 onions, chopped
1kg/2lb 4oz/10 cups diced tomatoes
2 carrots, chopped
5 tbsp tomato purée (paste)
2 tsp ground cumin
1 tsp ground turmeric
½ tsp ground paprika
¼ tsp ground chilli powder, or to taste
2 garlic cloves, finely chopped
1 tbsp fine sea salt
organic tortillas or Romaine lettuce hearts, to serve
Greek yogurt, guacamole or grated Cheddar cheese,
    to serve

If cooking dried beans, put the beans, double the amount of warm water and 2 tablespoons cider vinegar in a large saucepan and leave to soak, covered, at room temperature, overnight.

Put the barley in a medium saucepan with 700ml/ 24fl oz/3 cups water and 1 tablespoon yogurt, kefir or lemon juice.

Rinse the beans, add 950ml/32fl oz/4 cups water and bring to the boil. Boil the beans hard for 10 minutes and skim the scum from the surface. Reduce the heat to low, add the kombu, if using, and simmer, covered, for 1½ hours until soft.

Put the oil in a large saucepan over a medium heat. Add the onion and sauté for 10 minutes until beginning to brown. Add the beans, barley, water or broth, tomatoes, carrots, tomato purée (paste), cumin, turmeric, paprika and chilli powder and bring to the boil over a high heat. Reduce the heat to low and simmer, covered, for 1 hour until everything is soft and the beans are creamy. Add the garlic and salt and mix until combined.

Serve with Greek yogurt, guacamole or grated Cheddar and organic tortillas or Romaine lettuce hearts to make chilli baots.

Spelt

Spelt is an ancient predecessor of modern durum wheat and has been cultivated for 5,000 years. It is one of the original, ancient grains that nature, in her wisdom, created. When used in salads, soups and risottos, spelt has a tasty, nutty chewiness. Modern wheat, on the other hand, has been hybridized over centuries and is no longer considered even a good food by many modern nutritionists.

Benefits

Spelt has more protein, a higher profile of amino acids, lipids, vitamins and minerals and is easier to digest than modern wheat varieties. Spelt contains gluten, but it is shorter and more fragile, making it easier for the body to digest. Spelt provides slow-releasing energy, is a good source of protein and nutrients and supports your heart, blood and bones.

Compared to wheat, spelt is also low in a group of short-chain carbohydrates named FODMAPs (Fermentable Oligosaccharides, Disaccharides, Monosaccharides and Polyols). Because FODMAPs are badly absorbed in the small intestine, they ferment and cause wind and bloating, which many people experience with wheat.

Ways to Eat

- Look for spelt bread, breakfast cereals, biscuits, crackers, grissini, pasta and grains.
- Use the whole grain in salads, soups and as sides to replace pasta, rice and potatoes.
- Make risotto with spelt grains.
- Swap white flour with wholegrain spelt flour in your favourite baked goods.

How to Use

Like all grains, spelt is most nutritious and easiest to digest after soaking (see page 143).

Replace regular flour for ancient wholegrain equivalents like spelt (and Kamut or Khorasan). You can swap white flour for wholegrain spelt flour in any recipe, including in baking.

Spelt Soup

A classic Tuscan soup, this makes a warming and well-balanced lunch. The soup starts with *odori*, the base stock of many Tuscan soups, which is a mix of finely chopped onion/red onion, carrot, celery, parsley and sometimes garlic sautéed in olive oil. When the soup is ready it should not be too thick or too thin. If you use cooked beans, you can reduce the cooking time to an hour.

Serves: 4
Prep: 30 minutes, plus overnight soaking
Cook: 2 hours 40 minutes

200g/7oz/1 cup dried cannellini or borlotti beans or
    425g/15oz/2¾ cups cooked beans
1 tbsp cider vinegar
180g/6¼oz/1 cup spelt grains
1 tbsp plain yogurt, kefir or lemon juice
350ml/12fl oz/1½ cups water
1 kombu strip, cut into small pieces (optional)
2 tsp chopped sage
2 tsp chopped rosemary
4 garlic cloves, 2 crushed and 2 chopped
4 tbsp extra virgin olive oil, plus extra for serving
1 onion, diced
1 carrot, thinly sliced
1 celery stick, diced
3 small tomatoes, diced
30g/1oz pancetta, chopped (optional)
240ml/8fl oz/1 cup water
1 tsp fine sea salt or 1 tbsp miso
4 tbsp roughly chopped parsley

Put the beans in a saucepan, cover with double the amount of warm water and add the vinegar. Soak, covered, at room temperature overnight. Put the spelt in another saucepan and add the yogurt, kefir or lemon juice and water. Soak, at room temperature, overnight or for 8 hours.

Drain the beans, rinse, add 1.4l/48fl oz/5½ cups fresh water and bring to the boil over a high heat. Boil hard for 10 minutes and skim any scum from the surface, then add the kombu, if using, 1 teaspoon of the sage, 1 teaspoon of the rosemary and the crushed garlic cloves. Reduce the heat to low and simmer, covered, for 70 minutes. Add the spelt and simmer, covered, for 20 minutes.

In a large saucepan, heat the olive oil over a medium heat. Add the onion, carrot, celery, tomatoes, pancetta, if using, chopped garlic and remaining sage and rosemary, and sauté for 10 minutes until beginning to brown. Add the beans (including water and everything). Bring to a simmer and cook, covered, for another 30 minutes.

Add the salt or if you are using miso, dissolve it in some of the soup water and stir in (do not boil once you have added miso). Just before serving, add the parsley. Immerse a hand-held blender in the soup and part purée, then serve drizzled with a little oil.

Quinoa

An ancient grain from South America, quinoa (pronounced keen-wah) is renowned for its high protein content. Quinoa comes in white, red or black colours. It is easy to cook and easy to use.

Benefits

Quinoa is famous for the overall nutrients it provides. A pseudocereal, as it is not a grass, quinoa contains all nine essential amino acids, and is especially rich in lysine, which is necessary for growth and repair in the body. It is a valuable source of healthy fats and a good source of recommended daily allowance nutrients such as folate, zinc and phosphorus. It is also gluten-free.

Ways to Eat

Once quinoa is cooked, try this:
• Add it to smoothies.
• Use it like porridge (oatmeal).
• Create a breakfast parfait with yogurt, fruits, nuts and seeds.
• Stuff it into vegetables.
• Replace the meat in chilli con carne or tempeh in chilli non carne.
• Mix with sautéed veg in burritos.
• Put in savoury fritters.
• Mix into beef, chicken or veggie burgers.
• Use in place of rice or pasta to include another whole grain in your diet. It's also a great replacement for couscous or bulgur wheat.
• Swap with breadcrumbs as a binder or as breading/coating.
• Make quinoa pudding with non-dairy milk, coconut sugar or Manuka honey, cinnamon, nuts or berries.
• Include in traybakes.

How to Use

Quinoa is most nutritious and easiest to digest after soaking (see page 143) or toasting. If you're thinking ahead, soak quinoa overnight, but if you're in a hurry and haven't soaked it, simply toast it to neutralise the phytic acid (see page 143).

Quinoa Salad

My favourite way to eat quinoa is in a salad packed with a combination of steamed and raw veggies and sprouts, with a fabulous dressing. It's a great way to use any veg you have in the house. For a change, serve this as a wrap with nori rolled around the outside.

Serves: 4
Prep: 30 minutes
Cook: 20 minutes (while you're chopping)

150g/5½oz/¾ cup red quinoa, soaked or toasted, then cooked (see page 143)
150g/5½oz broccoli, chopped and lightly steamed
50g/1¾oz spinach or kale, chopped and lightly steamed
1 avocado, peeled, stoned (pitted) and chopped
1 large carrot, grated
50g/1¾oz seed sprouts
50g/1¾oz parsley, chopped

For the dressing:
1½ tbsp grated ginger
2 garlic cloves, crushed
2½ tsp soy sauce or tamari
6 tbsp extra virgin olive oil
3 tbsp cider vinegar

In a medium bowl, put the cooked quinoa, broccoli, spinach or kale, avocado, carrot, seeds sprouts and parsley.

In a small jar, mix all the dressing ingredients and shake until combined. Pour over the quinoa mix and toss until combined.

Teff

Teff is the tiniest grain in the world – and it's gluten-free. It is native to Ethiopia and used there to make injera, their fermented sourdough flatbread. Teff grain and teff flour are wonderful alternatives to wheat, barley and rye for those on a gluten-free diet.

Benefits

Teff has a low glycaemic index, so it gives long-lasting, slow-releasing energy. Teff is high in copper, a mineral that is important for many systems in the body. It is also high in protein with eight essential amino acids, and high in calcium and vitamin C, normally not found in grains. Teff is also rich in iron, which is easy to absorb. It fills you up, strengthens your bones and keeps you regular.

Ways to Eat

- Make teff porridge (oatmeal) with warming spices, soaked nuts, seeds and other super ingredients.
- Swap half of your gluten flour for teff flour.
- For gluten-free pastry, mix 280g/10oz/2 cups teff flour, ½ tsp fine sea salt, 90ml/3fl oz/⅓ cup extra virgin olive oil, 2 tbsp yogurt, kefir or lemon juice and 8–9 tbsp water, and leave to soak for 8 hours or overnight, then press into a pie tin, fill and bake.
- Use for gluten-free brownies.
- Make cookies and pancakes.
- Find recipes for teff burgers.

How to Use

Like every grain, teff is most nutritious and easiest to digest after soaking (see page 143). Teff can be soaked overnight, but if you have time, 24 hours is best.

Teff Spice Cookies

Cookies are very forgiving of gluten-free flour. Teff, with its chocolatey, nutty flavour, is perfect for cookies that provide nutrients as well as delight. These are nicely spiced with a delicate sweetness. They are gluten- and dairy-free.

Makes: 30 cookies
Prep: 15 minutes, plus overnight soaking
Bake: 12 minutes per batch

140g/5oz/1 cup wholegrain teff flour
100g/3½oz/1 cup jumbo oats
135g/4¾oz/generous 1 cup almonds, soaked (see page 169) and ground
75g/2½oz/⅓ cup organic sugar or 75g/2½oz/generous ½ cup coconut sugar
½–1 tbsp grated ginger
1 tbsp ground cinnamon
½ tsp dried mace
1 tsp baking powder
½ tsp fine sea salt
1 egg, beaten with a fork
80ml/2½fl oz/⅓ cup molasses
125ml/4fl oz/½ cup extra virgin olive oil or other healthy oil
1 tsp vanilla extract

Preheat the oven to 170°C/325°F/gas mark 3. In a medium bowl, mix the teff flour, oats, almonds, sugar, ginger, cinnamon, mace, baking powder and salt. In a small bowl, mix the egg, molasses, oil and vanilla. Add the egg mix to the teff mixture and mix until just combined.

Scoop the dough by the tablespoonful into balls and place on a cookie sheet. Flatten with a fork into 5cm/2 inch circles, making a criss-cross pattern on top. Bake for 12 minutes until lightly browned. Remove from the oven and put on wire racks to cool.

Wild Rice

Distant cousins to Asian rice, wild rice is not a grain but is the seed of marsh grasses from North America. The plants grow in shallow water in slow-moving streams and small lakes. They were harvested by Native Americans travelling in canoes and using sticks to knock the long, slender, black seeds into their boats.

Benefits

Cup for cup, wild rice outpunches wholegrain rice because it has less carbohydrate and more nutrients. It has more folate, zinc, and vitamin E than wholegrain rice. It is also high in fibre, magnesium, phosphorus, manganese, vitamin B6 and niacin.

Research on the health benefits of wild rice is scarce as it such a small part of people's diets, but the studies that have been carried out show that wild rice is extremely high in antioxidants.

Ways to Eat

- Add to omelettes.
- Use in savoury pancakes.
- Make pilaf or wild rice salads to accompany fish, chicken or meat.
- Use in casseroles or bakes.
- Bake into frittatas.
- Mix with chopped dried fruits, nuts, onion, herbs and more, and stuff into birds and vegetables.
- Cook and toss with nut oil and salt.
- Create wild rice pudding with chopped apricots, figs and/or cranberries.

How to Use

Mix it with other rice to make it more economical.

Like all grains, wild rice benefits from soaking (see page 143).

Wild Rice Chicken Soup

Chicken noodle soup is usually a winner. This version replaces those mushy white noodles with chewy, slightly nutty wild rice. If you've made your own chicken or fish broth, use it here for added flavour and nutrients. If there's any soup left over, this is great the next day, too. Refrigerate and eat within three days.

Serves: 8
Prep: 20 minutes, plus overnight soaking
Cook: 50 minutes

2 tbsp healthy oil
2 onions, chopped
100g/3½oz mushrooms, chopped
950ml/32fl oz/4 cups chicken broth (see page 122) or water
150g/5½oz/1 cup wild rice, soaked (see page 143)
1 tsp dried dill or thyme or sage
1 tsp fine sea salt, if not using stock
450g/1lb chicken breasts or thighs, cubed
4 celery sticks, chopped
2 carrots, grated
4 garlic cloves, roughly chopped
2 lemons, cut into wedges

Heat the oil in a large saucepan over a medium–high heat. Add the onion and sauté for 10 minutes until soft and beginning to brown. Add the mushrooms, chicken broth or water, wild rice, herbs and salt and bring to the boil over a high heat. Reduce the heat to low and simmer, covered, for 30 minutes. Stir, add the chicken, celery, carrots and garlic, and simmer for another 10 minutes until the chicken is cooked through.

Serve with lemon wedges to squeeze over the soup.

Wholegrain Rice

Some see rice as the perfect grain, in which yin and yang are equally balanced. Rice is the staple food in the Orient and the Japanese and Chinese eat about ten times more rice than Americans and English people. Interestingly, compared to westerners, Asians have a larger pancreas and salivary glands in relation to body weight, making them better suited to eating grains.

Benefits

Wholegrain or brown rice retains the nutrient-dense bran and germ, with only the inedible outer hull removed. It is the highest of all grains in B vitamins; it also contains iron, vitamin E and some protein, but no gluten.

If wholegrain rice is good for you, black rice is even better. The bran hull contains significantly higher amounts of vitamin E, which bolsters the immune system and protects cells from free radical damage. And black rice contains more anthocyanin antioxidants than blueberries, according to a recent study. Black and red rice add beauty to simple meals.

Although wholegrain rice is relatively low in phytic acid compared to other grains, it will still benefit from soaking overnight or for 8 hours (see page 143). You can put it to soak in the morning, then it will be ready to cook that evening for dinner. Even if you forget to soak it, it's still much better for you than white rice.

Ways to Eat

- Make endless varieties of rice salads with meats, fish and vegetables.
- Make rissoles.
- Fry leftover rice with eggs.
- Add cooked rice to tomato soup.
- Enjoy different types of rice with meats, fish or tempeh.
- Make risotto.
- Create sushi.
- Stir-fry vegetables to have over rice and top with toasted seeds, nuts and/or soaked arame seaweed.
- Serve gumbo over rice.
- Stuff into vegetables.
- Create your own egg-fried rice with water chestnuts and bamboo shoots.
- Make rice pancakes.
- Make paella.
- Eat jambalaya.
- Enjoy with dhal or curry.
- Stuff into birds at Christmas.
- Create countless casseroles.
- Whip up some rice pudding.

How to Use

Eat wholegrain rice that has only the husk removed. This is also known as brown or unpolished rice and it is packed with vitamins, minerals, protein and fibre.

Arborio: perfect for risotto because it is firm, chewy, creamy and holds a lot of liquid. Brown Arborio must be soaked prior to cooking or it takes hours to make risotto.

Basmati: aromatic, elegant rice grown in the Himalayas, good for scented Indian dishes.

Black: thought to be an incredibly nutritious mutation of Japanese rice, black rice has an earthy, nutty flavour with a texture like white rice once it's cooked. It is a sticky rice and it turns the cooking water a beautiful deep purple.

Jasmine: commonly used in Southeast Asian cooking, jasmine rice is a long-grain rice from Thailand that has a delicate floral aroma and a soft, sticky texture when cooked. The grains are shorter and thicker than basmati rice.

Red Camargue: from the South of France, this rice has a nutty, rich flavour. When cooked, it is softer than wholegrain brown rice, so it is a good rice to start with if you only eat white rice. It marries well with cinnamon and cardamom.

Brown short grain: starchier and stickier than long grain.

Brown sushi: a lightly sticky rice, but not a 'glutinous rice' (a very sticky rice that does not actually contain gluten, which is too gummy for sushi).

Brown sweet: for puddings and sushi as it is sticky.

Brown Rice Paella

Paella is like a less-stirred Spanish version of Italy's risotto. The flavours in this are absolutely wonderful for such a simple dish. I use fish, prawns (shrimp) and scallops, but you can swap out those shellfish for clams and mussels or try with fish and strips of chicken or beef and sausage. If you use chorizo, reduce the salt.

Serves: 4
Prep: 20 minutes, plus overnight soaking
Cook: 30–40 minutes

4 tbsp extra virgin olive oil
1 large tomato, chopped
1 red (bell) pepper, chopped
1 onion, chopped
8 garlic cloves, chopped
1 tbsp chopped thyme
2 tsp sweet paprika
750ml/26fl oz/3 cups water or fish stock
3 pinches of saffron
1¾ tsp fine sea salt
200g/7oz/1 cup short-grain brown rice, soaked (see page 143) and drained
200g/7oz firm fish (hake or monkfish is great), cut into bite-sized pieces
16 king prawns (shrimp), about 150g/5½oz, shell on and deveined
12 scallops (about 200g/7oz), sliced in half around the equator if they are very thick
2 spring onions (scallions), sliced
2 tbsp chopped parsley or more
lemon wedges, to serve

Additional ingredients (optional):
12 mussels
12 clams
200g/7oz chorizo or any sausage, thinly sliced
200g/7oz chicken or beef, cut into thin strips

Put the oil in a large frying pan or paella pan and heat over a medium heat. Add the tomato, red pepper and onion and sauté for 10 minutes until soft and beginning to brown.

Add the garlic, thyme and paprika and sauté for another minute. Add the water, saffron, salt and rice and bring to the boil. Reduce the heat to low and simmer, stirring occasionally, for 15–25 minutes (it will depend on your type of rice, so you need to check) until the rice is al dente. You may need to add a little more water, depending on the rice you are using. The final dish should be wet, but not soupy, but if it is, just serve in bowls.

Put the fish and shellfish, if using (or mussels, clams or meat, if using), on top of the mixture, cover and simmer, stirring once or twice, for another 5 minutes until the fish is just cooked. Sprinkle the spring onions and parsley on top and serve hot with lemon wedges.

Nuts

Nuts

Nuts are nature's little storehouses – a combination of protein, fibre and great fats mixed with minerals and vitamins. These three macronutrients unite to form a filling and satisfying snack. If you're hungry in-between meals, enjoy a handful of nuts or some nut butter on a wholegrain cracker or oatcake.

Benefits

Nuts are low in carbs, but high in healthy fats, protein and fibre, making them a perfect choice for diabetics. Studies show that eating nuts can increase satiety and help you eat fewer calories, and the monounsaturated fats reduce your risk of heart disease. Although some people avoid nuts because of the fear of weight gain, a study published in the journal *Obesity* shows such fears are groundless. In fact, people who ate nuts at least twice a week were much less likely to gain weight than those who almost never ate nuts.

Ways to Eat

- Add chopped or ground nuts to plain yogurt, porridge (oatmeal) or American-style pancakes.
- Spread nut butter on wholegrain toast instead of jam.
- A tablespoon of nut butter added to your morning smoothie, chia pot, breakfast parfait or smoothie bowl adds creaminess and protein.
- Eat an apple and a handful of soaked nuts or sliced apple with nut butter.
- Put nut butter on oatcakes.
- Create your own trail mix.
- Chop or grind and add to raw balls, bars or pies.
- Slice or chop nuts and add to sautéed vegetables, green salads, grain salads or pasta.
- Grind or finely chop and add to soup.

How to Use

In keeping with the idea that it is always best to eat whole foods, nuts should be eaten with their skins on. Nut skins are full of nutrients and fibre, and when eaten with the nut, they increase the nutrient value making the whole nut greater than the sum of its parts.

Nuts are best for you if you eat them raw, but they contain enzyme inhibitors that can be hard on your digestive system and phytic acid that binds to minerals in your large intestine, preventing you from absorbing them. To remedy this, you should soak nuts (see opposite) to make them easy to digest and more nutritious. Soaked nuts must be kept in the fridge and eaten quickly because they develop mould – unless you crisp them (see opposite). You can buy activated (soaked and dehydrated) nuts in some specialist stores.

Nuts vary in terms of the quantity of their oils. The higher the oil content, like pecans, the more quickly they spoil. Pale nuts mean fresh nuts. Picked off the tree and cracked open, pecans are actually pale – even with their skins on. Always keep raw nuts in the fridge to preserve their oils.

BASE RECIPE
Soaked Nuts

Soak 50g/1¾oz/½ cup of any kind of nut in 120ml/4fl oz/½ cup water and
¼ teaspoon fine sea salt for 8 hours or overnight. Drain and store in
an airtight container in the fridge. Eat within 5 days.

BASE RECIPE
Soaked & Crisped Nuts

Use the combination of nuts below or other varieties if you prefer. This
makes a large quantity because they keep well and you can use them for
snacking, breakfasts, salads, grain dishes, and raw balls and bars. If it looks
like too many for you, just cut the recipe in half.

Makes: 4 cups
Prep: 5 minutes, plus overnight soaking
Bake: 9–10 hours

1 tbsp fine sea salt
650ml/22fl oz/2¾ cups water
135g/4¾oz/1 cup almonds, skins on
100g/3½oz/1 cup pecans
100g/3½oz/1 cup walnuts
135g/4¾oz/1 cup hazelnuts, skins on

Put the salt and water in a large bowl and mix to dissolve the salt. Add
the almonds, pecans, walnuts and hazelnuts. Leave to soak for 8 hours or
overnight.

Preheat the oven to 50°C/120°F (or the lowest setting, but no more than
65°C/150°F). Drain the nuts and spread them out in a large baking dish or on
a large baking sheet. Bake, or dehydrate, for 9–10 hours or overnight until dry
and crispy. Store in an airtight container. If the container shows moisture on
the inside, dry the nuts for a bit longer.

Brazil Nuts

Brazil nuts come from a South American tree. They are actually seeds, but most people think of them as nuts because of their brown shell and nutty texture. Brazils are a deliciously fatty and creamy nut, making them a lovely snack and a great addition to other dishes. They are hugely popular in Latin America and beyond.

Benefits
Brazil nuts' claim to fame is that they are one of the richest food sources of selenium. Selenium is vital for anyone with an underactive thyroid. Just a few Brazil nuts each day will provide enough selenium to produce thyroxine or thyroid hormone. Selenium is also good for immune system support and the healing of wounds. The wonderful, unsaturated, polyunsaturated and omega-6 fats in Brazils makes for a happy heart, as well.

Ways to Eat
See the suggestions on page 168.

How to Use
Brazils are the fattiest nuts, up there with pecans and macadamias, so buy raw Brazils as pale as you can find them (paler nuts mean fresher nuts) and keep them in the fridge to preserve their precious oils.

Like all nuts, Brazils should be eaten raw, with their skins on, and soaked (see page 169).

Brazil Nut Balls

Quick and easy to make, these give a lovely energy boost. Although they have a lot of fructose from the dates, the balls also have nutrients, while the protein and fibre in the Brazils balances out some of the fructose.

Makes: 15
Prep: 20 minutes, plus overnight soaking

135g/4¾oz/1 cup pitted dates, chopped
150g/5½oz/1 cup Brazil nuts, soaked (see page 169)
75g/2½oz/½ rounded cup dried cherries
2 tbsp raw cacao powder
¼ tsp fine sea salt

Put all the ingredients in a blender and blend until combined. Take a tablespoon of the mixture and squeeze and press into a ball. Repeat with the rest of the mixture. Store the balls in an airtight container the fridge.

Walnuts

Walnuts, cultivated for thousands of years, are treasured as a food and medicine. Of the three types, black walnuts and white walnuts are native to North America and played vital roles not only for Native Americans, but also for early settlers in the New World. It's interesting that a shelled walnut looks like the human brain, which it feeds with its essential fats.

Benefits

Walnuts are 65 percent great fat. Something particularly interesting about walnuts as a high fat food is that they are beneficial to the almost 25 per cent of American adults with Metabolic Syndrome. The Metabolic Syndrome combination of high blood fats, high blood pressure, low HDL (High Density Lipoprotein) cholesterol plus obesity is actually benefitted from eating walnuts over only a few months. Eating walnuts also seems to reduce muffin tops or fat around the middle, so start munching!

New research is pointing toward walnuts as being helpful for memory and cognitive processes. They naturally contain melatonin, which regulates sleep, and daily rhythms, and is used in some countries to overcome jet-lag.

Ways to Eat

See the suggestions on page 168.

How to Use

Walnuts, like all nuts, should be eaten raw, with their skins on, and soaked (see page 169).

Raw Walnut Cherry Pie

This is a wonderful combination of cherry, walnut, chocolate and coconut. It is rich and satisfying, so individual ramekins are the perfect size. You can swap in other stone or soft fruits for a change.

Serves: 4
Prep: 10 minutes, plus overnight soaking

100g/3¼oz/1 cup soaked walnuts (see page 169), ground
pinch of salt
2 tbsp coconut oil
300g/10½oz pitted cherries, fresh or frozen
2 tbsp chia seeds
2 tbsp cacao nibs
1 tbsp Manuka honey (optional)

In a small bowl, mix the ground walnuts and salt. Add the coconut oil and mash it into the mixture with a fork. Divide the mixture between 4 ramekins and press into the base of each.

In a medium bowl, mix the cherries, chia seeds and cacao nibs. Leave to set for 5 minutes. Divide the cherry mixture between the 4 ramekins and serve.

Macadamia Nuts

Like little butterballs, these nuts grow on macadamia trees native to Australia. Sometimes called the Queensland nut, macadamias are high in fat and low in protein compared to other nuts. They are so unctuous that they make a wonderful addition to breakfast foods and are a great snack.

Benefits

Macadamias are unique in their essential fatty acid makeup. The majority of the total fat content is stable monounsaturated fat, containing a large portion of omega-7 palmitoleic acid that protects us from viruses, harmful bacteria and yeast in the gut. A Chinese study published in 2006 found that about 80 per cent of the fat is monounsaturated, which benefits the cardiovascular system.

Also, the ratio of omega-3 to omega-6 is equal, which is excellent.

Ways to Eat

See the suggestions on page 168.

How to Use

Macadamias are the fattiest nuts, up there with pecans and Brazils, so buy raw macadamias as pale as you can find them (paler nuts mean fresher nuts) and keep them in the fridge to preserve their precious oils.

Like all nuts, macadamias should be eaten raw and soaked (see page 169).

Macadamia Breakfast Parfait

I'm always looking for more breakfast ideas as I prefer my family not to eat boxed cereals. Put the nuts and seeds to soak the night before and then it's just a case of assembling everything the next morning. This breakfast is beautiful and my kids love to prepare and eat it, choosing different fruits, nuts and seeds to rotate in throughout the week.

Serve: 4
Prep: 20 minutes, plus overnight soaking

100g/3½oz/¾ cup macadamia nuts
480ml/16fl oz/2 cups water
½ tsp fine sea salt, plus a pinch
4 tbsp sunflower seeds or other soaked seeds
4 tbsp shredded coconut
120g/4¼oz pomegranate seeds (1 pomegranate)
360g/12¾oz/1½ cup Greek yogurt
2 tbsp milled linseeds (flaxseeds)
180g/6⅓oz/1½ cups blueberries or mixed berries or sliced bananas
  or any fruit

Optional toppings:
Manuka honey
cacao nibs
ground cinnamon

Put the nuts, 350ml/12fl oz/1½ cups of the water and ½ teaspoon of the salt in a bowl and leave to soak overnight. Put the sunflower seeds, remaining water and pinch of salt in a small cup or bowl and leave to soak overnight.

Layer 1 tablespoon shredded coconut, 3 tablespoons pomegranate seeds, 3 tablespoons yogurt, 1 tablespoon soaked sunflower seeds, ½ tablespoon milled linseeds (flaxseeds), 3 tablespoons blueberries and 2½ tablespoons soaked macadamia nuts into each of 4 serving glasses or bowls. Serve as is or top with Manuka honey, cacao nibs and/or ground cinnamon.

Pecan Nuts

According to the USDA, pecans are in the top 15 foods known for their antioxidant value. Pecan nuts are one of the oiliest nuts, with a buttery flavour, making them unctuous to eat. The nuts are from the hickory tree, which is found in Central and Southern North America. In the South, pecans are traditionally used in pies and pralines.

Benefits

Pecans are full of protein and great oils, make a tasty snack and are easy to carry around. They are full of antioxidants, essential fats and lots of fibre, and they contain over 19 vitamins and minerals that support heart function, digestion, immune system, joints and diabetes.

Remember that the fat in nuts is great fat – fat that your body needs – so it's a great idea to include them in your weekly diet.

Ways to Eat

- Grind, chop or use whole in breakfast foods like yogurt, bircher muesli, chia pots, smoothies, smoothie bowls, breakfast parfaits or porridge (oatmeal).
- Use in raw energy balls.
- Make pecan butter.
- Finely chop or grind and add to soups for flavour and nutrients.
- Chop or use whole in green, pasta, rice, grain and mixed salads.
- Add to fruit salad.
- Mix chopped pecans with steamed, sautéed or roasted veggies.
- Include in raw pastry (see page 90) and raw tarts.
- Take on hikes, bike rides, picnics and to the beach as a snack.

How to Use

Remember when buying pecans, the paler the nut, the fresher it is. They should not be dark brown.

Because pecans are high in oils, they are more likely to become rancid, so keep them in the fridge or freezer to preserve their precious oils.

Like all nuts, pecans should be eaten raw, with their skins on, and soaked (see page 169).

Spinach Pecan Salad

This salad works with a nice chunk of wholegrain bread or oatcakes if you need carbs. You can add chopped sundried tomatoes for a little more depth of flavour or use them to replace the feta for a dairy-free version.

Serves: 4
Prep: 10–15 minutes, plus overnight soaking

200g/7oz spinach, roughly chopped
100g/3½oz feta cheese, chopped
75g/2¾oz/½ cup pitted Kalamata olives, quartered
50g/1¾oz/½ cup soaked pecans (see page 169)
50g/1¾oz/½ cup sultanas
50g/1¾oz/½ cup dried cranberries
80g/2¾oz/¾ cup sundried tomatoes, chopped
　　(optional)

For the dressing:
1½ tbsp Dijon mustard
3 tbsp balsamic vinegar
6 tbsp extra virgin olive oil

Put the spinach, feta, olives, pecans, sultanas, cranberries and sundried tomatoes (if using) in a large bowl and mix. Put the mustard, vinegar and oil in a small jar and shake until combined. Pour the dressing on the salad and mix well.

Pecan Squares

Although pecans are best eaten raw, here you do still retain most of their goodness because they are baked quickly at a lowish temperature. My kids regularly make these because they are so easy and quick – and wonderful to eat. It makes a small amount, but once you fall in love with them, you might want to double it.

Makes: 20 x 15cm/8 x 6 inch baking tin
Prep: 10 minutes, plus overnight soaking
Bake: 15–18 minutes

healthy oil, for greasing
1 egg, beaten with a fork
80g/2¾oz/generous ⅓ cup organic sugar
1 tsp vanilla extract
60g/2¼oz/½ cup wholegrain spelt flour
½ tsp baking powder
¼ tsp fine sea salt
100g/3½oz/1 cup soaked pecans (see page 169)

Preheat the oven to 180°C/350°F/gas mark 4. Grease a 20 x 15cm/8 x 6 inch or equivalent baking tin.

Put the egg, sugar and vanilla in a medium bowl and mix until combined. In a small bowl, put the flour, baking powder and salt and mix until combined. Coarsely chop the pecans. Add the flour mixture to the egg mixture and stir just until combined. Add the pecans, mix until just combined and spread in the baking tin. Bake for 15–18 minutes until lightly browned. It should be soft in the centre. Leave to cool for 20 minutes, then cut into bars. Eat warm or at room temperature.

Almonds

Almonds, prized around the world and popular since the Ancient Egyptian era, are valued for their delicate flavour and versatility in savoury and sweet foods. They are available all year, but are freshest mid-summer at harvest time. Ancient Indian Ayurvedic practitioners believe that almonds contribute to increased brain capacity, intellectual prowess and long life. They are sometimes called a perfect food.

Benefits

Almonds are the most nutritionally dense nut, prized for their healthy fats, fibre, protein, magnesium and vitamin E (one of the world's best sources), a heart-happy vitamin. In addition, they have high levels of magnesium and potassium. Magnesium is a mineral involved in over 300 bodily functions. Potassium is involved in nerve transmission and the contraction of muscles, including the heart, and is essential for maintaining normal blood pressure.

Although there is some debate about eating almonds without their skins, stick with the whole food theory and eat them with skins on. The antioxidant flavonoids in almond skins combine with vitamin E in the almond to more than double the antioxidants delivered to your body, which can protect your cells from oxidative damage, a major contributor to ageing and disease. Almonds are also an excellent source of calcium.

Ways to Eat

See the suggestions on page 168.

How to Use

Almonds, like all nuts, should be eaten raw, with their skins on, and soaked (see page 169).

Almond & Nut Crostata

Like many Italian baked goods, this pastry is made with extra virgin olive oil instead of butter, but I've given the choice of both. With its wholegrain crust, a crostata makes a delicious, protein-rich and not-too-sweet treat. If you buy activated nuts, you can skip the soaking instructions and save time. Feel free to swap out any nuts you don't like.

Makes: 25cm/10 inch tart
Prep: 25 minutes, plus overnight soaking
Bake: 15–20 minutes

20g/¾oz almonds, skins on
20g/¾oz pine nuts
25g/1oz pecans
30g/1¼oz walnuts
40g/1½oz hazelnuts, skins on
240ml/8fl oz/1 cup water
1 tsp fine sea salt
3 tbsp unsweetened jam or chia jam

For the wholegrain pastry:
120g/4¼oz/1 cup wholegrain spelt flour, plus extra for rolling
155g/5½oz/1 cup wholegrain Kamut flour
¼ tsp fine sea salt
100g/3½oz butter, cubed or 75g/2¾oz sweet (not spicy) olive oil
60g/1¾oz/scant ¼ cup organic sugar
2 tbsp plain yogurt, kefir or lemon juice
7–8 tbsp water

Put the almonds, pine nuts, pecans, walnuts and hazelnuts in a small bowl.
Add the water and salt and mix until dissolved. Leave to soak overnight or for
8 hours.

To make the pastry, put the spelt flour, Kamut flour and salt in a medium bowl
and mix well. Add the butter or olive oil and mix with a fork until the mixture
resembles breadcrumbs. (If you're using butter, rub between your fingers until
the mixture resembles breadcrumbs.) Add the sugar and mix well.

Add the yogurt, kefir or lemon juice and sprinkle with about 5 tablespoons
water. Toss with a fork. Add the remaining water a tablespoon at a time
and mix again with the fork until the mixture easily holds together without
crumbling apart (this is critical), then gather it together into a ball, wrap in
clingfilm (plastic wrap) and refrigerate overnight (or for at least half an hour).
If you're using olive oil, the pastry can be left at room temperature.

Preheat the oven to 180°C/350°F/gas mark 4. On greaseproof paper, roll the
pastry out to 26cm/10½ inches and smooth the edges into a tidy circle with
your fingers. To make a good circle, trim it with a knife and then 'glue' cut
pieces where needed by using a little water and then a little dusting of flour.

Fit the pastry into a 25cm/10 inch tart tin with your fingers, fold the edge
backwards over itself so it comes halfway up the side of the tart tin and then
squeeze the pastry between your thumb and index finger to make a pretty
edging pattern. Prick the sides and bottom with a fork.

Bake for 15–20 minutes until the pastry is lightly browned. Leave to cool,
spread the jam on the pastry base and then sprinkle the nuts evenly, pressing
lightly onto the jam so that they stick.

Coconuts

The various products from coconuts are a dietary and beauty staple in many nations. Coconuts, a drupe from the coconut palm, are incredibly versatile. We use the milk, oil, flesh, shell and husk.

Benefits

Coconuts are high in dietary fibre, improve heart health, help with digestion and absorption, boost brain function, suppress appetite, give energy and reduce sweet cravings. Amazingly, they are also antiviral, antifungal, antibacterial and anti-parasitic. Coconut oil is nature's best source of lauric acid, an essential fat that aids the immune system and protects against pathogens in the gut.

The Organic Advantage

The most widely available form of coconut oil is often bleached and deodorized. Make this great food even better by buying organic.

Ways to Eat

- Include it in your breakfast foods.
- Use coconut oil for frying or roasting.
- Bake with coconut oil, replacing butter with 20 per cent less oil.
- Use coconut sugar in place of regular sugar in baking (see right).
- Add coconut oil to coffee.
- Use coconut oil for dairy-free pastry.
- Make popcorn in coconut oil.

How to Use

When substituting coconut sugar for regular sugar, measure by weight, not volume (i.e. cups) as it is lighter than regular sugar and you need more.

We refer to coconut fat as oil, even though it may be sold as a solid. This is fine to use – in recipes, you don't have to melt it unless specified.

Coconut Lime Squares

A coconutty take on Key Lime Pie, this wonderful recipe uses coconut oil, coconut milk, coconut sugar and coconut flakes. The unctuousness of the coconut is contrasted beautifully with the tartness of the lime juice. You can buy lime juice, but you'll need at least 1 lime for the zest. Coconut sugar is dark and makes the filling brown.

Makes: 12 squares
Prep: 15 minutes
Chill: 1–1½ hours

4 tbsp melted coconut oil, plus extra for greasing
120g/4¼oz digestive biscuits, crushed to fine crumbs
290ml/10fl oz/1¼ cups coconut milk
125ml/4fl oz/½ cup lime juice
70g/2½oz/generous ½ cup coconut sugar
⅛ tsp fine sea salt
4 tbsp agar agar
1 tsp lime zest
50g/1¾oz/⅔ cup shredded coconut, lightly toasted in a frying pan

In a small bowl, mix the coconut oil and biscuit crumbs until combined. Press firmly with the back of a spoon into the bottom of a 25cm/9 inch pie plate or 15 x 20cm/6 x 8 inch baking dish. Refrigerate for 30 minutes while you make the filling.

In a medium saucepan, whisk together the coconut milk, lime juice, sugar and salt. Sprinkle the agar agar over the surface of the liquid and let it dissolve. Bring the mixture to a simmer and then let it bubble gently for 5 minutes, stirring occasionally. Remove from the heat and allow to cool while the base is still chilling, then stir in the zest and pour gently onto the biscuit base. Sprinkle the shredded coconut on top and refrigerate for 1 hour until set. Store in the fridge.

Seeds

Seeds

Seeds are tiny, but mighty. They contain everything needed for the plant, so they are a complete food. Nutrient dense, seeds are satisfying, tasty and versatile.

Benefits

Seeds are packed with protein, vitamins, minerals, essential fats and fibre. With slow-releasing energy, seeds help keep blood sugar levels steady and keep you feeling full for longer.

Seeds are known for their B vitamins, among them B5, or pantothenic acid, which supports brain function. They support bone health – with phosphorus, magnesium, zinc and manganese – and strengthen the immune system with B6, folate, iron and zinc. They also support the heart with vitamin B1 or thiamin. They protect cells from oxidative stress with vitamin E and zinc, and they support vision with high levels of B2, or riboflavin, and zinc.

Ways to Eat

- Add to yogurt, Bircher muesli, porridge (oatmeal), breakfast parfaits, smoothie and smoothie bowls.
- Sprinkle on fruit salads.
- Mix into green, mixed, pasta, noodle, rice, bean and grain salads.
- Include in egg, tuna and chicken mayo salads.
- Have in mash and Colcannon.
- Put in guacamole and hummus.
- Sprinkle on sandwiches.
- Toss with vegetables before serving.
- Mix into potato and sweet potato salad.
- Add to raw energy bars and balls.

How to Use

Seeds should be eaten raw and soaked or sprouted (see opposite) to neutralize the enzyme inhibitors that can be hard on your digestion and the phytic acid that binds to minerals in your large intestine, preventing you from absorbing them. Soaking seeds makes them easy to digest and more nutritious.

Soaked seeds will develop mould, so make small quantities, keep them in the fridge and eat within 3–5 days.

Soaked seeds that are dried in a dehydrator or oven can be kept at room temperature and will stay fresh for much longer. You can buy activated (soaked and dehydrated) seeds in some specialist stores or you can dry soaked seeds easily at home (see opposite).

Raw seeds are best kept in the fridge to protect their oils.

BASE RECIPE
Soaked & Sprouted Seeds

To help you eat lots of seeds, this recipe for soaking is simple so that you can remember it without having to continually look it up. Simply soak equal parts of seeds to water (whether it's 2 tablespoons or ½ cup), with a pinch of salt, as this helps the process.

To soak:
Put 70g/2½oz/½ cup/8 tbsp seeds and 120ml/4fl oz/½ cup/8 tbsp water in a sprouting jar or jar or bowl. Add a pinch of fine sea salt and leave to soak for 8 hours or overnight. Rinse until the water runs clear and drain, either through the sprouting lid or a colander. You can use these as soaked seeds or keep going for sprouts.

To sprout:
For the next 2–3 days, rinse and drain the seeds at least twice a day and leave them in a sprouting jar or a regular jar with mesh over it. They should be well-drained and have air circulating. Keep sprouts in the fridge and use within 2–3 days to avoid mould.

BASE RECIPE
Soaked & Crisped Seeds

It's easiest to use a dehydrator and just follow the instructions on the machine, but if you don't have one, you can very slowly dry seeds in the oven to crispness. It's worth drying quite a large quantity, as these will keep out of the fridge for much longer than raw or soaked seeds.

Preheat the oven to its lowest setting, about 50°C/120°F. Spread any quantity of soaked seeds on a baking sheet and let the seeds dry for about 1 hour until crisp.

Sunflower Seeds

Not just for the birds, sunflowers are one of the first plants to be cultivated in the US and have been used for over 5,000 years by Native Americans for food, oil, dye and more. Inside those black-and-white-striped shells are seeds so rich in oil that they are one of the main sources of polyunsaturated oil and one of the most popular oils in the world.

Benefits

Sunflower seeds are loaded with nutrients, particularly calcium, iron, magnesium, phosphorus and potassium. Good sources of B vitamins and carotenoids, they are also 50 per cent fat, including omega-6 in a very stable form. Eating sunflower seeds will take care of your heart with vitamin E, magnesium and selenium, take care of your hunger with protein, oil and fibre and take care of your head with tryptophan, which helps to release serotonin, relieve tension and relax you. Add to that the choline in sunflower seeds that improves memory and cognitive function.

Ways to Eat

- Add to yogurt, Bircher muesli, porridge (oatmeal), breakfast parfaits and smoothies.
- Use sprouted seeds in salads and sandwiches or sprinkle on hummus.
- Include in sweet potato, egg, chicken, and fish salads.
- Mix into green, pasta, rice, bean, grain and mixed salads.
- Sprinkle on mash.
- Toss with vegetables before serving.
- Use in raw protein or energy balls.

How to Use

Eat raw and soaked (see page 183) for best nutrition.

Raw Sunflower Seed Crackers

Raw crackers are great to have around the house for breakfast, lunches and snacking, with all kinds of toppings. These contain a wonderful combination of seeds that have been soaked and dried slowly on a low heat to preserve their nutrients. Use a dehydrator to dry them if you have one.

Serves: 4
Prep: 15 minutes, plus overnight soaking
Bake: at least 5 hours

65g/2½oz/½ cup sunflower seeds
60g/2½oz/¼ cup milled linseeds (flaxseeds)
30g/1¼oz/¼ cup pumpkin seeds
4 tbsp sesame seeds
3 tbsp poppy seeds
2 tbsp hemp seeds
240ml/8fl oz/1 cup water
1 tbsp lemon juice or cider vinegar
1 tsp ground turmeric
¼ tsp fine sea salt

Put the sunflower seeds, linseeds, pumpkin seeds, sesame seeds, poppy seeds, hemp seeds, water, lemon juice or vinegar, turmeric and salt in a bowl and soak overnight.

Preheat the oven to 50°C/120°F or your oven's lowest setting. Add any extra ingredients, if using, and mix well. Put greaseproof paper over a baking sheet and spread the seed mix into a thin rectangular layer. Use a sharp knife to score into crackers.

Bake for 2 hours, then turn over and bake for at least another 3 hours, until dry and crisp. Break into crackers along the scoring marks.

Linseeds

Seeds, which are nature's storehouses, are great nutrition and we should all eat more of them. Linseeds (also known as flaxseeds) are perhaps the easiest to include in your diet because they are the only seed that you don't have to soak and that you can bake with because their nutrition is heat stable.

Benefits

Linseeds (flaxseeds) have three major benefits: (a) they are the greatest source of lignans, which give us antioxidant and fibre benefits, (b) they are the number one plant source of omega 3 and (c) they are unique in their mucilage or gum content, which support the intestinal tract and improve absorption.

In addition, linseeds are good for your heart, joints, digestion, hair, skin, mood and brain.

Ways to Eat

- Sprinkle on yogurt, porridge (oatmeal), Bircher muesli or cereal.
- Blend into smoothies.
- Mix into soups, stews and chilli con carne (or non carne) after serving.
- Toss into salads.
- Include in egg, tuna or chicken mayo salads.
- Add to coatings for chicken and fish.
- Incorporate into nutloaf and meatloaf.
- Add into bread, banana bread, muffins, cookies, traybakes, brownies and more.

How to Use

Unlike other seeds that benefit from soaking because of their phytic acid content, linseeds don't need to be soaked to be at their optimum. But because they are small and can pass through your body without being properly chewed and digested, it is best to eat them ground in order to access the goodness inside.

Raw linseeds are ripe when they are amber, yellow, gold, brown or reddish brown. White, green or black are either under ripe or overripe and should be avoided.

Linseeds are stable when baked, so adding them to all kinds of baked goods, from breads to brownies, is an excellent way to eat them.

Raw linseeds are best kept in the fridge to preserve their oils.

BASE RECIPE

Egg Replacer for Cooking & Baking

Grind 1 tablespoon of linseeds (flaxseeds) into
fine powder in a coffee or spice grinder. Whisk in
3 tablespoons of water until the texture is gelatinous.
Use in a recipe as you would use for 1 egg.

Zesty Linseed Muffins

Perfect for breakfast or snacks, these muffins – made
with wholegrain flour and oat flakes – are low in sugar,
high in flavour and goodness, and absolutely packed with
seeds. Because they are dairy-free, there's no creaming
of butter and sugar. Instead, the time is in the soaking
and zesting.

Makes: 12 regular muffins
Prep: 25 minutes, plus overnight soaking
Bake: 20–25 minutes

35g/1¼oz/3 tbsp linseeds (flaxseeds)
35g/1¼oz/3 tbsp sunflower seeds
20g/¾oz/2 tbsp poppy seeds
10 tbsp water
pinch of fine sea salt
300g/10½oz/2½ cups wholegrain spelt or other flour
75g/2½oz/¾ cup porridge (rolled) oats or other flakes
175g/6oz/1½ cups organic sugar
4 tbsp finely grated orange zest (about 2 oranges)
1½ tsp bicarbonate of soda (baking soda)
½ tsp fine sea salt
3 large eggs, beaten with a fork
185ml/6fl oz/¾ cup extra virgin olive oil
150ml/5fl oz/scant ⅔ cup juice of the oranges
1 tbsp cider vinegar

Put the linseeds, sunflower seeds, poppy seeds, water
and salt in a small bowl and soak overnight or for 8 hours.

Preheat the oven to 180°C/350°F/gas mark 4. Line
12 regular muffin cups with paper cases.

In a medium bowl, mix the flour, oats, sugar, zest,
bicarbonate of soda (baking soda) and salt. In another
medium bowl, put the seeds, eggs, oil, orange juice and
vinegar, and mix well. Add to the flour mixture and fold
with a spatula just until moistened – about 20 strokes.

Spoon the mixture into the muffin cups. Bake for 20–25
minutes until the muffins are domed and a toothpick
(cocktail stick) inserted in the middle comes out clean.

Poppy Seeds

Poppy seeds are tiny, kidney-shaped blue-black oil seeds taken from the dry fruit pods of the opium poppy. They have been harvested for thousands of years and used whole, ground, in foods and for their oil. In America, they are used in or on baked goods and are often ground and made into a delicious paste with butter and sugar for pastries.

Benefits

Like other super seeds, poppy seeds contain many plant compounds that have antioxidant, disease-preventing and health-supporting properties. About 50 per cent of their weight is made up of wonderful fatty acids and essential oils, especially oleic and linoleic acids, which are known to help prevent coronary artery disease and strokes. Poppy seeds are a good source of dietary fibre, B-complex vitamins and many minerals. With high amounts of calcium – 13 percent of your daily value in one teaspoon – they help keep bones and teeth healthy.

Ways to Eat

- Add to yogurt, Bircher muesli, porridge (oatmeal), breakfast parfaits and smoothies.
- Use in salads and sandwiches or sprinkle on crackers with hummus.
- Include in sweet potato, egg, chicken and fish salads.
- Mix into green, pasta, rice, bean, grain and mixed salads.
- Sprinkle on mash.
- Toss with vegetables before serving.
- Add to raw bars and energy balls.
- Use in fritters and burgers.

How to Use

Eat raw and soaked (see page 183) for best nutrition.

Lemon Poppy Seed Balls

The great thing about this recipe is that you combine almost everything in advance and leave to soak, before adding the last few ingredients and rolling. So most of the work can be done the night before or first thing in the morning. The oats, poppy seeds and chia are activated by the warm water and lemon juice. The sumac (see page 96) adds extra citrusy flavour and goodness.

Makes: 20 balls
Prep: 15 minutes, plus overnight soaking

100g/3½oz/1 cup rolled oats
50g/1¾oz/⅓ cup poppy seeds
3 tbsp chia seeds
1 tbsp grated lemon zest
1 tbsp lemon juice
pinch of fine sea salt
125ml/4fl oz/½ cup warm water
3 tbsp coconut sugar or organic sugar
1 tsp vanilla extract
1 tsp sumac

Put the oats, poppy seeds, chia seeds, lemon zest, lemon juice, sea salt and warm water in a medium bowl and mix well. Leave to soak for 8 hours or overnight.

Add the sugar, vanilla and sumac and mix well. Roll by the tablespoonful into balls, discs or squares. Store in the fridge.

Hemp Seeds

Tiny hemp seeds are so incredibly good for you that they are described as 'heroic'. They are the seeds, technically nuts, from the hemp plant or *Cannabis sativa*. They won't get you high, but they are loaded with nutrients that really make it worth including them in your diet.

Benefits

Hemp seeds are a perfect protein with all 20 amino acids and all nine of the essential aminos. They are a great source of vitamin E and provide a wonderful spectrum of minerals and vitamins. Hemp seeds are a perfect ratio of essential fatty acids, in which pretty much everyone is deficient. Hemp seed oil is the only seed oil that meets all of our essential fat needs.

When it comes to hemp seeds. I think there is value in eating hulled and unhulled. Hulled seeds give you a higher percentage of protein and fats, whereas unhulled seeds provide more carbohydrate, fibre and minerals.

Ways to Eat

- Blend in or add to smoothies and smoothie bowls instead of protein powder.
- Enjoy with yogurt, Bircher muesli, chia pots, breakfast parfaits or porridge (oatmeal).
- Blend hulled hemp hearts with water for hemp seed milk or soak unhulled seeds overnight and blend with water until smooth.
- Stir whole into hummus or blend with the hummus ingredients if you're making your own.
- Sprinkle a few tablespoonfuls on green or mixed salads.
- Toss on top of pasta, rice and grain salads.
- Mix in with egg mayo and sweet potato salad.
- Mix with mash.
- Add to tabbouleh..
- Include in raw energy balls and bars.

Raw Hemp Balls

Nice for lunchboxes, snacking or a sweet treat, these protein balls are sweetened with dates and Manuka honey, and have a lovely cinnamon edge. When you roll them in coconut, cacao or sesame, you add another flavour and additional nutrients. These are quick and easy to make.

Makes: 20
Prep: 20 minutes, plus overnight soaking

150g/5½oz/1 cup pitted dates, diced
75g/2¾oz/½ cup hulled hemp seeds
30g/1oz/¼ cup milled linseeds (flaxseeds)
20g/¾oz/¼ cup desiccated (shredded) coconut
1 tsp ground cinnamon
¼ tsp fine sea salt
3 tbsp water
1 tbsp Manuka honey
1 tsp vanilla extract
desiccated (shredded) coconut, raw cacao powder or sesame seeds, for rolling (optional)

Put the dates, hemp seeds, linseeds, coconut, cinnamon and salt in a bowl and mix until combined. Mix the water, honey and vanilla in a small bowl or cup. Add the water mixture to the date mixture and mix well. Leave to soak overnight or for 8 hours until they are sticky enough to form into balls.

Store in the fridge in an airtight container. If you would like to coat the balls before serving, roll them in one of the ingredients suggested above.

Cacao

Cacao is thought to be the highest source of antioxidants and magnesium of all foods. Cacao trees, which are native to Mexico, Central and South America, produce pods that hold around 50 seeds. The seeds are fermented and then dried. Cacao butter is removed from the bean and the remainder is ground to produce raw cacao powder that contains nutrients from the whole bean. Cacao nibs are chopped-up beans that retain the fibre, nutrients and the fat.

Benefits

Cacao is an excellent source of fat, vitamins, minerals (especially iron), fibre, carbs and protein. It also contains a compound called theobromine that helps stimulate the central nervous system, relax muscles and dilate blood vessels, giving a shot of energy similar to caffeine. Components in cacao increase the circulation of serotonin and other neurotransmitters in the brain, helping to improve mood.

The Organic Advantage

Conventional chocolate is the most highly sprayed food crop in the world. Choose raw, organic, unroasted cacao.

Ways to Eat

- Mix cacao powder into smoothies.
- Put cacao nibs into porridge (oatmeal) and smoothie bowls.
- Layer nibs into breakfast parfaits.
- Include in raw energy balls.
- Mix into nut butters.
- Top fruity desserts with nibs.
- Put on raw cheesecakes.
- Make raw chocolates.
- Stir into warmed nut milk for healthy hot chocolate.

How to Use

Eat cacao uncooked in order to get the maximum benefits.

Cacao Nib Cookie Dough Porridge

I'm not normally a fan of chocolate for breakfast, especially oversweet cereals aimed at kids, but I make an exception for raw cacao nibs. This porridge (oatmeal) really tastes like raw cookie dough. And it doesn't have to be a breakfast food – you'll love it as an afternoon snack.

Serves: 2
Prep: 10 minutes, plus overnight soaking
Cook: 5 minutes

100g/3½oz/1 cup porridge (rolled) oats
455ml/16fl oz/2 scant cups rice milk
1 tbsp plain yogurt, kefir or lemon juice
¼ tsp fine sea salt
3 tbsp chopped walnuts
2 tbsp coconut sugar
25g/1oz butter or healthy oil
2 tbsp cacao nibs
1 tsp ground cinnamon

Put the oats, rice milk, yogurt (or kefir or lemon juice), salt and walnuts in a small saucepan and leave to soak, covered, overnight.

Bring to a simmer over a medium–high heat, reduce the heat to low and simmer for 5 minutes, stirring occasionally. Remove from the heat and stir in the sugar, butter, cacao and cinnamon.

Pumpkin Seeds

Pumpkins are native to the Americas and their seeds were valued by Native Americans for their dietary and medicinal goodness. It is said that they have been treasured since the Aztec times of 1300–1500AD. Pumpkin seeds, or *pepitas*, are flat, dark green seeds from various kinds of pumpkins, so when you carve that Halloween face, save those seeds!

Benefits

Pumpkin seeds have an excellent range of minerals, vitamins and antioxidants. They are known for their vitamin E content, which they contain in different forms, and for their zinc content. Pumpkin seeds are also antifungal and antiviral, which make them an excellent addition to everyone's diet.

People with diets rich in pumpkin seeds have been linked with lower rates of cancers such as stomach, breast, lung, prostate and colon, and eating pumpkin seeds has been linked with a reduced risk of postmenopausal breast cancer.

Ways to Eat

- Use with yogurt, Bircher muesli, chia pots, smoothies, smoothie bowls, breakfast parfaits or porridge (oatmeal).
- Add to raw bars and energy balls, whole or ground.
- Put little bowls out for snack time.
- Add to green, pasta, rice, bean, grain and mixed salads.
- Use in fritters and burgers.

How to Use

When you eat pumpkin or squash, pick the flesh off the seeds, rinse them and leave to dry on paper towels overnight. Eat raw and soaked (see page 183) for best nutrition.

Pumpkin Spread

This is a brilliant recipe for eating more pumpkin seeds. It uses activated seeds that are very nutritious, and it's tasty on pasta, as a dip with vegetables, or spread on oatcakes, wholegrain or raw crackers. Play with the spices if you want more cumin or some turmeric, sumac or paprika.

Serves: 4
Prep: 5 minutes, plus overnight soaking

280g/10oz/2 cups raw pumpkin seeds
240ml/8fl oz/1 cup water
¾ tsp fine sea salt
60g/2oz/1 cup coriander (cilantro) leaves
30g/1oz/½ cup chopped parsley
1 garlic clove, roughly chopped
5 tbsp lemon juice
1½ tsp grated lemon zest
4 tbsp extra virgin olive oil
½ tbsp ground cumin

Put the pumpkin seeds, water and salt in a small bowl and stir until the salt has dissolved. Soak overnight or for 8 hours.

Put the soaked seeds, soaking water, coriander, parsley, garlic, lemon juice and lemon zest in a food processor or blender. Pulse until the mixture is a paste.

Put into a serving bowl and mix in the olive oil and cumin. Spread on crackers, use as a sandwich spread, dip crudités into it, use as pesto or thin with water and use for salad dressing.

Spicy Pumpkin Seeds

Perfect for snacking or adding to salads, these spicy seeds are good to have on hand.

Makes: 140g/5oz/1 cup
Prep: 2 minutes, plus overnight soaking
Cook: 1 hour

140g/5oz/1 cup soaked pumpkin seeds (see page 183)
½ tbsp extra virgin olive oil
½ tsp ground cumin
½ tsp ground turmeric
½ tsp ground paprika
¼ tsp fine sea salt

Preheat the oven to 50°C/120°F or its lowest setting. Put all the ingredients in a bowl and mix until combined. Spread in a single layer on a large baking sheet and bake for about 1 hour until crisp.

Chia Seeds

Chia, native to South America, is the ancient Mayan word for 'strength'. The seeds were valued by Aztecs and Mayans for their energy, especially for warriors and runners. Chia are prized today for their nutritional profile and health attributes, which are very dense per calorie.

Benefits

Chia seeds are tiny black or white seeds that are loaded with protein, fibre, essential fats, antioxidants and much more. They are good for the heart, hair, skin, energy, mind, brain, bones, diabetes, metabolism and fighting cancer. Their antioxidants are not only good for you, but protect the essential fats they hold. Chia seeds contain all of the nutrients essential for bone health, and early studies show they can lower blood pressure and are anti-inflammatory. Happily, they are usually grown organically, are always sold as a whole food and they are gluten-free.

Ways to Eat

- Add to yogurt.
- Add soaked seeds to your morning smoothie or smoothie bowl.
- Stir into breakfast foods like porridge (oatmeal), Bircher muesli and breakfast parfaits.
- Add to guacamole, tzatziki and other dips.
- Mix with salad dressings.
- Make pudding with soaked chia, coconut milk and Manuka honey, and serve for breakfast, snack time or dessert.
- Use in raw bars and balls.
- Make chia jam (see opposite).
- Create chia and fruit ice lollies.
- Find a chia truffle recipe.

How to Use

Like most seeds, chia seeds should be eaten raw and soaked (see opposite). If you're in a hurry, soak them for at least 15 minutes.

When mixed with liquids, the outer layer of the seed swells and forms a gel. This can be used as an effective binder/egg replacement (see opposite).

Raw seeds are best kept in the fridge to preserve their oils.

BASE RECIPE
Soaked Chia

Put 3 tbsp chia seeds and 240ml/8fl oz/1 cup water or
non-dairy milk in a small bowl and mix well. Mix after
a few minutes and then again after a few more minutes
until they start to thicken, in order to prevent clumping.
Leave to soak, covered, for 8 hours or overnight. If they
do clump together, simply scrape loose with a fork.

Chia Breakfast Pot

Surprisingly filling and satisfying for breakfast,
chia can be soaked the night before and mixed up
in the morning with your preferred nuts and fruits.
Blueberries work particularly well. Whisking the chia
into the liquid for a few minutes seems to help them
distribute better.

Serves: 2
Prep: 5 minutes, plus overnight soaking

360ml/12fl oz/1½ cups rice milk or other non-dairy milk
50g/1¾oz/scant ⅓ cup chia seeds
4 tbsp pecans or walnuts
2 tbsp hemp seeds
1 tsp vanilla essence
2 tbsp desiccated (shredded) coconut
½ tsp ground cinnamon

Put the rice milk, chia seeds, pecans, hemp seeds and
vanilla in a small bowl and leave to soak, covered, for
8 hours or overnight.

Add the coconut and cinnamon and mix until combined.
Divide between 2 bowls and serve.

BASE RECIPE
Egg Replacer for Raw Foods

Put 1 tbsp chia seeds and 3 tbsp water in a small
bowl and mix until there are no lumps. Leave to sit
for 15 minutes, then add to recipe to bind.

Chia Berry Jam

When there's an abundance of fruit, don't think of
traditional jam-making, which cooks the fruit to death
and uses lots of sugar. Think of chia jam, which is raw,
gorgeous and adds no sugar.

Makes: 1 pot
Prep: 5 minutes, plus overnight resting

115g/4oz/1 cup raspberries, fresh or frozen, thawed
115g/4oz/¾ cup cherries, fresh or frozen and thawed
1½ tbsp chia seeds
Manuka honey, to taste (optional)

Mash the fruit in a bowl and add the chia seeds. Leave it
to sit for 15 minutes and if watery, add a little more chia
until it is a bit thicker. Cover and leave it to sit for 8 hours
or overnight. Add honey if it's not sweet enough. Put in a
jar and store in the fridge for up to 2 weeks.

Tahini

Tahini is the name for ground sesame seeds, which are possibly the oldest condiment used by people, dating to around 5,000 years old. These tiny seeds are a powerhouse of minerals and are one of the best sources of calcium you can eat. Tahini is used in much Middle Eastern cooking.

Benefits

Tahini can be made with sesame seeds that are whole or hulled, toasted or untoasted. Tahini made from whole sesame seeds is best, because hulling them removes about 60 per cent of the calcium, and although the calcium in the hull is in a less absorbable form, it is still worth having. Sesame seeds support bone and general health, and are an alkaline food. Eating tahini is probably better than eating sesame seeds, because when the seeds are crushed, they break down easily and are more absorbable during digestion.

Sesame seed oil, which is beneficial for skin, oral health, heart health and more, is a stable oil that is resistant to going rancid.

Ways to Eat

- Spread on toast for breakfast or snacking.
- Mash 2 teaspoons with an avocado and lemon juice to taste for a nutritious dip.
- Spread on a corn cake and top with a fresh or sundried slice of tomato.
- Stir a teaspoon into your bowl of soup to add texture and taste.
- Mix into lentil or bean dishes with cumin and lemon juice.
- Mix a couple of teaspoons into a stir-fry for creaminess.
- Make a tahini dressing with 85g/3oz/⅓ cup well-mixed tahini, 4 tablespoons extra virgin olive oil, 4 tablespoons lemon juice, 2 tablespoons water, 1–2 crushed garlic cloves and ¼ teaspoon fine sea salt. Put all the ingredients into a jar and shake until combined. Use on mixed leaves or steamed or roasted veggies.

Chocolate Tahini Balls

It's wonderful to enjoy a decadent dessert that is also doing you good. These very rich treats combine the charm of chocolate with a hint of nuttiness for a healthier and more elegant version of the American chocolate and peanut butter combo. Your hands will get chocolatey if you roll them, but it's the most effective method.

Makes: 20 balls
Prep: 30 minutes, plus 20 minutes chilling time
Cook: 15 minutes

200g/7oz dark (bittersweet) chocolate (at least 70% cocoa solids)
200g/7oz/generous ¾ cup well-mixed tahini
3–4 tbsp granulated organic sugar
1 tsp vanilla extract
¼ tsp fine sea salt
sesame seeds or cocoa powder for rolling (optional)

Put the chocolate in the top of a double boiler. Cook over gently simmering water until the chocolate has melted. Remove from the heat and add the tahini, sugar, vanilla and salt and mix until combined. If you have silicone chocolate moulds, spoon into the moulds and freeze until ready to use.

If you are rolling them by hand, pop the mixture in the freezer to harden for 15–20 minutes. Break the mixture up with a blunt knife and roll into balls in your hands. They are sticky, but they do hold together. Either place on a plate for serving or, if you like, roll in sesame seeds or cocoa powder. Refrigerate until ready to serve and serve cold.

Other
Ingredients

Water

You'd think that the human body was more solid than liquid, but we are on average 60 per cent water, making water the main component of our bodies. People can live for weeks without food, but you can only go about three days without water and then you must have a drink to survive.

Benefits

Drinking water helps maintain fluid balance and is needed for digestion, absorption, circulation, saliva, transporting nutrients and regulating body temperature. Water affects energy levels, mood, brain performance and memory. Dehydration can cause headaches and migraines, constipation and hangovers. Water is important during exercise, for skin and to detoxify and to excrete toxins and water through sweat, urine and bowel movements.

Ways to Drink

- Make a large jug of diluted green, black or jasmine tea to enjoy through the day at room temperature.
- Infuse your water with fruits, vegetables or herbs.
- Enjoy water in soups, especially miso soup, with meals.

How to Use

Drink water away from meals. Sip hot water with food.

Think of your stomach as a simmering cauldron where the flame is needed to digest your food. Don't down a glass of icy water while you're eating.

Buy the best filter you can afford. Use the cleanest water you have to cook grains, beans, soups and stews.

Fill your bottle from home and buy fewer plastic water bottles when you're out.

Avoid plastic bottles for your water or at least get BPA-free.

Stay hydrated while you exercise.

Take special care to drink enough water if you're pregnant.

If your kids say they're hungry during the night, try a small glass of water first. Sometimes little kids get confused and say they're hungry when in fact they are thirsty.

You don't have to force down 6–8 glasses of water a day, which is tough on your kidneys. Less is fine.

Flavoured Water

Don't get bored drinking water! There are so many ways you can make it even better. In the morning, just take a pretty jug, fill it with good water, take an idea from below and set the jug in the sun for extra infusing (except the first one). You can eat the fruit that falls in your drink – and the lavender.

Cucumber slices or curls • Strawberry, cucumber and lime • Sliced strawberries and oranges • Pineapple • Citrus trio of sliced oranges, lemons and limes • Fresh mint leaves with or without lemon • Apple slices or apple and mint • Grapefruit • Lavender and blueberry • Kiwi

Oils

Our bodies love good, cold-pressed oils. Oils give us concentrated energy and are building blocks for cell membranes and hormones. Fats are satisfying, making us feel full for longer, carry fat-soluble vitamins and are necessary for mineral absorption and other important processes in the body. And remember, two-thirds of your brain is fat.

Benefits

Oils support our heart, joints, hair and skin, and are anti-cancer. Essential fatty acids are oils that our bodies can't make from other foods. They are essential to health and it is important that we eat them regularly. You can find essential fats in oily fish, nuts, seeds and some vegetables.

You should only ever buy extra virgin olive oil, because virgin oil is made by mixing lower-grade oils.

Ways to Eat

- High-heat frying: butter, coconut and ghee.
- Light frying/roasting: almond, avocado, olive, coconut, sesame and toasted sesame.
- Baking: coconut, macadamia and olive.
- Low heat/no heat: argan, linseed, hazelnut, hemp, pecan and walnut.

How to Use

Good-quality organic, cold-pressed oils are fragile. It's a good idea to have a few in your kitchen, but keep them in the fridge, except for olive oil, which solidifies. If you want to experiment with more specialist oils, try them one at a time. If you buy several at once, they're more likely to get old before you finish them.

Oil Dressing

Pour 4 tablespoons extra virgin olive oil (or other good oil) and 2 tablespoons balsamic vinegar, cider vinegar or lemon juice onto your salad and toss. If you're adding mustard or miso, it makes sense to put in a jar and shake, to dissolve and distribute those added ingredients. Add crushed garlic, fresh herbs or mustard for variation.

Courgette Carpaccio

This simple Italian side dish is elegant and delicious. It goes with any meal or is a beautiful starter with fresh, wholegrain bread to soak up the olive oil and lemon juice. The Parmesan cheese is traditional, but the dish is excellent without it if you're looking for something dairy-free.

Serves: 4
Prep: 15 minutes

2 courgettes (zucchini), green or yellow or one of each, sliced thinly into rounds (with a mandolin if you have one)
2 tbsp lemon juice
3 tbsp extra virgin olive oil
½ tsp fine sea salt
freshly ground black pepper
50g/1¾oz Parmesan cheese, grated (optional, but reduce salt to ¼ tsp if using)

Lay the courgette slices in lines on a large serving plate overlapping each other in one layer. Sprinkle the lemon juice, olive oil, salt, pepper and cheese, if using, over the top. Serve immediately or leave to marinate for a while.

Salt

Salt is necessary to human health. We are saline and our bodies can't make salt, so we do need to eat it. Sea salt is from evaporated sea water; table salt is usually refined from mined rock salt, both of which originate from the sea. Sea salt undergoes little processing, contains natural iodine, macro-minerals and trace minerals. Salt isn't only sodium, but is 40 per cent sodium and 60 per cent chloride, both of which are needed in the body.

Benefits

Salt is necessary for essential functions in the body, such as to help maintain the fluid balance in our blood cells, transmit information in our nerves and muscles, take up nutrients from our small intestine, regulate blood pressure, balance the pH of body fluids, make hydrochloric acid and for processes in the brain.

We often hear that we should eat less salt, but the problem may be the quality of salt we are eating and the over-salting of processed foods and ready meals. Table salt is refined, dried at very high temperatures and can contain anti-caking agents, potassium iodide, bleaching agents and additives.

It is very possible that if you eat good food that you cook at home and use sea salt to lift the flavour, that you do not need to worry about your salt consumption. It is interesting that the body is put off by overly salted foods; there is only so much you can take.

How to Use

The following is a basic guide to adding salt to foods at home:

1 teaspoon fine sea salt = 5g/⅛oz

200g/7oz/1 cup wholegrain rice	1 tsp
200g/7oz/1 cup any whole grain	½–1 tsp
200g/7oz/1 cup beans	1 tsp
4 eggs	¼ tsp
240g/9oz/2 cups wholegrain flour	½ tsp
100g/3½oz/1 cup porridge (rolled) oats	¼ tsp
950ml/32fl oz/4 cups stock	1 tsp
100g/4½oz/1 cup nuts (for soaking)	1 rounded tsp
seeds to soak	a pinch

Manuka Honey

Manuka honey is made by bees in New Zealand that pollinate the manuka bush, a prolific, hardy, scrubby tree with white flowers. Honey is made when nectar in the bee's mouth mixes with enzymes. Manuka honey is particularly rich in enzymes, which produce hydrogen peroxide, an anti-inflammatory. Manuka honey applied topically can soothe and reduce inflammation.

Benefits

Manuka honey also contains methylglyoxal (MG), made from a compound found in manuka nectar. MG is a natural antibiotic. When you buy Manuka honey, it will have a rating for UMF on the label, which is a measure of MG and other beneficial compounds. To be considered therapeutic, Manuka must have a minimum UMF of 10.

What's fascinating is that harmful bacteria has the ability to change and become resistant to antibiotics, but Manuka kills bacteria by drawing the water out of it, making it impossible for the microbes to survive. Of course, sugar is sugar, but if you want something sweet, Manuka is beneficial.

Ways to Eat

• Instead of buying sweetened yogurt, buy plain yogurt and stir in a spoonful of Manuka honey.
• Take a tablespoonful a day when you have a sore throat (mix with 1 teaspoon ground cinnamon for optimum effect for throats) and for general good health.
• Use in porridge (oatmeal), Bircher muesli, chia pots, smoothie bowls or breakfast parfaits if you want to add some sweetness.
• Spread on toast instead of jam.
• Add to herbal infusions, after adding the boiling water.

How to Use

Heat destroys the beneficial qualities of honey, so enjoy it raw.

Wellness Warmer with Honey

For immune system support through the autumn and winter months, enjoy this warming drink.

Pour 290ml/10fl oz/1 cup plus 3 tablespoons water that has just come off the boil into a mug. Add 1 tablespoon chopped ginger, the juice of 1 lemon, 1 teaspoon Manuka honey (UMF 10+ or higher) and ½ teaspoon ground cinnamon and mix well. You can eat the ginger once you've enjoyed the drink.

Honey Spread

We all know we should eat less sugar – whatever the type – but if you have a craving that you can't ignore, try this lovely mix on wholegrain bread, toast, crispbreads, oatcakes or crackers. It will satisfy your sweet craving while giving you the many benefits of Manuka honey and tahini (see page 196).

Mix 1 teaspoon Manuka honey (UMF 10+) and 1 teaspoon unhulled, roasted tahini in a small cup or bowl and use as a spread.

Manukamacacocoa

Warm 240ml/8fl oz/1 cup rice milk or nut milk, then add 1 tablespoon raw cacao powder, 1–2 teaspoons maca powder (see page 208) and 1 teaspoon Manuka honey, or to taste. Add a tablespoon of cream or coconut oil to add richness.

Acai Berries

Pronounced ah-sigh-ee, this reddish purple fruit is an inch-long berry from the acai palm tree, native to Central and South America. It's pretty impossible to export the berries and keep their nutrients intact, so we usually see acai in powdered, drink or frozen pulp form. Look for freeze-dried powdered acai, which is more widely available and retains nutrients and flavour.

Benefits

Acai berries contain antioxidants, fibre and heart-healthy fats. They are widely thought of as a healing- and immune-supporting fruit. Brazilians eat acai to help with skin problems and generally improve their skin. So far, research on acai berries is limited and many claims about the health benefits have not yet been proven. Like other brilliant berries, acai are packed with vitamins and minerals, though.

Ways to Eat

• Stir 1 teaspoon into porridge (oatmeal), which makes a nice purple colour, too.
• Add to smoothies and smoothie bowls.
• Mix into yogurt and use in breakfast parfaits.
• Add to chia pots.
• Use if you're making chocolates.
• Mix into raw energy balls or bars.
• Stir a tablespoon into your salad dressing.
• Make sorbets.

How to Use

Eat acai uncooked to enjoy maximum benefits.

Acai Smoothie Bowl

If you prefer chewing your breakfast, then try smoothie bowls instead of smoothies. For a variation, you can thicken this with soaked oats or yogurt. And if you use sliced, frozen bananas (good to do when they're getting old), it becomes an ice-cream alternative.

Prep: 10 minutes
Makes: 4

300g/10½oz/2 cups fresh or frozen cherries or mixed berries
2 bananas
240ml/8fl oz/½ cup Greek yogurt (or 2 tbsp nut butter)
120ml/4fl oz/½ cup non-dairy milk
4 tbsp acai powder
2 kiwis, peeled and sliced
1 mango, peeled and chopped
50g/1¾oz/½ cup walnuts, soaked if time (see page 169)
50g/1¾oz /⅓ cup pumpkin seeds, soaked if time (see page 183)

Optional toppings:
fresh fruit/berries, hemp seeds, pollen granules, Manuka honey, matcha powder, cacao nibs, shredded coconut (or toasted if you prefer), goji berries, sunflower seeds

Put the cherries or mixed berries, bananas, yogurt, milk and acai powder in a blender and blend until smooth.

Divide between 4 bowls and top with the kiwi, mango, walnuts and pumpkin seeds.

Maca

Maca is a vegetable crop that grows in the high plateaus of the Andes Mountains in central Peru. A relative of the radish, it has been cultivated for over 3,000 years, and its root is used to make medicine. It is generally taken for energy, stamina, athletic performance, memory, female hormone imbalance, menopause, PMS, fertility, osteoporosis and to boost immune function.

Benefits

Because it is from Peru and is a fairly new export, there is no research on maca and its proven benefits. It is, however, loaded with vitamins and minerals, essential fats and amino acids. Maca contains over 55 beneficial and naturally occurring plant chemicals and is a natural stimulant, but quite powerful.

Ways to Eat

- Use 1–2 teaspoons with yogurt, Bircher muesli, chia pots, smoothies, smoothie bowls, breakfast parfaits or porridge (oatmeal).
- Mix into raw or protein balls.
- Blend into frozen bananas for a soft-serve ice-cream substitute.
- Add a teaspoon to fruit salads.

How to Use

Maca is best eaten raw.

It affects people differently, so start with ½ teaspoon a day and build up to 1–3 teaspoons for a healthy adult weighing 65kg/140lb. For raw premium maca, take 1–2 teaspoons.

It doesn't blend easily, so you may need to use a chasen (bamboo whisk) or shake jar to blend.

Macasquares

This no-bake bar makes a great mid-afternoon snack or treat yourself to a square with a morning smoothie. You can add protein powder if you want a more balanced snack. Store in the fridge and eat within 3 days.

Serves: 4
Prep: 10 minutes
Wait: 8 hours or overnight

coconut oil, for greasing
40g/1½oz/⅓ cup raw coconut flour
40g/1½oz/⅓ cup raw, milled linseeds (flaxseeds)
60g/2¼oz/⅓ cup chia seeds
60g/2¼oz/½ cup coconut sugar
1 tbsp raw maca powder
1½tsp ground cinnamon
240ml/8fl oz/1 cup water or non-dairy milk
1 tsp vanilla essence

Grease a 18 x 13cm/7 x 5 inch baking dish or similar. Mix the coconut flour, linseeds, chia seeds, coconut sugar, maca powder and cinnamon in a medium bowl. Add the water or non-dairy milk (slowly and allow to thicken/absorb with the chia). Add the vanilla and mix well. Pour into the dish and level. Leave to sit at room temperature for 8 hours or overnight until the chia and linseeds have soaked up the water and will hold the bars together. Cut into pieces and serve.

Macamilk

Mix 1–2 teaspoons maca powder in 240ml/8fl oz/1 cup rice milk or nut milk and add ½ teaspoon ground cinnamon.

Sea Veg

Unlike land vegetables, which come from tired and depleted soils, sea veg are fed by never-ending passing currents. They are said to be the most mineral-dense food available and contain important trace elements that our land vegetables just don't provide anymore.

Benefits

In a nutshell, sea veg are rich in minerals, vitamins and protein. They are also high in a stable form of iodine, necessary for thyroid hormone, which can be difficult to obtain from other foods. Sea veg contribute to the overall wellness and health of your endocrine and nervous systems. They are one of the richest plant sources of calcium. They also have antiviral, antibacterial and anti-inflammatory properties. But perhaps most important is the alginic acid in sea veg that cleanses your body of toxins.

Ways to Eat & How to Use

Arame: With its lovely black colour and mild flavour, this sea veg creates a beautiful contrast when combined with brightly coloured vegetables. Rinse to remove any shells or sand, then cover with water to soak for only 5 minutes. The volume will triple when soaked. Once soaked, arame must be cooked for 25 minutes, so add it to brown rice when you reduce the heat to a simmer.

Dulse: Slightly spicy, dulse is a popular seaweed from the North Atlantic. Rinse it, soak it just until soft and cut it up before adding to soups and salads. Or sauté it in oil straight from the package.

Kombu: See page 210.

Nori: See page 211.

If you like these sea veg and in time want more variety, try wakame and hijiki, which are more strongly flavoured sea veg.

Wakame: For a milder-flavoured wakame, which is excellent in salads, look for a wild variety, grown in the cold waters of northeastern Japan. Soak in water for 10–15 minutes. Remove, squeeze excess water out, cut away the hard ribs and slice.

Sea Veg Salad

Mixed with avocado, cucumber and tomato – and then combined with this beautiful dressing – here wakame is transformed into a wonderful salad. Wakame is not a very strongly flavoured seaweed (it is the one usually in miso soup), so works well as a side dish with other foods, but especially fish.

Serves: 4
Prep: 30 minutes

25g/1oz wakame, soaked for 15 minutes, drained and squeezed
1 avocado, peeled, stoned (pitted) and chopped
1 cucumber, thinly sliced
10 cherry tomatoes, quartered

For the dressing:
1½ tbsp soy sauce or tamari
1 tbsp raw tahini
1 tbsp Manuka honey
½ tsp toasted sesame oil
1 tsp finely chopped ginger root
½ garlic clove, pressed

Cut the tough stems from the wakame and slice the leaves. Put the sliced wakame, avocado, cucumber and tomatoes in a medium bowl. In a jar or small bowl, mix the soy sauce or tamari, tahini, honey, sesame oil, ginger and garlic until combined. When you are ready to eat pour on the dressing and mix well.

Kombu

Kombu, also known as kelp, is a brown algae that grows from the ocean floor like a thicket. It is sold dried in strips and high-quality kombu is broad and flat with a deep, even colour. Kombu is brilliant for cooking dried beans and with its umami taste, it is the basis for Japanese stocks for soups, stews and sauces.

Benefits

Kombu adds nutrients, flavour and digestibility to your cooking. Two abundant minerals found in kombu are calcium and iron. Kombu has more iodine than any other sea vegetable. Iodine is essential for hormone production and normal thyroid function. The umami taste in kombu comes from glutamic acid, which also can improve brain, muscle and prostate function.

Ways to Eat

- Always use when you cook your own beans (see page 131).
- Sprinkle roasted and ground kombu on soups, salads and grain and bean dishes (see below).
- Make dashi (see right), Japan's multi-purpose stock for soups, stews and sauces.

How to Use

Try roasted and ground kombu as a condiment. Simply cut 6 kombu strips (16 x 10cm/6½ x 4 inches) into small pieces with scissors, put them in a large saucepan and dry fry over a medium heat, stirring constantly, for 10–12 minutes until they are very crisp. Remove from the heat and allow to cool, then use a pestle and mortar or *suribachi* and *surikogi* to grind the pieces into a powder.

Miso Soup with Kombu Stock

This is a great superfood recipe, combining several excellent ingredients. Miso soup is based on kombu stock or *dashi*, which is great to have in the freezer any time you want a vegetarian stock. For leafy greens in the soup, use any of the following alone or in any combination: beetroot (beet) greens, broccoli rabe, Brussels tops, cabbage, collard greens, dandelion greens (go outside and pick them), kale, mustard greens, turnip greens, spinach or Swiss Chard. The soup makes a great light lunch or starter.

Serves: 4
Prep: 15 minutes
Cook: 15 minutes

For the dashi:
1.4 litres/48fl oz/6 cups warm water
8 dried shiitake mushrooms
1 kombu strip (16 x 10cm/6½ x 4 inches)

200g/7oz leafy greens
2½ tbsp barley or red rice miso
3–4 spring onions (scallions), sliced

Put the water and dried shiitake in a large saucepan and leave to sit for 10 minutes. Remove the shiitake, cut off the stems and leave whole. Finely chop the shiitake caps and return them and the whole stems to the pan. Cut the strip of kombu into small pieces with scissors and add the pieces to the pan. Bring the water to a simmer over a medium heat. Simmer gently for 10 minutes, then remove the shiitake stems and throw them away.

Add the leafy greens to the stock and simmer for another 5 minutes. Remove from the heat, dissolve the miso in a cup with some of the liquid, then mix thoroughly into the soup. Serve topped with the spring onions.

Nori

If you want to incorporate sea vegetables into your diet, then start with nori. It has a delicate flavour, is versatile and easy to use. Nori is best known for its use in sushi and is a favourite with children because they can wrap it around rice or just eat it as a snack. If you like nori and want to try other seaweeds, look for arame, dulse, wakame, hijiki, kombu and more.

Benefits

Like other seaweeds, nori is high in calcium and iron, with vitamin C to help digest it and an impressive amount of iodine in a very absorbable form. Nori is about one-third protein and one-third fibre. It is high in vitamins A and B, and includes more vitamins than fruits and vegetables. Nori is good for your heart, hair, skin, immune system, digestion, detoxification, teeth, bones, joints, allergies, brain and blood pressure, and it also helps fight cancer.

Ways to Eat

- Sprinkle nori flakes on soups, rice or noodle dishes or salads.
- Cut into strips for a snack and add to lunches, lunchboxes, picnics and beach parties.
- Liven up your wraps by dampening the edge of a sheet of sushi nori, place it under the wrap and stick it to the edge, add your favourite fillings in, then roll the wrap and nori around the goodies.
- Use for onigiri (see page 232), sushi maki and nori hand rolls.
- Wrap strips around warm rice balls and dip in umeboshi paste.
- Steam greens, cabbage, kale or spinach, lay on nori sheets and roll for a side dish or green snack.
- Sprinkle nori flakes on savoury pancakes and fishcakes.

How to Use

The easiest sea veg to eat, nori has been dried and pressed into fine sheets. Either buy sushi nori, which has been pre-toasted and you can eat straight from the package, or carefully toast sheets of nori over a burner until they go bright green. Toasted nori can be used to wrap or decorate food.

For toasted crispy nori sheets, preheat the oven to 130°C/250°F/gas mark 1. Fold 4 sheets of nori in half. Use a pastry brush to brush the inside with sesame oil. Sprinkle lightly with salt. Fold, press, cut into strips and place on a baking sheet. Bake for 10–12 minutes until crisp. Cool on wire racks. Store any leftovers in an airtight container.

One-pan Noodles with Nori Flakes

Quick, beautiful, warming and satisfying, this brothy noodle dish is a great recipe that you can vary according to what veg you feel like or what's in the fridge. The recipe is delicious as is, but you could add some garlic or fresh herbs to vary the flavours or use scallops or calamari instead of king prawns (shrimp).

Serves: 4
Prep: 15 minutes
Cook: 7 minutes

1.2 litres/40fl oz/5 cups water or broth
1 tsp fine sea salt
250g/9oz buckwheat or wholegrain noodles
350g/12oz king prawns (shrimp), peeled and deveined (or you could use chicken or beef strips)
300g/3½oz broccoli, cut into small florets
100g/3½oz mushrooms, trimmed and chopped
1 leek, sliced lengthways and chopped
4 tbsp olive oil or toasted sesame oil, to serve
2 tbsp nori flakes, to serve
2 tbsp furikake (optional), to serve

Put the water and salt in a large frying pan or medium saucepan and bring to the boil over a high heat. Add the noodles slowly – it takes about 2 minutes to do this – so that the water continues to boil or they will clump together. Stir and separate the noodles, then add the prawns, broccoli, mushrooms and leek.

Reduce the heat to low and simmer for 5 minutes, stirring occasionally, until the shrimp are no longer translucent and the vegetables are tender. Remove from the heat, divide between 4 bowls and top with oil, nori flakes and furikake, if using.

Bee Pollen

Bee pollen is the pollen that bees collect from flowers, mixed with a little salivary nectar and brought back to the hive. There it is packed in honeycomb cells, covered with honey and wax, and it ferments. This incredible food provides protein for the hive. Since ancient times, bee pollen has been used for energy and endurance. In Chinese medicine, it is considered a tonic, giving energy and many nutrients. Herbalists consider bee pollen to be exceptionally nutritious. And health-food stores have sold it for decades as a tonic.

Benefits

Bee pollen is a complete food, containing vitamins, minerals, carbohydrates, lipids, fat and protein. It is considered to be a nourishing and enriching food, but there is little or no research on bee pollen.

If you have (or suspect you have) a bee allergy, bee pollen should be avoided.

Ways to Eat

- Use to top yogurt and Bircher muesli.
- Mix into chia breakfast pots and breakfast parfaits.
- Add to smoothies/smoothie bowls.
- Put on yogurt.
- Sprinkle over nut butter or tahini on toast.
- Sprinkle on fruit salad.
- Toss into green and mixed salads or mix into salad dressing.
- Include in raw and protein balls.
- Mix into raw desserts.

How to Use

Eat it raw and sparingly: adults can eat ¼–2 teaspoons a day; children should start with a few granules and not have more than ½ teaspoon per day.

Blueberry & Bee Pollen Smoothie

Here is a great smoothie to have in your repertoire. You can use different nuts or fruit (pitted cherries are great), swap soaked seeds for linseeds (flaxseeds), add other super powders (cacao, baobab) and/or thicken it with amazake or yogurt. If you reduce the dairy-free milk, it works well as a smoothie bowl, too.

Serves: 2
Prep: 5 minutes

350ml/12fl oz/1½ cup rice milk or other non-dairy milk
100g/3½oz/¾ cup fresh or frozen blueberries
25g/1oz/¼ cup pecans, soaked if time (see page 169)
1 banana
2 tbsp bee pollen
1 tbsp linseeds (flaxseeds)
1 tbsp acai powder

Put all the ingredients in a blender and blend until smooth.

Baobab

Baobab is the common name of the *Adansonia* genus of trees, which grows in Madagascar, mainland Africa, Australia and Arabia. Revered in Africa, there are myths and legends that surround the trees, some of which are over 1,000 years old. The fruit is found inside a hard, strange, greenish pod that hangs upside-down from the tree. It has a tasty, lemony, sherbety flavour.

Benefits

Baobab is not organic, but wild-harvested, although there doesn't seem to be any chemical spraying. The fruit dries naturally on the branch, the seeds are then removed and the pulp is ground into a citrusy powder.

Baobab is being hailed as a nutrient-rich African superfruit. Like a few of these superfoods that are being imported from far-flung countries, there is very little research on them, but it is an interesting ingredient to have in your cupboard. Baobab is an excellent source of vitamin C and other antioxidants. It is high in potassium, which is good for muscle efficiency and recovery. And it is 50 per cent fibre.

Ways to Eat

- Use with yogurt, Bircher muesli, chia pots, smoothies, smoothie bowls, breakfast parfaits or porridge (oatmeal).
- Sprinkle on pancakes, waffles and French toast.
- Add into salad dressings.
- Mix into fruit salad.
- Include in raw and protein bars and balls.
- Blend into homemade ice-cream or blended frozen bananas.
- Include in raw fruit pie (see page 90) mixing to your taste.
- Mix with amazake (see page 240) for dessert.
- Add to raw pudding recipes or cooked ones like rice pudding after it has cooked.
- Combine with hot water for a citrusy warm drink.
- Mix 480ml/16fl oz/2 cups water or juice with 1 tablespoon powder to make a refreshing citrus drink.

How to Use

Baobab powder is best eaten raw to preserve its nutrients.

Carrot Cake Baobab Bircher

This is such a scrumptious breakfast that you could eat it every day.
Swapping the walnuts for pecans or almonds make a nice change, and
you may like it with more grated carrot or raisins instead of currants.
When you make your own Bircher, you can play around with spices and
other ingredients.

Serves: 4
Prep: 10 minutes, plus overnight soaking

200g/7oz/2 cups rough oats
3 tbsp baobab powder
2 tsp ground cinnamon
1 tsp ground nutmeg
700ml/24fl oz/3 cups water or non-dairy milk
2 carrots, grated
70g/2½oz/⅔ cup walnuts
2 tbsp currants
2 tbsp plain yogurt, kefir or lemon juice
1 tsp vanilla essence

In a medium bowl, mix the oats, baobab powder, cinnamon and nutmeg.
Add the water or non-dairy milk, carrots, walnuts, currants, yogurt (or kefir
or lemon juice), vanilla and ginger and mix well. Leave to soak, covered,
overnight at room temperature. Serve the next morning.

Matcha

Matcha is high-quality, powdered, whole-leaf, bright emerald green tea that only comes from Japan. It is enjoyed as tea, used in tea ceremonies and used as an ingredient in foods like sweet and savoury sauces, noodles, baked goods and other drinks. It is rich in antioxidants – partly owing to the special way it is grown and harvested. In the spring, tea cultivators in Japan cover fields of sencha tea for a number of weeks before harvest so they don't get direct sun. This stimulates the production of chlorophyll, creating many nutrients and the vivid green colour. Later, the leaves are picked, steamed, dried, cut, sorted, mixed, and then ground into a fine powder. It can take an hour to make 30g/1oz.

Benefits

Matcha contains green tea flavonoids that have an antioxidant effect on our bodies. Compared to drinking a cup of ordinary green tea, matcha is like drinking 10 cups, providing super antioxidants because you are drinking the whole leaf tea rather than an infusion of its leaves. It is rich in an amino acid that relaxes the mind and gives matcha its unusual flavour. Amino acids help create the umami taste – that creamy mouthfeel, in matcha – which is aromatic, a little bitter and slightly sweet.

Matcha does contain caffeine, but it releases slowly into the bloodstream. And matcha caffeine is alkalizing as opposed to caffeine from black teas and coffee, which is acidic. The Samurai warriors of Japan drank matcha tea before going into battle for the energy it provided.

Ways to Eat

- Dust onto pancakes.
- Stir into porridge (oatmeal).
- Put in your Bircher muesli.
- Mix into yogurt for breakfast parfaits or add to your breakfast.
- Add to chia breakfast pots.
- Use in fruity or green smoothies and smoothie bowls.
- Mash into guacamole.
- Include in dressings.
- Add to baked goods.
- Toss with popcorn.
- Blend with frozen bananas and eat as a dessert.
- Make matcha ice-cream, frozen yogurt lollies or frozen matcha banana lollies.
- Drink matcha tea (see right).

How to Use

To make matcha tea, put 1 teaspoon matcha into a cup with a little cool water. The easiest way to incorporate the matcha into the liquid is to use a *chasen*, or bamboo whisk, which is worth getting if you drink matcha regularly. The bamboo filaments are so fine that they smooth out all of the pockets and bubbles of matcha. Otherwise, leave to absorb, then incorporate with a small whisk. If you don't have one of those, sift the powder into the liquid and whisk with a fork.

Top up with water that has boiled and sat for 2–3 minutes.

To make matcha latte, use your favourite warmed non-dairy milk – rice milk is delicious as its natural sweetness complements the matcha. Whisk or sift as above.

Or drink it cold, whisked or sifted into rice milk or water.

Matcha Cupcakes

Matcha is versatile and commonly used in Japan for confectionery, although a lesser grade is used for baking. Matcha adds such a wonderful flavour and beautiful colour to these cupcakes. I've provided dairy and dairy-free versions on this page.

Makes: 12
Prep: 25 minutes
Bake: 20 minutes

125g/4½oz/½ cup butter, salted
150g/5½oz/⅔ cup organic sugar
2 large eggs
300g/10½oz/2½ cups wholegrain spelt flour
1½–2 tbsp matcha green tea powder
1 tsp bicarbonate of soda (baking soda)
¼ tsp fine sea salt
240ml/8fl oz/1 cup rice milk or other non-dairy milk
1 tbsp cider vinegar
1 tsp vanilla extract

Preheat the oven to 180°C/350°F/gas mark 4. Line 12 muffin cups with paper liners.

Cream the butter and sugar in a mixing bowl with an electric mixer on medium speed for 10 minutes until light and creamy. Scrape down the sides occasionally. Add 1 of the eggs, beat on a low speed until the egg is incorporated, then beat on medium speed for 5 minutes. Repeat with the second egg.

In a separate bowl, mix the flour, matcha, bicarbonate of soda (baking soda) and salt. In a measuring jug, mix the rice milk, vinegar and vanilla. Add about half the flour mix to the butter mix, then add the rice milk mix, beating on low until just moistened. Add the rest of the flour mixture and beat briefly.

Spoon the batter into the prepared muffin cups and bake for 20 minutes. Remove from the muffin tin and cool on a wire rack.

Dairy-free Matcha Muffins

Made with olive oil, these are more like muffins in texture than cupcakes, but are easier and quicker to make. You need a little more salt because you're missing the salt that would otherwise be in the butter.

Makes: 12
Prep: 10 minutes
Bake: 20 minutes

Ingredients as left, except the following:
100ml/3½fl oz extra virgin olive oil to replace the butter
½ tsp fine sea salt instead of ¼ tsp

Preheat the oven to 180°C/350°F/gas mark 4.

Line 12 muffin cups with paper liners.

In a large bowl, put the oil, sugar, eggs, rice milk, vinegar and vanilla and mix until combined.

In a separate bowl, mix the flour, matcha, bicarbonate of soda (baking soda) and salt. Add the flour mixture to the oil mixture and mix until just combined – about 12 strokes.

Spoon the batter into the prepared muffin cups and bake for 20 minutes. Remove from the muffin tin and cool on a wire rack.

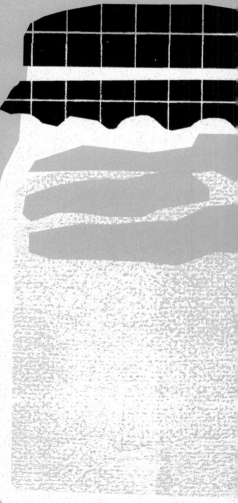

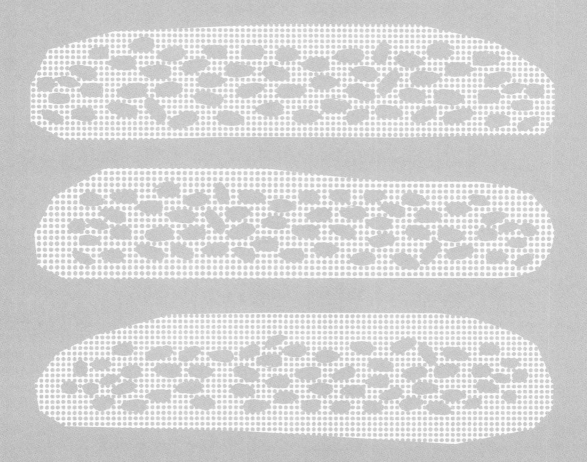

Fermented
Foods

Miso

There is goodness in food that takes time to make. Miso, a fermented soy food, is so nutritious that it is considered a medicinal food. It is a paste made from fermented soybeans, salt and koji (cultured barley or rice). We cannot prevent our exposure to heavy metals, toxins and radiation, but we can eat foods that help our body cleanse and detox. Miso is one of those foods.

Benefits

Miso is a complete protein with all the essential amino acids. It aids digestion and assimilation, it is loaded with lactic-acid bacteria, it is a good source of B vitamins, especially B12, and it strengthens the immune system.

But the most interesting fact about miso is that it removes heavy metals, such as radioactive strontium, from the body. This research was started at the Saint Francis Hospital in Nagasaki and later confirmed with the discovery of dipicolonic acid in miso by scientists at Japan's National Cancer Centre, Tohoku University in Hokkaido and Hiroshima University's Atomic Radioactivity Medical Lab.

Ways to Eat

- If you substitute miso for salt or add it to savoury dishes to create a richer flavour, you'll find many ways to incorporate it into everyday foods.
- There are two types of miso: sweet or mellow miso, which is shorter fermented and cream or yellow in colour, and dark miso, like red, brown rice and barley miso, which is saltier. Use sweet miso for a lighter flavour and dark miso in heavier stews and soups.

Here are ways to include miso in your meals:

Beans: If you cook your own beans, add miso after they are cooked. For 200g/7oz/1 cup dried beans or about 500g/1lb 2oz/2½ cups cooked beans, add 1 tablespoon miso. This is nice in beans that will be used in a dip, stew or quesadilla.

Burgers: Spread a thin layer on beef, chicken or veggie burgers. Same for fishcakes.

Coffee/Tea: Instead of reaching for another cup of coffee or tea, have a miso drink. It is satisfying, will do you good and gives you energy. Put 2 teaspoons miso in a mug, pour in some boiling water, mix until dissolved, then top up with more hot water.

Dressing: For salads or on steamed or raw vegetables, mix miso with oils such as olive, sesame, toasted sesame or flax. Add some lemon juice or brown rice vinegar, then other ingredients like crushed garlic, grated ginger or toasted sesame seeds.

Grains: After cooking grains like barley, buckwheat, millet, quinoa or rice, mix in miso instead of salt. For 200g/7oz/1 cup uncooked grain, use 1 tablespoon miso.

Grilling/Roasting: Slice a small aubergine (eggplant), courgette (zucchini), yellow squash or other vegetable in half lengthways, brush with miso and grill or roast on a high heat until tender. Try on prawns (shrimp), fish, chicken, meats and tofu or tempeh.

Marinade: Mix miso with chopped or grated ginger, toasted sesame oil and vinegar or lemon juice for a vegetable or fish marinade.

Mash: Instead of salt, mix a few teaspoons of sweet white miso into mashed vegetables like potatoes, sweet potatoes, celeriac and carrot.

Pesto: Replace Parmesan or salt with miso for pesto.

Sandwich/Toast/Wrap: Move over marmite! Try miso on toast – or miso and tahini on toast. For an easy snack or lunch, add slices of avocado, tomato, red onion, sprouts and/or grated carrot. Or put it all on a soft tortilla or wrap and roll it up.

Sauce: Whether it's spaghetti sauce or a marinade for fish or meats, put some of the sauce in a small cup, add miso and mix until combined. Return the cupful into the sauce and mix together well.

Soup/Stew: When soup or stew has finished cooking, simply put some of the stock in a cup, mix in miso until dissolved and add back into the pot (if you re-heat, miso may be simmered briefly).

How to Use

Miso is best not boiled as this will change the flavour and reduce the beneficial enzymes and microorganisms. It is good to add it to some of what you are cooking, and mix until it dissolves. Once added, don't bring to the boil as this destroys the amazing enzymes. Generally, use 1 tablespoon miso instead of 1 teaspoon salt or 1 tablespoon miso to 480ml/16fl oz/ 2 cups water, but it does depend on the saltiness of the miso.

'Moromi' Miso

Moromi miso, which is difficult to find for sale, is a gorgeous, mild, chunky spread that is less salty than miso and is eaten as a condiment. This is a mock moromi miso that you can make at home. You can also add grated ginger, to taste, as a variation.

Serves: 4
Prep: 10 minutes

4 tbsp dark miso
5 tbsp amazake
2–4 tsp mirin
4 tbsp water
35g/1¼oz/⅓ cup walnuts, soaked if time (see page 169), roughly chopped
2 cucumbers, sliced into rounds
1 pointed red or green cabbage, quartered

In a small bowl, mix the miso, amazake, mirin and water until the miso has dissolved. Add the walnuts and mix well. Spread with a knife onto the cucumber rounds and on cabbage leaves peeled off the stem.

Miso Dressing

Miso used in dressing increases the enzymes in salad for a more nutrient-dense mix. Toss this with lettuce leaves or with steamed vegetables. For a creamier version, use a tablespoon of tahini instead of sesame seeds.

Serves: 4
Prep: 5 minutes

2 tbsp sesame seeds
2 tsp miso (any kind)
1 tsp lemon juice
2 tsp brown rice vinegar
3 tbsp sesame seed oil

Put the sesame seeds in a small frying pan over a medium heat and sauté for 2 minutes until the seeds begin to pop. Grind using a pestle and mortar.

Put the seeds in a small jar, add all the other ingredients and mix well.

Kefir

Although Marco Polo mentioned kefir in his travel logs, it was unknown outside of the Caucasus Mountains in Russia where it was kept secret for a long time. Kefir is a slightly effervescent, fermented milk product. Tart and refreshing, it tastes like a drink-style yogurt and similarly to yogurt contains healthy and beneficial probiotics. In addition, however, kefir contains beneficial yeasts.

Benefits

Kefir is made with kefir 'grains' – a yeast and bacteria fermentation starter that looks like miniature cauliflower the size of grains. The fermentation creates a mineral- and vitamin-rich drink with easily digestible complete proteins. It is said that even people with lactose intolerance can enjoy kefir as most of the lactose is consumed by the enzyme lactase during the fermentation.

With its beneficial yeast and beneficial bacteria, kefir has antibiotic properties. Although it is considered mucous forming, this mucous coats our digestive tract, creating the perfect surface for good bacteria to establish and multiply.

The Organic Advantage

It is best if you buy organic dairy products. Organic dairy contains around 50 per cent more beneficial omega-3 fatty acids than conventionally produced equivalents. Organic dairy contains 40 per cent more conjugated linoleic acid (CLA), which has been linked to a range of health benefits, such as reduced risk of cardiovascular disease, certain cancers and obesity, although evidence is mainly from animal studies. Organic dairy contains slightly higher concentrations of iron, vitamin E and some carotenoids.

Conventional dairy is infamous for containing antibiotic residues and bacteria levels.

How to Use

You can buy kefir 'grains' and make your own kefir at home. If you would like a non-dairy version, simply substitute coconut milk or coconut water for cow, goat or sheep milk.

Simply put 480ml/16fl oz/2 cups whole organic milk (or coconut milk or coconut water) and 1 tbsp kefir grains in a measuring jug or open-mouthed storage jar. Stir, cover loosely and leave at room temperature. Over the next day or two, stir occasionally and taste the mixture until it achieves a tartness and thickness that you like.

Strain and drink or refrigerate the kefir, and re-use the kefir grains for another batch. If you don't want more kefir straight away, rinse the grains well and store in a small jar in the fridge in a small amount of water for several weeks and re-use as needed.

Yogurt

Yogurt is a fermented product with rich probiotic content. Although most people think of yogurt as milk-based, you can find non-dairy 'yogurts' that give you the same digestive support. Traditionally, milk is heated, cooled and mixed with friendly bacteria. It then ferments, producing lactic acid and a thick, slightly sour product.

Benefits

Health benefits from the lactic bacteria in yogurt include immune system support, improved digestion and decreased constipation. The lactobacilli, lactic acid and enzymes protect against infection-causing bacteria like salmonella and E. coli. Yogurt provides protein, plus calcium, B vitamins including B12, potassium and magnesium.

Milk is not a healthy food and is difficult for people to digest. Fermenting milk into yogurt makes it easier for people to eat as the majority of the lactose is transformed into lactic acid.

The Organic Advantage

Organic dairy contains around 50 per cent more beneficial omega-3 fatty acids than conventionally produced equivalents. Organic dairy contains 40 per cent more conjugated linoleic acid (CLA), which has been linked to a range of health benefits such as reduced risk of cardiovascular disease, certain cancers and obesity. Organic dairy contains slightly higher concentrations of iron, vitamin E and some carotenoids.

Ways to Eat

- Add to smoothies.
- Put on porridge (oatmeal) and Bircher muesli.
- Have for breakfast mixed with seeds, nuts and fruits.
- Add to pancake and pastry batter for overnight soaking.
- Make raita with cucumber, yogurt, cumin, garam masala, fresh coriander (cilantro), lemon juice and salt to have with curry.
- Mix into guacamole.
- Use instead of soured cream for dips and dressings.
- Make tzatziki.
- Use instead of cream in soups or dollop onto soups when serving.
- Make chilled yogurt, cucumber, dill, spring onion and walnut soup.
- Use in instead of mayonnaise in Waldorf salad.
- Create sauces with yogurt for vegetables, fish and meats.
- Halve large tomatoes, scoop out the inside, mix with crab or lentils, spring onion (scallion), pine nuts, lemon juice and yogurt, stuff back into the tomatoes and eat raw.
- Replace mayo and make yogurt slaw instead of coleslaw.
- Dollop on chilli con carne.
- Make frozen yogurt pops by mixing equal amounts of yogurt with fruit juice or smoothies.

How to Use

If you like sweet yogurt, it's an idea to buy plain Greek yogurt and sweeten it yourself with Manuka honey, baobab powder, coconut sugar or super fruits instead. You can then reduce your sugar intake.

Make sure the yogurt you are buying is live.

At 4 per cent fat, yogurt is not a high-fat food, so go for plain full fat products. If you reduce the fat, yogurt has little flavour and tends to have increased sugar.

Full-fat Greek yogurt is so thick and creamy that it doesn't need sugar, and is a great substitute for cream or soured cream.

Yogurt Dip

In a large bowl, mix 240ml/8fl oz/1 cup plain Greek yogurt, 2 tablespoons fresh, chopped basil, 1½ tablespoons lemon juice, 1½ teaspoons finely chopped garlic and ½ teaspoon salt. (If you like cumin, for variation, you can also add ½ teaspoon ground cumin.) Refrigerate until ready to use. Great with crudités.

Lentil & Spinach Pie with Yogurt

This beautiful and tasty pie can be made with or without the pastry depending on how much time you have. Try another strong, melting cheese like Cheddar or Monterey Jack if you prefer. You can substitute yogurt for milk in any quiche or savoury tart.

Makes: a 20cm/8 inch pie
Prep: 20 minutes
Cook: 55 minutes

For the wholegrain pastry:
90g/3¼oz/⅔ cup wholegrain spelt flour
115g/4oz/⅔ cup wholegrain Kamut flour
⅛ tsp fine sea salt
75g/2½oz butter, cubed or 50ml/1¾fl oz extra virgin
    olive oil
1 tbsp plain yogurt
7–8 tbsp water

For the filling:
100g/3½oz/½ cup Puy lentils
350ml/12fl oz/1½ cups water
5 eggs
200g/7oz Greek yogurt
75g/2½oz spinach leaves, roughly chopped
1 leek, sliced lengthways, then chopped
2 tbsp Dijon mustard
2 tbsp extra virgin olive oil
1 tsp fine sea salt
150g/5½oz Gruyère cheese, grated (optional)

First make the pastry: mix the flours and salt in a medium bowl. Add the butter or olive oil and rub between your fingers until the mixture resembles breadcrumbs. Add the yogurt and water and toss with a fork.

Gather the dough together into a ball. If it is too crumbly to hold together, sprinkle a little more water until it easily forms a ball. Wrap in clingfilm (plastic wrap) and refrigerate overnight or for 8 hours.

To make the filling, cook the lentils in the water for 20 minutes until soft. Drain any excess water. Preheat the oven to 200°C/400°F/gas mark 6. Roll out the pastry and line the tin.

Beat the eggs in a large bowl with a fork. Add the yogurt, spinach, leek, mustard, oil and salt and mix well. Pour the egg mixture into a 20cm/8 inch pie tin and sprinkle the cheese evenly on the top, if using.

Bake for 35 minutes until the egg is cooked and no longer watery. Remove from the oven and cool on a wire rack for 15 minutes. Serve hot.

Kombucha

Kombucha originated in northeast China many centuries ago. It was known as a fountain-of-youth elixir in ancient China as part of its folk medicine. Kombucha is a refreshing, fermented tonic made with black or green tea, specific yeast cultures, acetic acid bacteria and sugar that ferments for at least a week. During this period, a strange-looking shape forms from the bacteria and yeast, known as 'mushroom tea'. This growth is not a mushroom, but a symbiotic colony of bacteria and yeast.

Benefits

Kombucha's fermentation produces vinegar, acidic compounds, a little alcohol, gases that make it sparkling – and a large amount of probiotic bacteria. We know that healthy bacteria means a happy gut with improved digestion and reduced inflammation. Kombucha also contains antioxidants, as does green tea, so you're getting a double antioxidant dose. Acedic acid, produced through the fermentation, kills harmful microorganisms like the polyphenols in tea, so this means a strong antibacterial hit. Interestingly, although kombucha is made with yeast, the antibacterial properties include the ability to fight *Candida albicans*.

Ways to Eat

- Soak 3 tablespoons chia to 240ml/8fl oz/1 cup kombucha.
- Use in smoothies instead of water or non-dairy milk.
- Drink it.

How to Use

You can buy the yeast and bacteria colony online and make your own kombucha at home, but it is worth a note of caution because contaminated or over-fermented kombucha can be dangerous. It is safer to buy kombucha from a good health-food store. Commercial products must contain less than 0.5 per cent alcohol, so are considered alcohol-free. Some people give it to their children watered down as a health tonic.

Sparkling Kombucha Mocktails

Forget the alcohol and go for a health tonic instead. Combine kombucha with other healthy ingredients like lemon or lime juice, fruit juices or smoothies for refreshing and uplifting drinks. All drinks serve 1.

Kombucha Lime

350ml/12 fl oz/1½ cups kombucha
1 tbsp fresh lime juice

Pina Kombucha

120ml/4fl oz/½ cup pineapple juice
120ml/4fl oz/½ cup coconut juice
120ml/4fl oz/½ cup kombucha

Berrybucha

100g/3½oz fresh or frozen berries
240ml/8fl oz/1 cup kombucha

Put the berries and kombucha in a blender and blend until smooth.

Umeboshi Plums

Umeboshi, which translates to 'dried plum', is a definite umami sensation. It is sour and salty and intense, waking up your taste buds and cleansing the palate. Umeboshi are used as a condiment with other foods (particularly rice), but are considered an ancient medicine in Japan and China. Some people in Japan start their day with one or two, as it is their preventative medicine, likened to our apple a day. Umeboshi are also said to be a great cure for headaches and hangovers.

Benefits

Umeboshi, which go through fermentation, contain citric acid and although they taste tart, the effect on the body is alkalizing. They stimulate digestion, cleanse and remove toxins and energise. They are also very high in iron. Along with rice and vegetables, pickled plums were carried by Samurai warriors as part of their food ration to add flavour and give energy.

Umeboshi are also good for nausea and stomach upsets, and have shown to prevent *Helicobacter pylori* – the bacterial infection that causes ulcers and is fairly antibiotic-resistant.

Ways to Eat

• Occasionally start your day with an umeboshi plum to stimulate digestion and provide energy.
• Mix a little umeboshi paste with salad dressings.
• Use as a salt substitute with grains, vegetables or soups.
• Spread umeboshi paste thinly on thick slices of cucumber.
• Serve with sushi and nori hand rolls.
• Finely dice umeboshi plums and mix with rice for sushi.
• Add ½ a large or 1 small pitted finely cut plum to green tea for a healthy drink.

How to Use

Umeboshi come as plums or paste. If you are adding umeboshi to other dishes, reduce or omit added salt. Salt is used in the fermentation process to protect against unwanted bacteria. Check the label to make sure the plums or paste only contain umeboshi plums, sea salt, shiso leaves and no colourings or preservatives. A skilled fermenter will use less salt, so choose a high-quality product when buying these plums.

Onigiri with Umeboshi

Onigiri are very easy to make. They are the Japanese equivalent of the sandwich, perfect for lunches or picnics. Make a bigger 'well' to fit in more of the fillings. Serve with a salad or some stir-fried vegetables, for a great, light meal.

Serves: 4
Prep: 15 minutes
Cook: 35–40 minutes

200g/7oz/1 cup brown sushi rice, soaked if time (see page 143)
480ml/16fl oz/2 cups water
1 tsp fine sea salt or 1 tbsp miso
umeboshi paste or plums, pitted and chopped
120g/4¼oz tuna mixed with mayonnaise
100g/3⅓oz smoked salmon, chopped
8 sheets toasted sushi nori, cut into 2.5cm/1 inch strips
2 tbsp white or black sesame seeds or furikake (optional)

If you're not soaking the rice, put the rice, water and salt (if you're using miso, mix into a little warm water and stir into the rice when it has finished cooking) in a small saucepan and bring to the boil over a high heat. Stir to distribute the salt, reduce the heat to low and simmer, covered, for 35–40 minutes until soft.

Put the rice, umeboshi paste or plums, tuna mayonnaise, smoked salmon, nori and sesame seeds or furikake, if using, in separate small bowls and place them on the table.

To make onigiri, take 2 tablespoons rice in one hand and press and shape into a triangle, ball or oval. Press the rice firmly so that it holds its shape. Make a well in the middle of the ball and put in a filling of tuna, salmon or umeboshi. Roll in sesame seeds or furikake if desired, wrap a strip of nori all the way or partially around the rice and enjoy.

Sauerkraut

Sauerkraut is made by the lactic fermentation of cabbage by the bacteria and yeast that live on the cabbage itself. Before refrigeration was invented, fermentation was used to preserve foods. But fermentation doesn't just prevent foods from going off, it also augments their nutritional value. Sauerkraut is often eaten with fatty meats that complement its mild acidity.

Benefits

The fermentation process packs sauerkraut with beneficial lactobacillus bacteria, the good gut bugs that support the healthy flora in our intestinal tract. Because of this, sauerkraut is valued as an aid for digestion, helping relieve upset stomachs and constipation. Sauerkraut is high in dietary fibre and is a good source of many vitamins and minerals. Fermenting can increase the vitamin C levels in cabbage by 100 percent and generally increases key B vitamins too. Sauerkraut is also valued as an anti-inflammatory, providing relief from sore joints and muscles.

Ways to Eat

- Mix into bean soups when serving.
- Add to sandwiches.
- Eat a Reuben sandwich – toasted rye bread, pastrami, Gruyere or Jarlsberg, sliced gherkins, non-spicy mustard and sauerkraut.
- Mix with tuna and mayo.
- Put on rye or wholegrain bread, add slices of Gruyère or Cheddar and grill for great cheese on toast.
- Mix with noodles or pasta.
- Find a good *pierogi* recipe (the Eastern Europe version of pasties).
- Add to toppings for baked potatoes and sweet potatoes.
- Serve with pork, other meats or meatballs (see page 120).
- Put on hamburgers and sausages.

How to Use

If you're buying sauerkraut, check the ingredients. Real sauerkraut only contains cabbage, salt and sometimes juniper berries or cumin seeds – never vinegar and certainly not preservatives. The presence of vinegar means it has not been fermented, but pickled. Watch sodium levels in ready-made sauerkraut, too. Or make your own, which is a breeze.

Like all fermented foods, sauerkraut is best eaten raw to preserve the beneficial enzymes and vitamins.

Homemade Sauerkraut

Sauerkraut is one of the easiest fermented foods to make at home. Fermenting cabbage boosts all of its beneficial qualities – vitamin C content, its ability to detox the liver, antioxidants and antibiotic and antiviral properties. Ferment it until the taste suits you (it will be mild after a week and then stronger the longer you leave it) and then refrigerate for up to 2 months.

Serve: 4
Prep: 15 minutes
Fermenting: 4–14 days

1 medium white or green cabbage (about 1.5kg/3lb 3oz)
1½ tbsp fine sea salt
1 tbsp caraway seeds (optional)
4 medium jars

Peel 4 leaves from the cabbage and cut into circles the size of the jar mouths. Cut the cabbage into 8 wedges, remove the core and thinly slice crossways by hand or with a mandolin.

Put the cabbage and salt in a large mixing bowl. Mix and massage the salt into the cabbage for 5 minutes until it softens and releases water. Pound the cabbage with the end of a wooden rolling pin or a potato masher for another 5 minutes. Add the caraway seeds, if using, and mix well.

Pack and push the cabbage into the jars, leaving a little room at the top. Pour in any liquid from the bowl. Put a leaf circle on top of the cabbage and push down to keep the cabbage submerged. Do not put the lid on because the pressure from the fermentation can cause the jar to explode.

Press the cabbage down a little more every day. If after a day the liquid has not risen above the level of the cabbage, dissolve 1 teaspoon fine sea salt in 240ml/8fl oz/1 cup water and add enough to cover.

After a week, the sauerkraut will be ready to eat, but will continue to ferment and develop for up to 2 weeks. If mould develops, skim it off and make sure the cabbage is under liquid. Taste the kraut every day and when you like the taste, put the lid on and refrigerate.

Kimchi

Kimchi, a traditional spicy fermented food, is Korea's national dish. Koreans eat about 18kg (40lb) pounds per person per year of it and apparently say 'kimchi' instead of 'cheese' when you take their picture. The main ingredients are Chinese cabbage, garlic, salt and chilli peppers (and sometimes radish) with other seasonings. Common seasonings include ginger, garlic, spring onion (scallion), shrimp sauce, oyster sauce and fish sauce. It is served at every meal with rice or noodles or as a side.

Benefits

Eating fermented foods that are teeming with beneficial microbes is a simple, effective way to improve the health of your gut. Good gut health is the foundation for physical, mental and emotional wellbeing and most English, European and American diets are lacking in beneficial lactobacilli.

Kimchi is part of the high-fibre, low-fat, enzyme-rich diet that is said to keep Koreans slim. It is a nutritious food, filled with various probiotic strains that promote healthy gut bacteria in the same way as yogurt, but without the dairy.

Because of the fermentation process, kimchi has high levels of vitamins (particularly vitamin C and beta-carotene), plus minerals, fibre and important phytochemicals.

Ways to Eat

- Make kimchi scrambled eggs.
- Swap for sauerkraut.
- Add to sandwiches.
- Make kimchi cheese on toast.
- Include in fish or crab cakes.
- Stir into fried rice with onion, garlic and chopped (bell) pepper.
- Mix with pork or chicken mince (ground pork or chicken) and make kimchi burgers or top your beef burger with it.
- Use on tacos.
- Eat as a side dish.
- Cook Japanese noodles in a little water and add kimchi.
- Create kimchi fried rice.
- Use in spring roll filings with crab or pork, a grated carrot and courgette (zucchini) and sliced spring onions (scallions).
- Chop and put on pizza (after the sauce and before the cheese).

How to Use

Like anything containing probiotics, kimchi should not be cooked or should be cooked very briefly or you will lose many of its benefits. As with miso, another excellent fermented food, kimchi is best stirred into something after it has cooked.

Kimchi is salty, so do not add salt when you include kimchi in a dish.

Kimchi Pancake

Kimchi is best eaten raw, but this delightful savoury pancake doesn't cook for long, so much of the nutrition is retained. It's a perfect light lunch or starter. If you mix the kimchi and flour in the morning, the flour will be nicely soaked by dinnertime. It's fun as one large pancake, but tricky to flip over, so you might prefer to make individual 10cm/4 inch ones.

Serve: 4
Prep: 15 minutes
Cook: 8–10 minutes

225g/8oz ground pork (optional)
400g/14oz/2 cups kimchi, drained and chopped, plus extra for serving
120g/4¼oz/1 cup wholegrain spelt or other flour
2 eggs, beaten with a fork
4–5 spring onions (scallions), sliced
1 garlic clove, finely chopped
½ tsp chilli flakes or cayenne pepper, optional
2 tbsp extra virgin olive oil
1 daikon, sliced into rounds, to serve (optional)

For the dressing:
50g/1¾oz watercress, finely chopped
2 tbsp cider vinegar
1 tbsp soy sauce or tamari
3 tbsp toasted sesame oil
2 tsp sesame seeds, soaked if time (see page 183)

In a large bowl, combine the pork, if using, kimchi, flour, eggs, spring onions, garlic and chilli flakes or cayenne pepper, and mix well.

Heat the olive oil in a large saucepan over a medium heat. Pour in the batter, spread to flatten and cook for 4–5 minutes until lightly browned. Meanwhile, in a small bowl, mix the watercress, vinegar, soy sauce or tamari, sesame oil and sesame seeds.

Flip the pancake over with a large spatula or slide it onto a plate and flip it over, cooking for another 4 minutes until lightly browned on the other side. Slide onto a large serving plate and cut into 8 pieces. Serve with extra kimchi, dressing and slices of daikon, if using.

Tempeh

Tempeh is thought to have come not from China or Japan, but from Indonesia. It is a whole fermented food in which the whole soybean interacts with various moulds, yeast and bacteria. Unfermented soy is not a great food. Soy products should not be eaten as a protein substitute, while soy protein and soy protein isolate are highly processed soy products that should be avoided.

Benefits

There is very little research relating specifically to tempeh as most studies are done on soy products like soy milk and tofu. But tempeh is a whole food and is fermented, both of which are good news. Fermenting soy transforms the carbohydrates, proteins, fats, minerals and vitamins. This makes the carbs and protein more digestible, the minerals more absorbable and increases the levels of vitamins.

Tempeh contains folate, vitamin K, calcium, magnesium, iron and fibre, all of which have proven health benefits. Eating tempeh instead of meat occasionally would increase your intake of these nutrients.

Ways to Eat

- Marinate and add to any kind of salad.
- Make mock tuna mayo salad with crumbled tempeh, a little red onion, spring onion (scallion), chopped celery, chopped gherkins and pickles, Dijon mustard and mayo.
- Buy marinated tempeh and use in a sandwich.
- Serve with sautéed leafy greens and wholegrain rice.
- Add to curry, stews and soups.
- Add to stir-fries.
- Use for chilli non carne and then use in tacos.
- Include in teriyaki skewers.
- Finely chop and use in Sloppy Joes (see page 62).
- Put in spring rolls.

Tempeh & Kimchi Noodle Bowl

This quick and easy meal is perfect for dinner when you're too tired to do much, but want something interesting, beautiful and delicious. The shiitake is fried separately, then the rest is cooked together and combined in a bowl for a lovely combination of colours and flavours.

Serves 4
Prep: 10 minutes
Cook: 15 minutes

2 tbsp extra virgin olive oil
225g/8oz shiitake, stems removed and sliced
¼ tsp fine sea salt
4 tbsp coconut oil or toasted sesame oil
1 onion, chopped
1.2 litres/40fl oz/5 cups water or broth
1 tsp fine sea salt
1 tbsp fresh ginger, finely chopped
250g/9oz wholegrain noodles – try wholegrain rice, buckwheat or black rice noodles
4 garlic cloves, chopped
200g/7oz tempeh, chopped
135g/4¾oz/1 cup kimchi, chopped
2 tbsp miso
100g/3½oz watercress, roughly chopped
nori flakes and furikake, to serve (optional)

Heat the olive oil in a medium frying pan over a medium heat. Add the shiitake and salt and sauté for 8 minutes until beginning to brown.

Heat the coconut oil or toasted sesame oil in a large saucepan over a medium heat. Add the onion and sauté for 10 minutes until beginning to brown.

Add the water or broth, salt and ginger to the saucepan and bring to the boil. Add the noodles slowly so that the water continues to boil or they will clump together. Add the garlic, reduce the heat to low and simmer for 5 minutes, stirring occasionally, until the noodles are al dente. Remove from the heat.

Add the tempeh and kimchi to the saucepan. Dissolve the miso in a few tablespoons of warm broth, then add to the saucepan and mix well.

Divide the noodles and liquid between 4 bowls. Divide the sautéed shiitake and place on top of the noodles, then add the watercress. Sprinkle with nori flakes and furikake, if using.

Amazake

Amazake is a traditional Japanese drink that translates to 'sweet sake', but is a thick, creamy, dairy-free, naturally sweet, traditional Japanese dessert. Amazake is produced by combining cooked brown rice with *koji*, a fermented culture called *Aspergillus oryzae*, whose enzymes convert the carbohydrate in the whole grains into sweetness.

Benefits

Amazake contains an abundance of active enzymes that help break down fats, complex carbs and proteins for your body to utilise. It is therefore excellent for anyone with poor digestion and is thought to be great for young children as it is simple to digest, easy on the stomach and naturally sweet. Amazake is high in B vitamins, calcium, phosphorus, iron and fibre, containing all of the beneficial nutrition of wholegrain rice. Make sure you are buying a quality product with no added sugar.

Ways to Eat

- Add to smoothies and smoothie bowls for protein and creaminess.
- Mix with porridge (oatmeal).
- Layer into breakfast parfaits and chia pots.
- Mix 1 part amazake to 1½ parts warm or cold water and some grated ginger, if you like, for a warm or cool refreshing drink.
- Mix with hot non-dairy milk.
- Swap 2 tablespoons amazake for 1 tablespoon sugar.
- Use instead of custard.
- Eat for dessert plain or add other super ingredients.
- Mix with raw, chopped fruit.
- Use it to sweeten your coffee or tea.
- Give to babies.

Amazake Pancakes

Wonderfully, naturally sweet from the fermented brown rice, these pancakes have a lovely texture. For a lighter version, use 300g/10½oz/2½ cups wholegrain spelt flour, sprouted if you like, instead of teff flour. If you don't want to soak the flour and seeds overnight, mix the dry ingredients in one bowl and the wet in another, then combine and mix well.

Serves: 4
Prep: 5 minutes, plus overnight soaking
Cook: 6 minutes per batch

300g/10½ oz/2 cups wholegrain teff flour
240ml/8½fl oz/1 cup amazake
240ml/8½fl oz/1 cup water or non-dairy milk
½ tsp fine sea salt
1 tbsp linseeds (flaxseeds) or 1 egg, beaten with a fork
2 tbsp extra virgin olive oil, plus extra for frying
1 tsp vanilla essence
1 tsp bicarbonate of soda (baking soda)
butter, Manuka honey, maple syrup and/or lemon juice, to serve

Put the flour, amazake, water or non-dairy milk, salt and linseeds in a medium bowl and mix well (if using egg instead, don't add until the following morning). Leave to soak, covered, overnight.

Add the olive oil and vanilla essence and mix well. Add the bicarbonate of soda (baking soda) and mix until combined. Heat a griddle or large frying pan with oil over a medium–low heat and drop in 2 tablespoons batter for each pancake. Cook for 3 minutes on each side until bubbles come through the surface and the underneath is lightly browned.

Serve the pancakes in a stack with your favourite toppings – Manuka honey, butter and a little sugar, maple syrup or lemon juice and sugar, for example.

Apple Cider Vinegar

It is said that Hippocrates, the father of medicine, used apple cider vinegar (ACV) for its cleansing and healing abilities. ACV is made by mixing chopped apples with water and sugar which then ferment to form alcoholic liquid, and then to acetic acid and malic acid. Organic, unpastuerised and raw ACV contains the 'mother' of vinegar, a natural chain of connected strands of protein, enzymes and friendly bacteria molecules.

Benefits

Although it seems acid, raw ACV is the only vinegar that is alkaline-forming in the body. The acetic acid in ACV is antibacterial and can be gargled with water to kill the bacteria that cause sore throats. There are many people who take ACV for relief from rheumatoid arthritis, which might be down to its alkalizing effect. There are lots of claims that ACV can help with your digestive system, reducing blood sugar spikes after eating, clearing up bad breath, acne, dandruff and more. ACV has a loyal following and is certainly better than harsh, cheap, commercial vinegars.

Ways to Eat

- Drink between 1 teaspoon and 1 tablespoon a day mixed with warm water.
- Use in salad dressings for mixed leaves and mixed, steamed vegetables.
- Use in place of other vinegars for marinades.
- Make salad Niçoise.
- Toss with roasted vegetables.
- Mix a little into guacamole.
- Make vinaigrette for bean salads.
- Use in slaws.
- Add 1 tablespoon to wet ingredients when baking with wholegrain flour and swap bicarbonate of soda (baking soda) for baking powder to lift the heavier flour.
- Pour a little into beef stew to lift the flavour and help tenderize the meat.
- Always use when making bone broth (see page 121).
- Use in chicken salad with extra virgin olive oil instead of mayo.

How to Use

The standard recipe for taking ACV on a daily basis is 1 tablespoon of vinegar in a glass of warm water. Some people add a teaspoon of Manuka honey to make it more palatable and add in even more health benefits (see Manuka honey, page 205).

Glossary

Acidophilus *Lactobacillus Acidophilus* (*L. Acidophilus*) is a beneficial bacteria that is naturally found in yoghurt, kefir and some other products where it has been added. It is a probiotic that helps to restore the balance of good bacteria in the gastrointestinal tract.

Alginic acid, also called **algin** or **alginate**, is an ionic polysaccharide distributed widely in the cell walls of brown algae, where through binding with water it forms a viscous gum. This gum binds to toxic metals in your body and eliminates them.

Amino acids are the building blocks of protein – they grow, repair and maintain our body tissues and are essential components of our diets. When protein is broken down by digestion, the result is 22 known amino acids that can be separated into two categories – essential and non-essential. Essential amino acids are those that cannot be manufactured by the body – it is essential that they are obtained through diet. Non-essential amino acids can be manufactured by the body. You need the right combination of essential amino acids and supporting nutrients to optimize healthy protein maintenance.

Anthocyanin is a compound that produces red, blue and purple pigments in plants. It is an antioxidant.

Antioxidants are substances (such as beta-carotene or vitamin C) that inhibit oxidation or harmful chemical reactions promoted by oxygen, peroxides or free radicals in the body.

Betalains are red and yellow pigments in plants such as beetroot. They have antioxidant and anti-inflammatory effects on the body.

Candida albicans is a species of yeast that occurs naturally in the gastrointestinal tract. An imbalance of the fungus can cause it to grow out of control and cause Candidiasis.

Dipicolonic acid is an alkaloid that chelates or binds with heavy metals that are toxic and removes them from the body.

Enzymes are the numerous complex proteins produced by body cells that help bring about or speed up bodily chemical activities, such as the digestion of food.

Fatty Acids are the building blocks of the fat in our bodies and in the food we eat. During digestion, the body breaks down fat into fatty acids, which can then be absorbed into the blood. They are important for energy storage. If glucose isn't immediately available to the body for energy, the body uses fatty acids to fuel cells instead.

Folate or vitamin B9 naturally occurs in a wide variety of foods, including vegetables (particularly dark green leafy vegetables), fruits and fruit juices, nuts, beans, peas, dairy products, poultry and meat, eggs, seafood and grains.

Folic acid is the synthetic form of folate.

Free radicals are especially reactive atoms that can be produced in the body by natural biological processes or introduced from outside sources (such as tobacco smoke, toxins or pollutants) and that can damage cells, proteins, and DNA by altering their chemical structure.

Furikake is a Japanese seasoning mix, composed of black and white sesame seeds with bits of nori and shiro leaves.

Glucosinolates are bitter sulphur-containing compounds found in cruciferous plants, such as broccoli, cabbage, or mustard, that when digested form bioactive compounds, some which are anti-carcinogenic.

Koji is a Japanese starter made from rice which has been treated with a fungus, Aspergillus oryzae. It is used to initiate fermentation in the production of soy sauce, miso, amazake and sake.

Heterocyclic amines (HCAs) are the carcinogenic chemical compounds formed when meat, including beef, pork, fish or poultry, is cooked using high-temperature methods, such as pan-frying or grilling directly over an open flame.

Inulin is a natural prebiotic present in numerous plant species that provides health benefits for our digestive tract, where it increases calcium absorption and promotes the growth of beneficial bacteria.

Methylglyoxal (MG) is made from a compound found in Manuka nectar. MG is a natural antibiotic and has antibacterial capabilities.

Macrobiotic is a diet of organic wholefoods based on Buddhist principles of yin and yang, that consists of whole cereals and grains supplemented especially with beans and vegetables.

Molybdenum is a trace element that acts as a catalyst for enzymes and helps facilitate the breakdown of certain amino acids in the body.

Organophosphate insecticides are a group of toxic phosphates and insecticides.

Phytochemicals are compounds occurring naturally in plants.

Phytonutrients are bioactive plant-derived compounds associated with positive health effects.

Polychlorinated biphenyls (PCBs) are toxic environmental pollutants that tend to accumulate in animal tissues.

Polyphenols are antioxidant plant chemicals.

Polysaccharides are carbohydrates whose molecules consist of a number of sugar molecules bonded together. They are used for energy storage and structural support in the body.

Pre-biotic is a substance and especially a carbohydrate that is nearly or wholly indigestible and that when consumed promotes the growth of beneficial bacteria in the digestive tract.

Shiso leaves, also known as perilla leaves, are an Asian culinary herb.

UMF stands for Unique Manuka Factor, which is a quality trademark and grading system for Manuka honey. Every jar of Manuka honey will display a UMF rating number, which represents the unique signature compounds characteristic of this type of honey, ensuring purity and quality. These include certain key markers, including Methylglyoxal (see above). To be considered therapeutic, Manuka must have a minimum UMF of 10.

Index

Resources & Bibliography

Authority Nutrition www.authoritynutrition.com
BBC Good Food www.bbcgoodfood.com
Clearspring Ltd www.clearspring.co.uk
Kitchn www.thekitchn.com
Medical and health advice www.webmd.com
Planet Organic www.planetorganic.com
The World's Healthiest Foods www.whfoods.com

John Belleme and Jan Belleme , *Culinary Treasures of Japan*, (U.S.,1993), Avery Publishing Group Inc.

Renée Elliott, *Me, You & the Kids Too,* (2012), Watkins Publishing Limited.

Sally Fallon, *Nourishing Traditions: The Cookbook That Challenges Politically Correct Nutrition and the Diet Dictocrats*, 2nd revised edition, (U.S., 2009), New Trends Publishing Inc.

Patrick Holford, *The Optimum Nutrition Bible*, (2004), Piatkus.

Pino Luongo, *A Tuscan in the Kitchen*, (1988), Crown Publications.

Roger Saul, *Spelt*, (2015), Watkins Publishing Limited.

Andrew Whitley, *Bread Matters: Why and How to Make Your Own*, (2009), Fourth Estate.

Acknowledgements

Writing a book affects everyone you are close to and some who you aren't. Researching, writing and testing recipes take over your kitchen and your life, and would be impossible without the support of a large group of people. I am grateful to everyone who helped.

Scarlett Knight, Amy Clinkard and Al Overton from the Buying Team at Planet Organic piled in at the beginning and helped the book take shape. Thank you for your input and especially you, Al, for all of the copy checking.

Thank you to Katie Cowan, the publishing director, who held the project together when things got complicated. Thanks to star designers, Gail Jones and Laura Russell, who made it flow so beautifully; and to the illustrator, Louise Lockhart, for her retro drawings that lift and complete the book. The photographer, Karen Thomas, was great to work with and captured the essence of the food perfectly. And thanks to home economist, Lizzie Harris, and prop stylist, Cynthia Inions, who brought style and colour to the pictures.

Huge thanks must go to the first editor, Krissy Mallett, who in her sweetness persuaded me to write the book and promised that it would be fun (!). Owing to unusual circumstances, there were three more editors, each of whom made valuable contributions: Ione Walder, Emily Preece-Morrison and Sarah Epton. I owe special thanks and big hug to Sarah, who came to the book when I was close to tears and forged a clear path forward.

Thank you to my gorgeous goddaughter, Laura Smith – my millennial muse, who guided me on what her generation would and wouldn't be bothered to do.

I owe a very special thanks to my recipes testers who re-tested dishes that needed a bit more work. Thank you to my brother David Jurgelon and my sister Lauren Jurgelon for their recipe ideas, for always saying yes and hitting my deadlines. And thank you to my friends who tested recipes: Julia Davies, Kate Handford, Anita Keogh, Natalie Bourne, Kate Ayling, Pagette Harrison and my son, Nix. Your feedback, opinions and enthusiasm were invaluable.

The most gratitude is for my husband, Brian, who is unwavering in his support of me and belief in me. And thanks and kisses to my children Jess, Nix and Cassie. My family tried over a hundred new dishes, remained excited about the book and managed without me when I was too busy working.

I couldn't have managed it without all of your help. It's a great book because you are all a part of it.

About the Author

I was born in Pascagoula, Mississippi, in the Deep South of America. I am the fourth child in my family, with ancestors on my mother Lucille's side from New Orleans, Louisiana. They were plantation owners along the Mississippi River. They grew sugar. My grandparents on my father Edward's side came on the boat from Lithuania to Rhode Island. My parents met on a paddle steamer on the Mississippi River.

Because I had no idea what I wanted to do or be, I studied English and Health at university. Already starting to question convention, I read a book about intensive beef production in America in my late teens. This nudged me into a search for another way of thinking and into a journey of self-discovery, spirituality and non-convention.

On a back-packing, train-riding trip across Europe while at uni, I met my future husband, Brian, on a night bus. I returned to America, finished my degree and moved to England. On my first day in my first job in England, I realized three things. One, as a passionate person, I have to love my work. Two, I really dislike being told what to do. And three, I wanted to do a Good Thing.

I worked in the wine trade from 1986–1990. Brian and I got married and then went to Connecticut to do a six-month course in personal growth. I came back on a mission to promote health in the community. I decided that a chain of organic supermarkets was the vehicle to achieve this. I had found my vocation.

I pioneered the UK's first organic supermarket, Planet Organic, in November 1995. We set the highest product standard in retail, sold the best quality foods and changed the face of retailing. No one knows how big a part we played in changing the food culture in England and bringing organic into the mainstream.

I gave birth to three children from 2002 to 2008, then stepped away from Planet, jumped off of the gerbil wheel and powered down. We moved the family to a small farm in Tuscany, put up solar panels, planted fruit and vegetables and grew olives. We slowed down, spent time together and grew closer.

While we lived in Italy, I transformed the way I bake, realizing that I wanted to give my kids treats that were enhancing their health, not detracting from it. We relished our Italian chapter for $3^1/_2$ years, and then returned to rural England. We chose Sussex and I kidded myself that the South Downs were *almost* like the Tuscan hills.

I've worked in the organic and health industry since 1991, during which time I have studied organic, food, ingredients and health. Now I write cookbooks, teach healthy cooking and baking, do inspirational speaking for budding entrepreneurs, lead groups of women to launch their businesses and raise my kids.

In spite of my ancestry, I have a healthy dislike of sugar. Because of my ancestry, I have a pioneering spirit. I will always do what I love. It's not work; it's my life. My tombstone will say, "I'm not done yet."

Renée

First published in the United Kingdom in 2017 by
Pavilion
43 Great Ormond Street
London
WC1N 3HZ

Text © Renée Elliott, 2017
Design and layout © Pavilion Books Company Ltd, 2017
Photography © Pavilion Books Company Ltd, 2017
Illustrations © Louise Lockhart

Photography by Karen Thomas

ISBN: 978-1-91121-618-6

A CIP catalogue record for this book is available from
the British Library.

10 9 8 7 6 5 4 3 2 1

Reproduction by Mission, Hong Kong
Printed and bound by 1010 Printing International Ltd, China

This book can be ordered direct from the publisher at
www.pavilionbooks.com